CASES IN MARKETING TECHNIQUES

Analysis, Alternatives, Action

ALAN WEST

P·C·P

Paul Chapman
Publishing Ltd

Acknowledgements

Creating a case study book requires an enormous amount of
information on a diverse range of topics. I am indebted to the
following individuals for providing much of the framework
for specific cases, many of which were dissertations for
degrees in business studies:

Andrew Burton – AFI
David Milne – Doorlarm
Andrew Firman – Adnams
Tessa Knight – Prestel
Bruce Dove – Yamazka
Abigail Carson – Drive in Liquor Store
Peter Omonseh – Axe Stores
Louise Mansfield – Twydale
Louise Simpson – Nestlé
Karen Gee – Club Méditerrannée

In addition I would like to thank colleagues and students at a
variety of institutions for suggesting improvements and
modifications to material

Dedication

To J & M in the hope that you will eventually read it.

First published 1988

Paul Chapman Publishing Ltd
London

British Library Cataloguing in Publication Data

West, Alan, 1951–
  Cases in marketing techniques.
  I. Title
  658.8

ISBN 1-85396-033-0

Typeset by Inforum Ltd, Portsmouth
Printed and bound by
St. Edmundsbury Press, Bury St. Edmunds

CONTENTS

Contents

Contents

PART I

INTRODUCTION

Chapter 1

THE ROLE OF CASE STUDIES IN MANAGEMENT DEVELOPMENT

INTRODUCTION

As business training becomes more systematic and widespread, the use of case study material appears to increase exponentially. It is often held that such cases should be handled in isolation and that the instructor or tutor should 'interpret' the material for the student. For the business student this has a number of disadvantages. First, it tends to decrease the amount of work that can be put into the material, and that boring old saying, 'you get out what you are prepared to put in', is especially relevant in the complex business world, with problems that require a substantial amount of initial preparation and analysis. The tendency to sit back and receive answers in a digested form is all too common and understandable but should, if possible, be resisted.

Second, the insistence on the student analysing the material should broaden the discussion from a single channel or model answer approach which will rapidly evolve when any teacher has to interpret the same material over a period of time, albeit with different groups of students.

Approaching case studies in this way does, however, mean that the current approach to the student needs to change from the classroom emphasis to one where much of the conceptual thinking about the issues involved in the case is completed on an individual basis by the student. In other words the case study manual must include the skeleton around which an individual can provide the flesh of knowledge provided by other textbooks and personal experience of the business world.

LOGICAL FRAMEWORK

The use of case studies or simulations encourages trainees to use a systematic approach or logical framework when dealing with problems. In each instance this will involve various issues.

1. The analysis of the problem.
2. The proposed solution.
3. The alternative methods for achieving the solution.
4. The best method for achieving the solution.
5. The way in which the best method will be implemented.

Teaching a standard approach to a particular problem so that it becomes second nature is not of course restricted to the business world. The armed services have, for example, carried out tactical exercises without troops (TEWTS) since the nineteenth century – long before the business school concept had surfaced. More recently, air crews use simulators to drum into individuals the need for system and method so that they will react quickly and correctly (one hopes!) to particular problems.

Though the planning and control issues in business are less immediate than those faced by the airline pilot, the same structured approach to problem-solving will minimize delay and hopefully maximize effectiveness, especially in the ability to handle events or problems in a more objective fashion. Close contact with any job or organization inevitably causes some loss of perspective which sometimes leads to situations where mundane issues achieve monumental proportions. We are often too well aware of minor issues such as the design of the office notepaper becoming major crises and totally overshadowing more important business or organization issues.

The standard structured approach to any problem is often criticized by practitioners in industry on the grounds that each particular company or market sector is unique; the cigarette industry is qualitatively different from the heavy engineering sector. Yet any brief study of the two industrial sectors will convince those who are interested that the same broad problems are faced in each area, though the emphasis or importance of the various elements will differ significantly. Since it is essentially vague, 'uniqueness' is obviously very convenient in explaining the different experiences of companies operating in the same sector where some will survive and grow, others will go to the wall. Analysing the experience of such companies using a structured approach will immediately demonstrate why it was that one company succeeded and another failed: perhaps by better forward planning or financial control, greater awareness of and response to changes in the market, appreciation of the potential for the company's balance sheet in new technological developments and decisive decision-making by management. In such a case the structured approach is basically a form of standardization, incorporating company experience within a common framework of knowledge designed so that others might learn from it.

The standard structured approach is therefore a training tool which is based essentially on the practical experience of others. It is optimistic, unlike the 'uniqueness' argument. It says, 'We can learn from the experience of others.' If used effectively it can be a very rapid method of familiarizing a trainee with analysing a variety of potentially complex data. The drawback of the standard approach – that it all too often involves the individual in unnecessary analysis – is again merely a matter of practice and understanding, as the key issues will rapidly become clear and the remainder can be discarded as of little relevance to *that particular case*. This minor drawback is outweighed by the considerable advantage that a structured approach provides, that of ensuring that the smallest number of important issues are ignored.

SCOPE

The use of a case study approach allows the individual to be trained in the potential problems and opportunities in whole areas which are currently outside his or her likely experience. For example, the officer in the armed services might take part in a simulated landing in hostile territory far from the home base; airline pilots learn the problems associated with total failure of all engines, business executives the effects of rapid inflation, diving exchange rates, the problems of service, consumer and industrial companies. The trainee is also given the opportunity to put forward his or her own ideas or pet solutions, to evaluate them and consider just how feasible they are; he or she will have the opportunity to see just how feasible it is to call upon personal experience in another area.

All this can be achieved in a brief time span which would not be matched in reality; for example, a company can be followed through a five-year period and problems and solutions analysed throughout this period during a short training session. This allows the individual to amass a considerable amount of knowledge in a short time, and is as a result a highly cost-effective method of training or teaching.

INTEGRATION

Marketing management is frequently accused of concentrating on tactical rather than long-term strategic analysis. Case study material can allow the manager to explore how strategy and implementation interact and to see the 'fine tuning' of the marketing mix within a broader concept, something that is often lost in day-to-day activity. The use of a structured approach is sometimes referred to as the 'audit' and serves the same function – ensuring that the entire range of the organization's activities is reviewed and reorganized. Again, the marketing manager is also accused of being unable to quantify effectively the impact of the decisions that are taken; the case study approach allows this discipline to be more rigorously enforced than other methods of learning.

THE ROLE OF INFORMATION IN DECISION-MAKING

Case studies or simulations have a vital role to play in developing an understanding of the information needed for effective decision-making. An army cannot invade another country in safety unless it has a clear understanding of the enemy's strength and intentions; a business cannot progress unless it is aware of factors that mitigate against success or failure and their relative importance in particular instances.

The classroom exercise can provide the whole range of information from the embarrassment of riches of too much information, which the individual is unable to use effectively, to that more akin to that of normal management – taking decisions on too little data and therefore having to minimize the large amount of risk inherent in the proposed action. Continuing use of simulations will therefore develop an awareness of the information issues and decision-making, and highlight the assumptions that individuals make on a day-to-day basis without often being fully aware of the possible impact should those assumptions be wrong.

COMPROMISE

Every decision is a compromise between often strongly competing issues: Should the company raise its price by 50p or increase promotion? Should it expand its sales in Europe or invest more heavily in new product development?

Case studies and simulations tend to identify the pay-offs that exist much more clearly because the participants are not corralled by perceived management wisdoms – that the company is sales led, or is never going to export. Participants in case studies are therefore more able to explore the whole range of possible solutions many of which in real life would be unacceptable to those individuals who would have to implement them. So while it may be said that case studies will have a slight air of unreality, they will still demand practical solutions; in other words the answer will have to be supported by the facts.

CONSENSUS

Case studies are a highly effective method of evaluating individuals and training them to develop inter-group skills. The classic army problem of providing a group with rope, barrels, tree trunks and other impedimenta out of which they are supposed to build some form of bridge, winch or other structure, identifies not only those who can think effectively under a degree of pressure but, more important, it clearly marks out those who are able to convince others of the most practical solution and then implement it.

PRESENTATION

One of the most frequent comments on skills shortages in managers is the lack of both oral and written presentation skills. Case studies and simulations can help to correct this weakness by requiring that individuals put forward effective and coherent presentations of their proposed solutions.

USING THIS BOOK

The object of this book is to fill one of the major gaps that exists in the provision of case study material for the business student and manager. Though many case study texts exist, far too often the comment will be: 'What are we supposed to learn from the material?'

Part I provides detailed introductory chapters which lead the student through the main strategic and marketing issues he or she will need to understand and evaluate. Each point is illustrated by use of examples from the twenty-seven case studies included in Part II for more detailed analysis. The reader is therefore able to turn to the case to see how each point discussed falls into the broader context of the entire problem.

From these notes each major topic area is provided with a checklist both for the assessment of the particular case and as a reference guide for future business or case problems.

Included with these point by point assessments are the key management techniques necessary for a full understanding of the issues involved, and which will vary in relevance according to the case studied, but are again included for broader reference reasons. These include:

(a) strategic analytical techniques;
(b) forecasting methods;
(c) planning tools;
(d) financial analysis;
(e) personnel analysis.

Chapters 4 and 5 continue through a standard approach to the setting of objectives and how these criteria can be used to develop action planning, and the various pay-offs that exist between the various elements of the plan, for example:

(a) product;
(b) price;
(c) promotion;
(d) place.

The key options are included for reference and to promote re-evaluation of the final solution as to whether the optimum has been achieved within the constraints of that particular case.

Chapter 6 concludes Part I, with presentation guidelines – what issues need to be considered in case study presentation and how a structured approach can provide a framework within which specific case studies can be developed.

Part II provides twenty-seven case studies which illustrate different aspects of the development of strategic and marketing planning. They have been designed to cover the main issues confronting the potential marketing or commercial manager. Topics include:

(a) consumer, industrial, service companies;
(b) small and large businesses;
(c) strategic (long-term broad issues) and tactical (price, promotion etc.) questions;
(d) implementation (resource allocation, timing, personnel).

The cases are broadly divided into three: analysis, alternatives and implementation reflecting their emphasis. However, the author is only too aware that cases can be used to illustrate a wide number of specific points and this division serves only to indicate the general direction of the material and should not be seen as prescriptive.

The book is designed as a teaching text for the undergraduate, postgraduate and practitioner wishing to improve their understanding or to maintain as a reference guide to the development and implementation of marketing techniques to a wide range of problems.

Finally, a warning. A recipe book slavishly followed never produces a great chef; and too much reliance on a standard format will never allow the individuality of solution often essential to produce the novel and innovative approach which will carry off the prizes.

Chapter 2

THE DEVELOPMENT OF AN ANALYTICAL SYSTEM

INTRODUCTION

For convenience the task of the case study analyst can be divided into a series of discrete steps to create a logical progression of activities:

Environmental analysis
Objectives
Alternative actions
Evaluating alternatives
Implementing

It should, however, be remembered that no issue can be dealt with in total isolation; each factor will interact to a greater or lesser extent with another, and appreciating the nature of the interaction is part of the skill required to handle effectively the often significant amounts of data and large number of factors involved in a complex case. Different individuals will approach the definition of a coherent plan in various ways, and understanding that there is no 'correct' plan or 'correct' system is an important part of the learning process. What the manager or the student should be aiming to achieve is consistency – that the final plan developed is logical and realistic within the bounds of the material provided.

The evolution of an action plan from the initial document is, in consequence, very similar to one of those games based on numerous pieces of differently shaped plastic which used to accompany superior Christmas crackers. All the pieces need to fit together to produce a coherent final shape – there may be more than one way of achieving the solution, but all the pieces must fit together.

ANALYSING THE ENVIRONMENT

Any organization will operate under a series of constraints. These are factors which will tend to determine the extent to which certain actions or certain directions can be followed. These constraining factors include the following.

1. The 'macro-environment' – government legislation, changes in the age and family structure of the population, communication, and so on.
2. The competitive environment – involving the current and future actions of competitors in the market.
3. The internal or 'resource' environment – the financial, production, product, and personnel factors within the company.

UNDERSTANDING LIKELY FUTURE CHANGE

The initial exercise of analysing the environment is a historical one. It tells the individual what has occurred in the past. For the development of an effective plan it is clearly important that the lessons of the past can be used to determine future trends and developments effectively.

To isolate the underlying trends and suggest possible successful approaches, a number of techniques have been developed to help the analyst. These include:

1. *Qualitative methods* that deal in concepts and likely outcomes of particular changes in the environment. These include competitive analysis, and techniques such as the PLC or product life-cycle.
2. *Quantitative methods* which include models that attempt to provide detailed figures for future planning rather than the general indications provided by the qualitative systems.

ADDITIONAL INFORMATION REQUIREMENTS

All decisions have to be taken without *all* the necessary information that should ideally be provided. Shortages of information will require one of two reactions. First, there will be the occasion where assumptions must be made; assumptions on the level of cost, on the effectiveness of distribution systems and the like. The problem with assumptions, of course, is that they may be unreasonable and unrealistic for particular industrial sectors or particular product areas. When dealing with a specific industry experience will often help to make assumptions far more realistic in comparison with those made by newcomers without the required level of knowledge. As stated in Chapter 1, much of the value in case study analysis is to be found in the exploration of new problem areas, and the solutions are often less important than the logical and systematic way in which the case is handled.

Identification of key assumptions will, however, be of considerable importance in the preparation of the final plan – this will enable others who have not taken part in the discussion or thought processes leading to the conclusions to understand the bricks out of which the final building was constructed

Where the assumptions are *absolutely crucial* to the success or otherwise of the plan the need to acquire additional information will need to be built into the final document. Managers are, however, employed to manage and the environment of the case study is not one that should encourage lack of proposed action because of data shortages.

CREATION OF OBJECTIVES

From an understanding of the environment in which the organization is operating objectives for future development can be defined. These will naturally vary from situation to situation, and from organization to organization.

There are four common features of successful objectives. They are consistent with both the external and internal environmental analysis; do not conflict with each other; and are achievable with the resources available. They will also provide specific action standards against which possible alternative channels of action can be judged.

Though the confines of the case study tend to encourage unreality in that the student is dealing with 'Monopoly money', the insistence on setting objectives that meet the above criteria helps to ensure that real problems are met with realistic solutions.

Setting objectives will also ensure that the interaction between the short and long term is fully understood – short-term objectives should always lead into, and be consistent with, the long-term direction of the organization. Case studies are a valuable method of emphasizing the need for objectives that are consistent over time and for short- and medium-term objectives to act as building blocks for the achievement of the long-term requirements.

Not all objectives will be of equal importance – part of the judgement involved in the establishment of objectives will be in ranking the factors defined, both in the short, medium and long term, in order to determine the best of the proposed alternative action plans.

The importance of various objectives will also vary over time and will depend on the approach adopted by the organization to achieve its long-term objectives. Taking the analogy of the Christmas puzzle further, the achievement of the final objectives can be produced by a variety of short and medium-term objectives. For example, a long-term market share objective can be achieved by:

(a) steady growth over the time period; or
(b) rapid initial growth followed by a period of stabilization; or
(c) slow initial growth followed by rapid gains.

ANALYSING ALTERNATIVE ACTION PATHS

Once the objectives have been defined the possible avenues of implementation can be explored. No action path will ever be ideal; comparing alternatives will demand an understanding of both the level of risk inherent in each of them, and how to weigh the acceptability of different action paths with the required objectives.

Short-term action will influence both the medium and long term; certain actions in the short term will make later developments either easier or more difficult. The development of branching action paths or decision trees will show these influences and how the final objectives can be attained.

IMPLEMENTATION

The implementation of the proposed action plan can again be approached in a structured fashion.

1. Segmentation. First, the plan will need to be translated into a statement of the exact nature of the customer or customer type that the organization is attempting to reach.
2. Product/physical/process decisions. Second, the product or service policy needed to service effectively the particular group chosen.
3. Distribution channels. The organization will then have to decide on how the operation will be supported in the market. This will require the definition of distribution channels and the necessary stockholding to service the particular channels.
4. Organizational issues. The way in which the company implements its plans will have a number of organizational implications needing attention; this will be especially important for service-based organizations.
5. Promotion (including salesforce). The way in which the organization is planning to promote its products will then need attention.
6. Price. The pricing structure for the product or service will have to be evaluated in the light of the financial demands, the level of promotion and the nature of the distribution system. The relationship of price to volume and the way in which important small changes in volume will affect total profit (marginal profitability) will often have significant effects on the way in which the marketing mix will be optimized.

Because of the large number of interacting factors involved in the implementation phase there will clearly be a number of pay-offs with one factor changing as a result of decision-taking in another area; changes in price, for example, being offset with changes in promotional activity. The process of optimization yields a number of options which should be considered in the completion of the final action plan.

All good planning should include in outline a suggestion as to what should be done if the original plan is unsuccessful. The creation of this fallback plan should be limited to the key issues and decisions that would need to be taken – together with the main criteria and time scale over which the initial plan will be judged to have succeeded or failed.

BUDGETING AND TARGETING

Once the plan has been finalized the budgets and revenue analysis will need to be completed. The degree of complexity will naturally depend on the amount of financial data provided, but even the roughest of projections will be obtainable from the majority of cases to show what effect the proposed plan will have on total revenues. For complex projects an understanding of the way in which the project will be completed and the interaction of various preliminary steps via network and critical path analysis will be a valuable addition to the completion of the final plan.

PRESENTING AND WRITING UP MATERIAL

Writing up the material is one of the keys to successful management. The crucial test is to show the reader that the conclusions are logical and consistent with the available material, and that the final plan shows a complete and realistic grasp of the problem posed by the particular case.

A useful mnemonic for judging case study presentation (and business plans generally) is SURE. Does the plan meet the following criteria?

1. Soundly based – is it likely to achieve long-term success or is it potentially fragile?
2. Understanding – does the plan show an understanding of the environment, both internal and external?
3. Realistic – are the objectives attainable with the resources and the marketing mix proposed?
4. Experience – are those most concerned in the plan's implementation sufficiently experienced to carry it forward?

Chapter 3

SITUATION ANALYSIS

DEFINING CURRENT COMPANY POSITION

Introduction

The first stage in any analysis is to identify *where* the organization is and *what* it is currently achieving. An understanding of the current position enables the individual to identify key strengths (S) and weaknesses (W) in the way in which the organization is operating, and from that to identify possible future lines of action or opportunities (O) that are open to it as well being aware of what likely constraints or threats (T) may appear to prevent the organization developing in a particular direction.

This method of analysis, called SWOT, is central to the theme of the initial analysis process discussed in this book. If carried through rigorously it will ensure that:

(a) all key elements of the environment that affect the organization will have been identified and their implications for future development understood;
(b) should there be important gaps in the information provided within the documentation, that necessary assumptions are made and recorded (the importance of assumptions is further underlined in Ch. 6, part IV);
(c) that targets for future development will be objectively based;
(d) a realistic time horizon is established over which the proposed plan can be achieved.

An important first stage

It is clear that organizations operating in different market areas will face very different problems; but this may be no less true of companies operating in what superficially appears the same market environment. To enable any analysis to proceed two issues will need to be clarified.

First, the exact market in which the company is operating (rather than the market that it thinks it is operating in). A useful technique to help this analysis is to consider the effects of raising or lowering price on the level of demand and the likely customers who will be reached. This will clarify who are the *real* rather than perceived competitors for the product or service the organization is providing.

The Club Méditerranée case (Case 4) illustrates the need to define the exact market in which the firm is operating. Is it providing a holiday camp? a sophisticated holiday? The definition of exactly what Club Med is providing is central to the issue of how it should proceed to expand its market share.

Second, the way in which the organization will be subdivided for the purposes of analysis. These will be different types of plan for the various levels within an organization, especially a complex one; one can define, for example, in a large multi-business firm at least four levels of planning each with different types of perspective.

Level	Decision type
Main board	Long-range vision
	Broad investment decisions
Subsidiary board	Medium term
	More detailed investment decisions
Senior management	Short-range concepts
	Detailed investment decisions
Departmental management	Short-term implementation

Nestlé (Case 12) shows clearly that in a diverse business any full understanding of the best marketing policy will require each section to be considered in isolation as an individual profit centre, or strategic business unit (SBU), and the interrelationship of these SBUs to corporate objectives to be taken fully into account.

Where it is possible, therefore, the division of an organization into component parts servicing distinctive areas of the market will be a prerequisite of the development of an overall marketing plan. It will, however, be important always to remember the interrelationships particularly where shared production facilities often make it difficult to identify the true underlying cost trends fully. The way in which the SBU is identified will therefore be one of the assumptions that the individual carrying out the analysis will need to make. Where the company has a complex structure with different divisions operating in distinct market segments the development of an integrated plan will be a complicated process, straying into the area of corporate strategy, which is largely outside the scope of this book. For each individual profit centre or SBU there will be a series of appropriate options, which should be the first that need to be considered for action. Should the central corporation then take the view that these are inappropriate for some other reason the initial analysis will still be the appropriate market response for a particular product group or business unit.

The initial anlaysis of the Technochem case (Case 9) should concentrate on what is the most appropriate marketing policy for the three separate divisions. Once this is complete the corporate strategy can be decided upon.

The nature of the environment

There are several methods by which the environment in which the organization operates can be defined. The simplest is to divide it into external and internal elements; more recently the tendency has been to separate out three factors – the macro-environment, which consists of overall trends within the overall market in which the firm is established, the task environment concerning the specific sector in which the firm is operating, and the resource environment relating to the assets which the organization possesses to progress with actions in the market. One can further subdivide these categories into a series of factors for ease of analysis.

1. The main features of the external environment – PESTG (politics, economics, social, technological, geography).
2. The competitive environment (how the organization is placed in relation to the competition).
3. The financial resource environment (what financial and other material resources including manufacturing resource are presently available and what are their current trends).
4. The personnel and production resource environment (skills, numbers, structure).
5. The product or service environment (what resources the company has available in products or services and what are their current trends in relation to the market).

Item 5 differs from the others in that it needs to be analysed in a slightly different way from the other factors, because products at different stages of development will demand different aproaches, and therefore an understanding of the strategic implications of each product development stage is important to determine effective action.

It must also be remembered that though these factors are dealt with apparently in isolation, each element will relate to all the others to a greater or lesser extent.

THE IMPORTANCE OF A STRUCTURED APPROACH

As has been stated earlier, not all the items will be relevant to all the case studies, but dealing with them in a structured fashion will ensure that factors are not missed, and will also highlight the areas of information shortage on which assumptions will need to be made. Sections I to V below each start with a checklist of factors which may be relevant in particular cases, and the most important factors are then analysed in relation to a specific case study included in the book to illustrate further the way in which a structured approach can be developed, the importance of the issue and how it interrelates to other planning issues.

In addition to developing an understanding of the underlying strengths, weaknesses, opportunities and threats posed by the current position of the organization, a structured approach will also determine those threats that cannot be easily *controlled*. This is because uncontrollable threats introduce a substantial amount of uncertainty into any planning process. They are also those factors about which the greatest number of assumptions will have to be made (see Ch. 6, part IV).

SECTION I: MACRO-ENVIRONMENTAL FACTORS

Political

Tax legislation
Attitude towards credit
Monopoly legislation
Regional incentives
Attitude towards education/health/unemployment expenditure
Capital transfer controls/tariff barriers
Promotion controls
Factory/consumer health controls
Attitudes towards foreign investment/control
Patent/copyright law
Legislation and control on distribution
Fiscal climate (depreciation rules, investment allowances)
Labour laws

Economic

Inflation rates
Monetary policy
Unemployment trends
Taxation emphasis
Growth trends
Trends in disposable income
Price and wage controls
Infrastructure investment: road/rail/air
Costs of borrowing
Currency stability

Social

Population age structure
Family sizes
Religion
Birth rates
Education levels
Consumer activism
Life-styles
Male/female roles
Savings ratio
Public holidays/gifting
Cultural heterogeneity
Environmental pressures

Technological

Government investment and focus
Speed of change
Technology transfer

Geographic

Population levels and concentration
Climate
Topography

Examples of key issues in macro-environmental analysis are discussed below (these include those factors that tend to be *most important*). It should be remembered that each case will vary as to the emphasis that will be placed on each particular factor.

Government investment in social infrastructure

One of the most important influences the political environment can have on the activities of companies, particularly those in the service sector, is the government's commitment or otherwise to social spending.

Strength: Service or product currently provided fits well with government expenditure proposals.
Weakness: Service or product at odds with trends in government expenditure.
Opportunity: To develop new services or products to meet changing government funding.

Threats: Rapid changes in government funding or changes in government expenditure allocation.

The Barnet Publications case (Case 26) highlights the importance of the level of government funding on the development of strategy as the number of people in higher education will have a fundamental effect on the level of future sales.

Government legislation

For large companies the likely effects of anti-monopoly action will be an important issue in the environmental horizon; safety and hygiene legislation may also have a very important bearing on future developmental plans.

Strength: Product range unlikely to be affected by government policy.
Weakness: Product range considerably influenced by government action.
Opportunity: To move into less problematic areas.
Threat: Sudden change in the external environment caused by government legislation that the company cannot control.

The Twydale case (Case 1) shows that the government can affect the business in a number of ways – especially by changes in the health regulations surrounding the issue of irradiation.

Tariff barriers

For the international company the nature and extent of tariff barriers and the control on capital transfer may form one of the central elements in the development of an investment strategy.

Strength: Majority of company's and/or subsidiaries' products not affected by tariff barriers or capital transfer.
Weakness: Company's and/or subsidiaries' products substantially affected by tariff barriers and capital transfer.
Opportunity: To develop into geographic or product areas less affected by tariff and/or capital transfer problems.
Threats: The imposition of stiffer tariff barriers and/or exchange control in some or all of the countries in which the organization operates.

The Sansui case (Case 2) illustrates the importance of considering tariff barriers and exchange control issues in the development of an international production and marketing strategy. The attitude of the United States towards the importation of silicon chips must be closely considered as part of the evolving business plan.

Costs of borrowing

For many companies changes in the cost of borrowing will be one of the most immediate and influential factors on the development of strategy.

Strengths:	Low borrowing/high equity ratio or borrowings designated in low-cost currencies.
Weakness:	High exposure to rising interest rates.
Opportunity:	Reduce borrowings by changing nature of capitalization.
Threat:	Lenders taking action against the company to recover high levels of indebtedness.

The Airfix case (Case 10) underlines the problems of high levels of gearing in periods of high bank rates. This issue also relates to financial ratios (see Section III below).

Disposable income

Growing levels of disposable income will have a significant effect on demand patterns, especially for luxury, sophisticated or unusual products, while reducing demand for staples such as basic foodstuffs.

Strength:	Product and/or service developed to meet changes in disposable income, or product that meets underlying and unchanging consumer requirements.
Weakness:	Basic product/service.
Opportunity:	To move into higher value products.
Threat:	Rapidly increasing disposable income leading to uncontrolled changes in demand.

The problem faced by Yamazka (Case 17) is initially to define which sector of the camera market on which to concentrate. As the purchase of cameras is closely tied to the levels of disposable income in the population, an understanding of the trends in this area will be important in defining realistic strategies.

Consumer activism

An understanding of developing consumer attitudes will often be important in determining strategic options for companies selling consumer goods.

Strength:	Product/service allied with consumer demands.
Weakness:	Product/service against consumer pressure group/trends.
Opportunity:	To change or introduce products to meet pressure group demands.
Threats:	Legislation preventing particular actions/intermediaries no longer stocking products/public relations problems.

The Adnams case (Case 14) illustrates the position of a company fortunate enough to take advantage of consumer activism – in this case the movement towards 'real' ale, which will affect the choice of product and choice of distribution methods in future planning.

Life-styles

For many products, especially those with a fashion content, the changing life-style patterns in the community will be important in defining the segment upon which the company should be attempting to concentrate.

Strength: Clearly definable life-style pattern relevant to company products/ services.
Weakness: Life-style patterns not relevant to company products/services.
Opportunity: To meet changing life-style patterns with new or modified products/ services.
Threat: Inability to meet rapidly changing life-style patterns.

The Fantsis case (Case 23) shows how important an understanding of life-styles can be in determining the market segment and the type of promotional investment that should be made.

Birth rates

For certain companies, particularly those supplying the education market, baby food, and other child products or services, trends in birth rates will often have important consequences.

Strength: Product range largely unaffected by changes in birth rates.
Weakness: Product/service adversely affected by birth rate.
Opportunity: To take advantage of changing age structures.
Threat: Dramatic change in market demand.

The changing nature of the population age structure has important implications for Transit (Case 5) as to how it should develop a future effective strategy.

Inflation/deflation

Environments will show two distinct general price trends; one which relates to the economy as a whole and the other specific to an industrial sector (many electrical goods, for example, have shown price reduction in both absolute and real terms, allowing for inflation, over the last ten years).

Strength: The ability to cope effectively with the demands of the general pricing environment.
Weakness: The inability to reduce or increase price sufficiently to compete.
Opportunity: To improve profitability by raising price/improving market share by holding price below general market trends/moving into areas with less price competition and more price stability.
Threats: Government price control/cash-flow problems caused by companies unable to meet payments.

The Technochem case (Case 9) shows the importance of understanding price trends for effective strategic analysis. In the electronic instrument division the need to buy all components from other manufacturers meant that the company was unable to match the price competitiveness of the integrated manufacturers in a market in which real prices continued to drop.

Technological speed of change

Where rapid technological change is taking place the company will need to be aware of the implications of continuing investment in new equipment and new products and the changes likely to occur. This also has obvious implications for the forecasting methods the firm adopts (see Chapter 4).

Strength:　　　High degree of technological expertise.
Weakness:　　Lack of ability to cope with technological change.
Opportunity:　To expand investment in technology to gain competitive advantage.
Threat:　　　　Faster and more effective handling of technology to gain competitive advantage.

The Prestel case (Case 7) illustrates the need for any organization operating in technical environments to be continually aware of the implications of rapid changes in technology on the current product or service.

Government investment in technology

Support for particular areas of technological development may be important in determining future direction.

Strength:　　　Product development designed to take advantage of government support for technology.
Weakness:　　Product development unable to take advantage of government support for technological development.
Opportunity:　Revise product development policy.
Threat:　　　　Competitors gaining technological edge through government-aided development work.

The Prestel case (Case 7) underlines the importance of government funding in technology for the progress of the company.

Climate

Climatic conditions will have an especially important role in many consumer goods markets.

Strength:　　　Product or service unaffected by climatic conditions.

Weakness: Product adversely affected by climate.
Opportunity: To provide added value with products/service that meet climatic conditions.
Threat: Loss of market share.

Part of the potential strength of the Gascofix product range (Case 13) is its ability to withstand working conditions which its competitors cannot, suggesting that a key element of the developing strategy should be to concentrate on these markets.

SECTION II: COMPETITIVE ANALYSIS

Throughout the major world markets the process of industrial concentration, the reduction in the number of firms competing in each sector, is an increasingly important factor in determining strategic direction. As a result, a detailed understanding of what the competition is currently achieving and likely trends, is essential for the planning process. With the growth of the service sector, additional factors such as the nature of the physical environment and the process by which competitive service is carried out will be increasingly important. Analysing the traditions and attitudes of management and employees will be important for understanding both the competition and the resources available to the company to develop.

Market position

Market size and growth
Market share
Distribution intermediaries
Nature of buyers

Capital investment requirements

Product

Quality
Width of range
Price position
Promotional policy
Packaging
Technical superiority
Uniqueness
Guarantees and servicing arrangements

Credit provision/leasing
Quality control
Level of investment in branding
Design
Distribution channels
Physical distribution

Substitutes

Possible entrants

Physical

Design of environment
Location

Process

Speed of service
Efficiency of service
Quality of service
Cost of providing service

Development

Research and development expenditure
Speed of product development
Acquisition or internal new product development
Sophistication

People (see Section IV below)

Information systems

Completeness
Usefulness
Accuracy

Financial (see Section III below)

Examples of key competitive factors and how they will be likely to influence
strategic development are considered below.

Customer base or nature of the buyers

The total number of customers and their relative importance can be vital to the way in which the company develops its strategy. Should one customer make up 70 per cent of a company's business it will naturally be more vulnerable than one whose largest customer provides only 5 per cent.

Strength: Wide customer base.
Weakness: Narrow customer base.
Opportunity: Broaden customer base.
Threats: Imposition of tight pricing constraints by major customers/effects on particular production lines.

In the Twydale case (Case 1) twelve customers supply 80 per cent of the total company business, and for certain product lines there is only one customer.

Market size and growth

The size of the company in relation to the market and the speed at which it is growing or declining will have important implications for the development of strategy. This is further discussed in relation to the resources the company has available to invest in particular markets, and is part of the PIMS study (see Section V below).

Strength: Strong position in growing or declining market.
Weakness: Poor position in growing market or, worse, a poor position in a declining market.
Opportunity: To maximize growth opportunities in expanding market or to maximize market share in declining sector.
Threats: Other entrants into the market in a growing sector or continuing speed of decline in market size.

The Nestlé case study (Case 12) clearly shows some of the issues confronting a company in a growing market sector. The pot noodle market expanded, numerous competitors entered the sector and the market then declined, forcing companies to withdraw.

Market share

The relationship between market share and market size will have important strategic implications. Those companies with high market shares in large markets will have the advantages of both *economies of scale* (as they will be able to produce product more cheaply) and of the *learning curve*, in that they have learnt to produce the goods more effectively, more rapidly and more cost effectively.

In consequence, market leaders in volume markets have a substantial edge over their competitors in terms of cost competitiveness.

Strength: Market leader in volume market or well established in fragmented market.
Weakness: Small market share in mass market.
Opportunity: To gain market leadership in mass market or to gain share in smaller, specialist sectors.
Threat: Loss of cost competitiveness in market increasingly dominated by large companies.

One of the issues on which Nestlé (Case 12) can build is the market leadership in coffee, powdered milk, in frozen food and snack products.

Capital investment levels

Different markets will exhibit different levels of capital investment. Some, such as the aircraft industry, will be very capital intensive; others will have low capital requirements, such as many companies offering financial services. The amount of capital investment required to compete effectively in a particular market will often be of particular importance in defining an effective strategy.

Strength: Ability to meet market investment requirements.
Weakness: Inability to meet market investment requirements.
Opportunity: To enter new markets with lower investment requirements.
Threat: Increasing investment requirements in current markets.

The Meon Packaging case (Case 15) illustrates the effect of high capital investment levels on a particular market sector, that of pallet construction, in which the company is operating.

Distribution channels

The nature of the distribution system and intermediaries that are used may be an extremely important part of current company operations. The implications of the type of distribution will vary according to the nature of the market and the stage of product development. It will be important to understand the nature of the distribution channels available to the organization to reach the target customers; what direct channels exist and what indirect opportunities there may be to use wholesalers and others to achieve distribution objectives.

Strength: Broadly based and flexible distribution system.
Weakness: Narrow and rigid distribution.
Opportunity: To widen market coverage and/or lower distribution cost.
Threat: Other companies competing more effectively in the chosen distribution channel.

The Doorlarm case (Case 16) illustrates the importance of the distribution policy on the proposed expansion of the firm.

Uniqueness

The degree to which the current product/service range is differentiated from the competition will have important implications for the way in which the organization progresses in the market. The ability to develop a product which can be patented will allow the firm to have a clear advantage over the competition for a substantial period. In contrast, the service company faces the problem that no service feature can be patented and that advantages over the competition are likely to be short-lived.

Strength: Products/services clearly differentiated from the competition.
Weakness: Similar product/service widely available from competition.
Opportunity: Create differentiated products/services.
Threat: Competitive entrants with unique and differentiated product/ service.

The Gascofix case (Case 13) shows that a company entering the market with a unique product clearly differentiated from the competition faces a different competitive position from a company with a fairly similar product in a crowded market; for example, compare the situation in the Nestlé case (Case 12). Gascofix was, however, unable to produce a product that was patentable – this is one of the development options available to Technochem (Case 9).

Servicing and guarantee system

Higher levels of servicing and an effective guarantee system can be important competitive weapons in a number of industrial and consumer markets. Naturally there is always a pay-off between servicing/guarantee levels and the level of investment in product quality (see below).

Strength: Well-organized and cost-effective servicing and guarantee system.
Weakness: Poorly organized/costly guarantee system.
Opportunity: To gain competitive advantage by redefinition of servicing arrangements.
Threats: New competitive designs/improved warranty arrangements.

The Technochem case (Case 9) illustrates the difficulties international companies, for example, may encounter within the markets in which they operate in seeking to achieve a product advantage over the competition.

Branding

The degree of investment competitors have made in building up a brand awareness amongst the consumer or intermediaries may have important consequences in defining future strategy.

Strength: Ability to match or surpass competitive investment where neces-
                 sary in the market.
Weakness: Unable to match competitive investment.
Opportunity: To enter new markets where branding investment is less highly
                 established.
Threat: Competitive expenditure in branding process leading to eventual
                 exclusion from current markets.

The Twydale case (Case 1) shows the importance of branding in defining some of
the opportunities open to the company when planning to compete in particular
sectors, especially that of the frozen further processed market.

Credit provision/leasing

Providing credit or making leasing facilities available will be particularly important
in many industrial sectors, where well-organized financing will often provide a
major competitive advantage.

Strength: Well-organized and competitive leasing arrangements.
Weakness: Poor and/or expensive leasing systems.
Opportunity: To gain competitive advantage through changing leasing adminis-
                 tration.
Threats: Changes in taxation/legislation on leasing.

The CupCo case (Case 19) shows how important leasing and credit provision
may be in certain industries – in this case, the drink vending sector – and how it can
be used to increase market share.

Product quality

Product quality will be one of the most important competitive advantages that the
company will need to consider when evaluating strategic directions, as the PIMS
study suggests (see Section V below).

Strength: Clear advantage in product quality over competition.
Weakness: Quality lower or the same as competition.
Opportunity: To improve quality.
Threat: New entrants coming into the market with higher quality product.

Product quality and how this will affect company objectives are part of the Clara
case (Case 21). One of the problems the company faces in taking over the Home
Foods organization is where the product range should continue to be positioned.

Price levels/elasticity

The degree of price competitiveness in the market sector will have a considerable bearing on the levels of investment required to remain price competitive, whether there is a close correlation between price and quality perceptions and how the pricing structure and eventual revenue to the firm fit in with the distribution system chosen.

Strength: Competitive price position in relation to market structure and segment requirements.

Weakness: Poor price position in relation to the market structure and segment requirements.

Opportunity: To improve market position and segment demand by changes in the pricing structure.

Threats: Loss of competitiveness through inadequate pricing or entry of cost-competitive company into the market.

The Cascade case (Case 27) shows how the price position chosen in the market will be directly affected by the competitive environment and the requirements of the chosen distribution system.

Packaging

For many consumer product companies the type of packaging chosen can have important competitive implications.

Strength: Cost-effective and well-designed packaging.

Weakness: Poorly designed/expensive packaging.

Opportunity: To improve market position by redefining the packaging.

Threat: Competitor gaining market share with innovative pack design.

The Airfix case (Case 10) shows that the failure to comprehend the importance of pack design can lead to a significant weakness in certain consumer sectors.

Physical distribution methods

The methods by which the company services its market will be a combination of the intermediaries employed and the exact type of physical distribution used. Changes in the type of physical distribution will not only affect cost, but also the company's competitiveness in the market.

Strength: Cost-effective physical distribution in the light of market requirements.

Weakness: Poorly constructed physical distribution support systems.

Opportunity: To improve competitiveness significantly through changes in the physical distribution system.

Threat: Improvement in physical distribution by a competitor, leading to eventual loss of market position.

The Technochem case (Case 9) shows how changes by competitors in the method by which they supply their markets can significantly reduce the competitiveness of specific products.

Design

For many companies the competitive issue of design will be especially important in two areas: the impact of the correct design as a means of promoting the product; and as an important means of reducing cost.

Strength: Product with highly cost-effective design.
Weakness: Product with poor and costly design.
Opportunity: To redesign to improve impact and/or reduce cost.
Threats: Reduced profitability/declining market share.

Design of product is a central part of the CupCo case (Case 19).

Promotional channels

The way in which the organization spreads its promotional expenditure will have important consequences as to the strategy that it can adopt. Thus, a consumer goods company will have to invest for a long period to build up brand awareness; an industrial company will need to build up a trained and professional salesforce. The important issue will be how closely the promotional expenditure structure meets market conditions.

Strength: Well-defined and consistent promotional policy related to market structure.
Weakness: Poorly defined and inconsistent policy.
Opportunity: To maximize on market by a well-organized promotional programme.
Threats: More efficient competitive activity/legislation.

The Fantsis case (Case 23) shows that the correct decision on which promotional channels (magazines, TV, radio) should be used will reflect the nature of the market and consumer.

Design of outlet

For companies in the service sector the design of outlets and their internal layout will be a vital factor in achieving profitable sales and repeat purchase.

Strength: Well-organized and up-to-date internal layout and design.
Weakness: Poor internal structure and dated layout.
Opportunity: To improve layout/refurbish.
Threat: Continuing loss of custom to better-equipped service providers.

The Axe case study (Case 25) underlines the problems posed by design in a service company, which become one of the major considerations of the development of a new strategic policy.

Location

The location of the outlet for a service provider will often have a prime influence on the nature of the strategy that can be developed.

Strength: Location ideal for market served.
Weakness: Poorly sited outlets.
Opportunity: Reorganize sites/change service provision.
Threat: New entrants into market.

Club Méditerranée (Case 4) with a wide range of locations faces problems in the UK market of relating location to service provided.

Substitutes

An important issue in the analysis of the competitive environment will be an understanding of the products or services which can act as substitutes. In many ways this will follow an accurate profile of the market in which the company is operating (see p. 14–15 above).

Strength: Few possible substitute products.
Weakness: Many possible substitute products.
Opportunity: To redefine products or services to reduce the threat of substitutes.
Threat: The introduction of other substitute products.

The Twydale case (Case 1) identifies clearly the problem of substitute products. Twydale is clearly not just operating in the turkey market – chicken products are clear substitutes. But are other convenience meal products, based on soya, substitutes or not?

Entrants

The ease with which the market can be entered by other competitors will have important implications as to the policies the company will need to adopt to maintain market share. The concept of barriers to entry, that is, the financial, legal, distribution and production problems a new company will need to overcome, will be particularly useful to define the problems the company is likely to encounter.

Strength: Established in a market with high barriers to entry.
Weakness: Market with low barriers to entry.
Opportunity: To increase barriers to entry in a particular market sector.
Threat: Large competitor entering the market.

The CupCo case (Case 19) illustrates the actions a company will need to take in a market where the barriers to entry are particularly low, and the continuing problems they pose.

Speed and effectiveness of service

For service companies speed of service may be one of the means of improving both customer satisfaction and profitability.

Strength: A service provided more rapidly than the competition.
Weakness: Slow service provision.
Opportunity: To invest in technology, pre-packaging or training to improve speed of service provision.
Threat: Competitive investment in improving speed of service provision.

Benjamin's (Case 18) faces threats from competitors in other towns providing faster service and will need to take account of these for future strategic development.

Research and development

The current policy towards research and development will often have important implications for long-term strategy.

Strength: High research and development expenditure in relation to the competition.
Weakness: Low or declining investment in research and development.
Opportunity: Expansion in research and development in profitable areas.
Threat: External competition.

Technochem (Case 9) illustrates the importance of competitive levels of research and development expenditure in the long-term development of the firm.

Speed of new product introduction

The effectiveness of a competitor will often be determined not only by the total expenditure on research and development, but also the speed at which innovation is brought to the market place.

Strength: Rapid rates of new product introduction.
Weakness: Failure to introduce new products into the market effectively.
Opportunity: Improve new product development performance or purchase companies with new product concepts.
Threat: Declining competitiveness because of lack of innovative capacity.

The Meon case (Case 15) shows the problems a rapid rate of competitive product introduction can cause a small industrial company and how it will need to react to the competitive environment.

Completeness of information systems

The nature and structure of the information the firm has available will be an important competitive issue, enabling it to understand the market more effectively than its rivals.

Strength: Well-organized and integrated information system.
Weakness: Inability to use information from the market effectively.
Opportunity: Improve competitiveness by more comprehensive information system.
Threat: Competitors responding more rapidly to market conditions.

The accurate definition of the trends occurring in the use of facilities is an important aspect of the management of the Northmouth Hospital Group (Case 8).

SECTION III: FINANCIAL AND PRODUCTION RESOURCES

Shareholders

Goals
Ease of raising finance
Price/earnings ratio
Dividends

Profitability ratios

Gross margin on sales
Net margin
Return on capital employed

Liquidity

Gearing ratio
Current ratio
Working capital ratio
Interest cover
Quick ratio
Cash flow

Activity ratios

Stock turnover
Creditors period
Debtors period

Fixed costs

Production

Nature of suppliers
Equipment sophistication
Production capacity
Production expertise
Product expertise (learning curve)
Inventory control
Raw material availability
Component costs

Goals of shareholders/lenders

The nature and goals of both the external shareholders and the current lenders of finance to the company are an important issue to determine company strategies and new directions.

Strength: Widely spread shareholding/lending with same goals as the company.
Weakness: Concentrated shareholding/lending at odds with company objectives.
Opportunities: To widen shareholding and/or source of finance.
Threats: Take-over or liquidation.

   The Barnet Publications case study (Case 26) illustrates some of these points. The attitudes of the major shareholders towards the way in which the group should develop will have an important bearing on the development of strategy.

ROCE *(return on capital employed)*

This is one of the key financial ratios, providing a measure of the underlying profitability and health of the business. Returns on capital employed are affected by investment in research and development and other factors, which need to be considered in turn, but a rule of thumb is that a 20 per cent ROCE is fair, anything above is good.

$$\text{ROCE} = \frac{\text{Profits after taxes}}{\text{Total assets}}$$

Strength: High rates of ROCE.
Weakness: Low rates of ROCE.
Opportunity: Improvement in ROCE from changed pattern of activity.
Threat: Action from shareholders/outsiders if ROCE remains low (take-over, etc.).

The Airfix case study (Case 10) illustrates the importance of ROCE. In the early days ROCE was very high, but by 1978/9 it had fallen to 6.5 per cent.

Margin on sales, or gross contribution

The margin on sales will vary from industry to industry and the key issues will be to compare if possible the rate of margin achieved by the company with that of its competitors. This ratio, otherwise known as the gross contribution level, is a particularly important factor when the company is selling a multiplicity of products with a high level of fixed overhead, in which case the net profit will be determined by the allocation of those overheads, which may lead to a fallacious understanding of the true contribution of various product groups to profit.

$$\text{Margin on sales} = \frac{\text{Profit after tax (VAT or sales tax)}}{\text{Total sales}}$$

Strength: Higher rates than competitors.
Weakness: Lower rates than competitors.
Opportunity: Change in product mix/pricing structure.
Threat: Inability to attract investment.

The Axe case study (Case 25) illustrates this point. When one compares the Axe margins with those of nearby competitors such as Sainsbury's, Makro and Safeway it can be seen that Axe is achieving a far poorer mix of sales of particular product lines.

Gearing ratio

The gearing ratio refers to the relationship of long-term or equity finance to short-term debt such as bank borrowings.

$$\text{Gearing ratio} = \frac{\text{Debt}}{\text{Total stockholders' equity}}$$

The gearing ratio reflects the vulnerability of the company to both changes in interest rates and reduction in cash flow. The acceptable level of gearing will vary from industry to industry but, overall, 40 per cent is often regarded as the highest continuing acceptable level.

Strength: Low levels of external debt.
Weakness: High and rising levels of debt.
Opportunity: To refinance with equity rather than debt.
Threats: Rising interest rates/sudden reduction in cash flow.

Meon (Case 15) is an example of a company with enormous problems caused by high levels of bank borrowings.

Cash flow

Whether the organization is generating enough cash quickly enough to fund its development will be an important issue especially for small companies with limited resources.

Strength: Positive cash flow.
Weakness: Prolonged periods of negative cash flow.
Opportunities: Changing product/distribution/pricing/credit procedure to ensure improved cash flow.
Threat: Financial failure.

Managing cash flow is of maximum importance in the Gascofix case (Case 13), and will have important implications for the distribution and pricing policy the company follows.

Stock turnover

The ratio of stock to total turnover reveals how quickly the organization manages to sell its stockholding during the year.

$$\text{Stock turnover} = \frac{\text{Sales}}{\text{Stock}}$$

Different industrial sectors operate on different stock turnover ratios but, generally, the higher the ratio the more efficient the organization is at controlling inventory levels and concentating on products that sell rapidly.

Strength: Rapid stock turn.
Weakness: Poor stock turn in relation to the industry.
Opportunity: Improve stock turn by changing product mix/improving stock control.
Threat: Reduced competitiveness.

Stock turn issues are particularly important in the Barnet Publications case (Case 26) as the very high stock levels of large numbers of titles in the publisher's list are one of the underlying problems of the organization.

Length of credit given

The length of credit given will affect the organization's cash flow – long periods of credit with low sales margins being of most concern.

$$\text{Length of credit given (days)} = \frac{\text{Debtors}}{\text{Total sales} \div 365}$$

Strength: Short credit period.
Weakness: Long credit period.

Opportunity: Change customer base or improve credit control.
Threat: Cash-flow problems if interest rates or trade conditions worsen.

The long credit period allowed by Doorlarm (Case 16) to many of its customers was a problem that needed to be resolved in future marketing plans.

Length of credit taken

The length of credit taken will also affect the cash flow – the longer the period of credit taken the greater the ability of the company to sell the goods before having to pay suppliers for them.

$$\text{Length of credit taken (days)} = \frac{\text{Total sales}}{\text{Creditors}}$$

Strength: Long credit period.
Weakness: Short credit period (especially when length of credit given is long).
Opportunity: To change suppliers to improve credit/order in larger quantities.
Threat: Cash-flow problems if sales turn down.

The Axe case (Case 25) illustrates some of the problems that the changing credit period involved in an altered customer base can cause.

Current ratio

The ability of the firm to meet its debts can be determined by the current ratio which is calculated by:

$$\text{Current ratio} = \frac{\text{Current assets}}{\text{Current liabilities}}$$

Current ratios below 1 are a sign of liquidity problems.

Strength: High current ratio.
Weakness: Low current ratio.
Opportunity: To improve liquidity by reducing liabilities.
Threat: Eventual severe liquidity problems.

The Western Hotel case (Case 11) shows the implications of steadily worsening liquidity ratios.

Fixed costs

The level of fixed costs will have an important role in determining the break-even point where the company will start to make a profit, calculated by the formula:

$$\frac{\text{Fixed costs}}{\text{Gross contribution per unit}}$$

What the company will need to consider as fixed will vary from case to case – in some instances wages can effectively be considered a fixed cost.

Strength: Low fixed costs.
Weakness: High fixed costs.
Opportunity: Reduce fixed costs to lower the break-even point.
Threat: Reduction in volumes by external factors that lead to significant reduction in profitability.

The Transit case (Case 5) illustrates the point at which a high level of fixed costs has a substantial effect on the development of strategy.

Relations with suppliers

How the company manufactures and how it maintains its relations with its suppliers are of considerable importance in the definition of future strategy.

Strength: Well-established and favourable relationships with suppliers.
Weakness: Poorly established and/or unfavourable relationships with suppliers/substantial fluctuations in raw material costs.
Opportunities: To establish new supplier links and/or production facilities.
Threats: New production processes/more efficient competitive production.

The Technochem case study (Case 9) illustrates the importance of the relationship between production and the suppliers.

Production expertise

The ability of the firm to produce a particular type of product will have an important influence on what can be achieved over the short term. The amount of expertise a firm has in a particular product or product field will have an effect on the production cost. This is the learning, or experience, curve effect, which leads to a steadily reducing unit product cost. This has an important role in forecasting competitive production costs (see Ch. 6, part IV).

Strength: High levels of production expertise and experience in specific market sector.
Weakness: Poor levels of production expertise for specific product.
Opportunity: To make products in line with production expertise.
Threat: More effective and expert production in competitive firms.

The Adnams case (Case 14) is an example of a company with specific manufacturing skills which will have an effect on the direction of the firm.

Manufacturing efficiency

Investment in manufacturing process will provide a substantial competitive edge which will be important in cost-competitive and volume industries.

Strength: High levels of manufacturing efficiency when compared with the competition.

Weakness: Poor levels of manufacturing efficiency or investment when compared with the competition.

Opportunity: To introduce improved manufacturing systems to improve profitability and product consistency.

Threat: Competitors with higher manufacturing efficiency producing a more cost-effective and satisfactory product.

The Technochem case (Case 9) illustrates the problem posed by the lack of manufacturing competitiveness within many areas of its product range.

Production capacity

The ability of the organization to meet the market demands effectively will have an effect on the strategy followed, as will the degree to which the company is prepared to consider third party manufacture or production under licence.

Strength: Sufficient production capacity to meet likely market demands.

Weakness: Limited production capacity for market demands.

Opportunities: To expand production to meet market demands/third party manufacture.

Threat: Increased competition due to failure to meet market demands.

The Fantsis case (Case 23) is an example of where third party manufacture may need to be considered to meet market demands.

Component costs

The degree to which a company is able to gain access to low-cost components or raw materials will have important consequences for the profitability of the products or services the company provides.

Strength: Low-cost components.

Weakness: High-cost components relative to competitive products.

Opportunity: To alter component sourcing or component type.

Threat: Diminished profitability from higher cost base.

The higher than industry average raw materials costs in the CupCo case (Case 19) are one of its weaknesses in relation to the competition.

SECTION IV: PERSONNEL RESOURCE

Staff

Management
Supervisory
Shopfloor
Salesforce
Turnover
Age

Style

Skills

Managerial
Technical
Market expertise
Salesforce
Training policy

Systems

Communication/control
Recruitment
Negotiation
Appraisal
Remuneration
Reporting

Structure

Departmental
Span of responsibility
Authority – central/decentral

Shared values

Management

The number of managers that a company has will be an important factor in determining whether it can carry through a particular strategic or marketing policy.

Strength: In-depth management for particular market policy.
Weakness: Poorly staffed management team for market policy.
Opportunity: Improve management pool either by training or recruitment.
Threat: Failure to manage change effectively.

The Airfix case (Case 10) is an example of a case in which there are clear weaknesses in the management team.

Salesforce

For companies depending on a high salesforce involvement the maintenance of a sufficiently large salesforce will be a vital ingredient in the successful implementation of market strategy.

Strength: Full salesforce team.
Weakness: Limited salesforce team.
Opportunity: To improve salesforce by training and/or recruitment.
Threat: Loss of market share because of inability to reach customers especially with technical products.

The Clara case (Case 21) illustrates the problems of the decline in salesforce numbers in implementing current and future policies.

Turnover

The degree to which the company loses employees will have an important effect on whether it can effectively implement complex tasks involving substantial skills and long-term contact with the market.

Strength: Well-established and long-serving workforce.
Weakness: Rapid turnover of personnel.
Opportunity: To improve working conditions for the workforce to lower turnover rates.
Threat: Steadily diminishing work performance due to high labour turnover.

Some of the problems facing Airfix (Case 10) can be seen to be caused by the high rate of labour turnover.

Style

The nature of the management philosophy operating through all the departments of the company will have an important bearing on the way in which implementation of strategy will be successfully or unsuccessfully achieved.

Strength: Management style in accordance with the previous experience of individuals.
Weakness: Management style in conflict with the individuals' previous experience and expectations.
Opportunity: To change management style, retrain or change employees.
Threat: Failure to implement changed strategy effectively.

The Zenith case (Case 22) is an example of largely conflicting management styles and the problems of implementing a changed strategy.

Market expertise

The skills that a management team can bring to bear on a particular market sector or problem area will be an essential ingredient in the effectiveness of a particular marketing policy.

Strength: Market expertise closely allied to current policy.
Weakness: Current policy not matched by management expertise.
Opportunity: To train or recruit individuals to improve knowledge of market sector.
Threat: Failure of plan due to inadequacies in market expertise.

The Meon case (Case 15) raises the important issue whether sufficient market expertise exists to handle effectively the market complications of the garden shed sector.

Communication/control systems

The ability of the department or the company to identify problem areas is a vital part of its ability to manage changing marketing policies.

Strength: An effective, wide-ranging control and communication system.
Weakness: Poorly structured and limited communication and control system.
Opportunity: To reorganize communication and control systems.
Threat: Failure to identify problems leading to poor performance or collapse.

The Transit case (Case 5) is symptomatic of a number of small businesses which fail to institute effective control and communication systems to identify problems.

Departmental/divisional structure

The complexity of the tasks the company is currently engaged in, or likely to become engaged in, will need to be reflected in its departmental structure so that authority is closely and effectively linked with responsibility and that the span of management remains fairly limited.

Strength: Departmental structure well designed in relation to task requirements.

Weakness: Departmental structure poorly designed in relation to task requirements.

Opportunity: To redesign organizational structure.

Threat: Failure to manage direction effectively.

The Sansui case (Case 2) is an example of a company with a poorly conceived management structure relating to its complex market activities.

Shared values

Whether the employees are in agreement with the aims of the organization will be central in determining the ease of implementation.

Strength: Common shared values throughout the organization.

Weakness: Disparate values throughout the organization.

Opportunity: To improve the level of shared values.

Threat: Internal conflict leading to substandard performance and achievement.

The Clara case (Case 21) illustrates some of the problems caused by divergent shared values within an organization.

SECTION V: PRODUCT RESOURCE ANALYSIS

There are a number of methods available to structure and identify strengths and weaknesses within the product portfolio of the firm.

Segmentation

Identifying the way in which the market is divided and matching the product to the respective segment compared with the competition are a basic first step to understanding the product portfolio.

Segmentation variables will vary according to the nature of the firm and the market serviced. For consumer goods the main subdivisions will be:

1. Demographic – age, sex, household size, location.
2. Economic – income, stage in family structure.
3. Psychographic – life-styles, attitudes, group influences.

For industrial products segmentation, subdivisions will concentrate on:

1. Size of organization.
2. Nature of buying process.

3. State of technological development.
4. Location.
5. Price sensitivity.
6. Type of activity.

BCG

The Boston Consulting Group portfolio analysis identifies four main subdivisions of products (or profit centres/SBUs) based on relative market shares and market growth.

1. Cash cows – products generating cash, which have high relative market shares and are established in slowly growing markets.
2. Dogs – products unlikely to be generating substantial positive cash flows due to the fact that they are in slowly growing markets with low relative market shares.
3. Stars – products generally with negative cash flows but with high relative market shares in rapidly growing markets.
4. Question marks – products also with generally negative cash flows but with low relative market shares in growing markets.

GEC

The General Electric portfolio defines products along the axes of market attractiveness and business position on a nine-grid basis. Products or SBUs with strong business positions in attractive markets will yield high returns on capital employed (ROCE). Those with medium positions will yield average returns and those with poor positions in relatively unattractive markets will yield poor returns on capital employed.

Business position and market growth

A further approach is to divide on a fifteen-grid square the products/SBUs on the basis of market growth and competitive position. Thus, products will be placed within one of five market development stages (development, growth, shake-out, maturity, decline) and one of three competitive or business positions (strong, average, weak). Products concentrated in the top left corner of the quadrant (market introduction stage/strong business position) will require concentration on growth, those in the mature market sectors will concentrate on profit.

Advantage/investment

Another available technique is to divide the product portfolio along the lines of the *ease of gaining competitive advantage* and the *investment requirements of the industry* with four main subdivisions:

1. Stalemate or commodity sectors, where the investment requirements are low and there are few ways to gain competitive advantage.
2. Volume markets, where the investment requirements are high but there are few ways of gaining competitive advantage.
3. Fragmented markets, where both the ease of gaining competitive advantage and the necessary investment are low.
4. Specialized markets, where the investment requirements are high and the ease of achieving competitive advantage is also increased.

All these analytical methods serve a purpose of defining the current product environment, and from that to determine strategic guidelines. There are two other approaches which also suggest strategic alternatives.

PIMS, profit impact on market strategy

This is a research programme based on an analysis of particular strategies and how they affect profitability. The findings, which mainly relate to consumer goods and are highly statistical in nature, need to be handled with caution.

The main conclusions are in line with the hypothesis put forward by the portfolio models:

1. That ROCE improves with:
   (a) increased market share;
   (b) improved product quality.
2. High product quality and high market share are to a degree interchangeable.
3. Research and development investment is most effective in strong market positions, where it should be increased, and least effective in declining markets or weak market positions, where product imitation is the most profitable route.
4. Companies with either poor market positions or lower-quality products should price keenly and reduce promotional expenditure.

Porter's competitive strategy concept

Porter considers that there are two basic types of competitive advantage, either low cost or differentiation, which can be applied across either broad or narrow targets. The conclusions reached are broadly similar to those of earlier commentators who saw the division into:

(a) market leadership;
(b) market followers/challengers;
(c) market specialists; and
(d) commodity manufacturers,

each of which had, as a result of their market position, particular market strategies that could be followed.

1. *Cost leadership* – low cost/broad target. The market leader route, achieving market domination by large economies of scale.
2. *Cost focus* – low cost/narrow target. The commodity producer route, achieving cost advantage in a narrow sector of the market.
3. *Differentiation* – product differentiation/broad target market. Specialization in particular market attributes.
4. *Differentiation focus* – product differentiation/narrow target. Producing specialized products for narrow target markets.

FUTURE TRENDS

Following the evaluation of the company's current position, the analyst must now examine the most likely changes during the future planning time period. Within the confines of case studies the information available will tend to be limited and the analyst will therefore be forced to make a series of assumptions about the future trends.

The most important issues will be those that may have a major impact on the firm especially factors which cannot be controlled. These include changes in such areas as the macro-environment, task environment and resource environment.

A distinction must be made between those evaluations which are qualitative – containing a varying degree of subjective assessment of the likely changes; and those which are quantitative – which involve some model relationship between the factors involved.

Macro-environmental factors

Political

Will future political/governmental/legal changes be important for the markets in which the firm will operate?

Changes in legislation, particularly in the health and hygiene area, will significantly affect Twydale (Case 1) and its future planning.

Economic

Will there be dramatic changes in economic circumstances that will affect the future activity of the firm?

Changes in the economic climate will have a substantial effect on the planning considerations of the Fantsis case (Case 23).

Social

Will the changes in the social environment be important for the future direction of the organization?

The way in which the population structure is changing will have important consequences for the decision of future development for the Western Hotel (Case 11).

Technology

Future changes in technology may have a very important impact on the planned direction for particular firms.

The rate and direction of technological development will be particularly important for Sansui (Case 2).

The majority of assessments concerning the macro-environment will be qualitative involving the subjective assessment of likely changes in the various factors. For the case study this will often involve a significant number of assumptions about future events. In many ways this reflects the real-world basis of case studies as many of the companies and organizations involved will have access to little more than the information already available in the case.

Task factors

Competitive direction

It will be important for the firm to be able to define the way in which competitors are likely to develop. This will involve an understanding of developments in the areas listed in Table 3.1.

To each category in Table 3.1 needs to be added the current investment policy – where the firm is recruiting, what patents have been filed, where production is being concentrated, what new plans have been made for production plants, purchase of new equipment, products currently in test market and speed of return on investment.

Table 3.1 The factors in competititive analysis

Resources	Manufacturing	Marketing	Finance	Management
Technical	Production expertise	Salesforce	Ratios	Key employees
Human	Equipment location	Distribution	Cash flow	Style
Funding	Sophistication	Promotion		Corporate plan
	Cumulative production	Product policy		Staff
	Production economies	Price		
		Market share		
		Market image		

Competitive reaction

How will the competitors react to particular market developments?

Much of the assessment of future competitive changes will also be qualitative though the use of the production or learning curve can be used to gain some sort of quantitative insight into the production costs of the competition.

Resource environment

The future progress of the resource environment can be analysed in a number of ways.

The use of the product life-cycle (PLC) provides a valuable qualitative method for defining future investment requirements, though it does suffer from a number of shortcomings.

Within the market the individual products or product groups will exhibit differing speeds of growth, decline and investment requirements. The earliest technique used to define this pattern was the product life-cycle or PLC. This suggests that products or product groups can follow paths independent of the market, with stages of introduction, growth, maturity and decline.

Each stage will have different marketing and financial requirements (Table 3.2). An understanding of the product trends in relation to the structure of the product life-cycle will help the analyst in defining possible investment requirements for the company in the short term.

It is clear from the review of the literature that the classic product life-cycle is far from the norm, with the market stabilizing and then declining after an initial period of rapid growth a fairly rare pattern of events. A more important investment analysis method is to consider the forward investment horizon in respect of the various factors that will adversely affect the product. Such a system is known as the product viability analysis and it concentrates on the problems that are likely to be encountered over the short, medium and long term (Table 3.3).

Quantitative methods are important in identifying changes in levels of sales activity, which is central to defining both the resource level required for future development and where resources should be allocated.

Table 3.2 Marketing and financial requirements at various stages of the PLC

	Introduction	Growth	Maturity	Decline
Sales				
Cash flow				
Distribution				
Type of buyers				
Promotion range				
Promotion				
Pricing				

Table 3.3   Product viability – planning horizons and product factors

Factor	Short-term	Medium-term	Long-term
Packaging			
Profitability			
Pricing			
Product quality			

Within the limitations of the data available in the case study only a few of the large number of quantitative techniques will be useful.

1. Straight line projection. Where the company has introduced a product with substantial benefits over the competition or entered a new market, straight line projections from the current level of activity may provide the best indication of *short-term* future demands.

   The introduction of a significantly new and improved product by Gascofix (Case 13) is an example of a company which in the early stages of its development could use straight line projections to define the short-term production requirements.

2. Moving annual totals. Where a number of years' data is available the use of moving annual totals will give some indication of likely future demand for a particular product or service.

   The sales experience of the Barnet company (Case 26) could be used to define the future demands for its titles in order to improve the company's planning.

   Where more information is provided more sophisticated quantitative models can be used to define likely future trends with greater accuracy.

   For example, the Northmouth Hospital (Case 8) could consider the causal relationship between the size of certain age groups in the local population and the increasing number and types of specific orthopaedic surgery.

Missing information – the need for assumptions

Once the case study data has been examined in order to evaluate the impact of likely future trends on the company's programme of action, there will, both in the case study and in the real-world environment of the manager, be substantial areas about which the analyst does not have sufficient information.

In most of these cases, assumptions will have to be made and specified, especially in the most important areas such as the external environment, and the way in which competitors are likely to react.

Missing information – the need for additional research

Where a lack of data will have a fundamental and far-reaching effect on the plans the company must make, and the level of risk inherent in taking a particular course of action without further information is unacceptable, there is a clearly defined need for additional research to fill the information gaps.

Within the confines of case study analysis the need for additional research should be extremely limited. Case studies exist to improve analytical and decision-making skills; the propensity of the student to put off action because of limited information must be rigorously challenged.

Chapter 4

CREATION OF OBJECTIVES

INTRODUCTION

The analysis of the environment in which the case study company is operating will clarify what the company has achieved, its position in relation to the market, what resources are available and what changes are likely to occur in the immediate future. Once this analysis is complete, the organization's future direction will need to be defined by the creation of objectives.

Setting objectives enables a company to:

(a) allocate resources more efficiently;
(b) supply management with a measure against which decisions and achievements can be judged;
(c) ensure consistency within the firm.

THE CRITERIA INVOLVED IN SETTING OBJECTIVES

Because of their special role in future development planning, there are certain criteria which must be applied to any exercise concerned with establishing objectives. These criteria are explained below.

1. *Specific and measurable.* Objectives need to be clearly stated in terms of measurable figures which can be used to determine the level of resources required to achieve them.
2. *Flexible.* The objective should be sufficiently flexible to be able to react to changes in the environment over the planning horizon.
3. *Attainable.* The objectives arrived at should be realistic in the light of the

resources available to the company and the external environment in which the company is operating.

4. *Consistent.* All the objectives should interrelate; areas of potential conflict should be minimized. The interrelationship of some specific factors should be closely considered for the development of an effective marketing plan.

(a) Short-run versus long-term profitability.

(b) Profit versus market share.

(c) Growth versus profit.

(d) Short-term payouts (dividends, wages) versus increased retained earnings.

In other case studies there will be other pay-offs for consideration, which will further complicate the setting of effective and consistent objectives.

The particular problems of Northmouth Hospital (Case 8) highlight the problems of ensuring consistency of objectives as the number of pay-offs deserving consideration are both numerous and ill-defined.

Consistency will need to be considered not only within the same time period, but also over the entire length of the plan.

5. *Acceptability.* The various groups employed within the company and the outside groups influenced by its activities will have different views about how attractive the objectives are. Some or all of the following groups will be involved, each with a different perspective:

(a) owners;

(b) shareholders;

(c) public;

(d) marketing;

(e) finance;

(f) production;

(g) sales;

(h) distribution;

(i) customers.

The acceptability of the new objectives in the Clara case (Case 21) is of particular importance to their effective implementation. Both the salesforce and the majority of current customers may find the probable new objectives unacceptable.

TIME SCALE AND DECISION CYCLES

The time scale over which realistic objectives can be set obviously varies from organization to organization and from industry to industry. The decision cycle is, however, central to the definition of the time scale.

Each industry has a particular decision cycle which can be defined as the length of time it takes to bring a new product into production from its initial inception. Short decision cycles are characteristic of fashion industries.

The speed at which Cascade (Case 27) can introduce new products is increased by the fact that it uses third party production.

Long decision cycles are found in industries with high levels of investment in research and development and manufacturing.

The length of time involved in Sansui (Case 2) effectively entering new areas of electronics manufacture would be substantial.

Though the length of the planning cycle varies, three main categories of time scale can be defined.

1. Long-term goals (for the typical company a three- to five-year horizon).
2. Intermediate goals (running from the end of short-term activity to the long term, say from the end of the current year to the end of year two).
3. Short-term goals (for the current year).

It is often useful to consider the long-term objectives first, and then to create short- and medium-term objectives which are related to these long-term goals, maintaining the maximum level of consistency.

KEY OBJECTIVES

The analyst will have to decide what are the central or key objectives for the particular problem under study. For the majority of purposes, Table 4.1. gives the most relevant of those that will need to be considered individually over the time horizon involved in the case. The objectives given in this table are most applicable for large organizations containing many profit centres or SBUs. Where a smaller company is considered a more detailed set of objectives might need to be drawn up. These would include factors such as those given in Table 4.2.

The more complex the list of objectives, the greater the problem in ensuring internal consistency and the less flexible the objectives will become. For the majority of companies, the list of objectives will need to lie between the two extremes.

Table 4.1   Key objectives/planning horizon for consideration

	Short term	Medium term	Long term
ROCE			
Gross contribution			
Cash flow			
Market share			
New product development/technology			
Productivity			
Employee relations			
Shareholders/owners			

Table 4.2 Objectives in the small firm

	Short term	Medium term	Long term
ROCE			
Margin on sales			
Market share			
Customers			
Geographic market			
Company reputation			
Product range			
Product quality			
Packaging			
Pricing levels			
Physical distribution			
Intermediaries			
Production efficiency			
Fixed costs			
Variable costs			
Suppliers			
R & D			
Promotion			
Management skills			
Salesforce skills			

ALTERNATIVE ACTION PATHS

A number of alternative action paths are available to the company, each having a number of broad implications.

1. Product abandonment.
2. Product maintenance or market consolidation.
3. Market penetration (current products, current markets).
4. Market development (current products, new markets).
5. Product development (new products, current markets).
6. Diversification (new products, new markets):
   (a) backward diversification (developments based on current production expertise or knowledge of intermediary activity);
   (b) forward diversification (developments based on current end-users or customers);
   (c) horizontal diversification (related products or services to current activities sold in current markets);
   (d) opportunity or conglomerate diversification (unrelated products or services to new markets).

In many instances the company or organization will follow a number of these paths simultaneously. This will be particularly true of large and complex companies with many divisions, profit centres or SBUs.

The Sansui case (Case 2) is an example of a company operating with many products in many markets. Each of the particular product groups faces a differing range of viable strategies.

Even within a single product group, or in a small company, a mixture of action paths may need to be considered. Therefore, it remains important that each major area of company operation should initially be considered in isolation to determine what would be most effective in that area before moving on to examine the overall position.

EVALUATING ALTERNATIVE ACTION PATHS

Defining in general terms the most effective action alternatives

The first stage of the process is to eliminate totally unsuitable alternatives. By considering each SBU or product group in relation to the company objectives, a ranking of alternative actions can be obtained ranging from the most suitable to the least suitable. This will supply a shortlist of the most acceptable alternative paths.

A chart such as that in Table 4.3. can be used to separate out the differing forces acting on each of the main divisions or SBUs.

Evaluating the risk inherent in each of the proposed action paths

Once the main realistic alternatives have emerged, the level of risk associated with each of the proposed action paths must be measured. The level of acceptable risk will vary from company to company, and will relate to the objectives which have been established. Rapidly changing objectives over the planning horizon will mean that the company will have to accept a higher degree of risk than one with conservative or little-changed objectives. The level of risk relates inevitably to the rate of return (however, this is measured in terms of the objectives of the company). High risks should relate to high rates of return and the pay-off between the two should be used to determine the appropriate action path.

Table 4.3 Divisional market forces summary chart

Division	Market growth	Market position	Market attraction	Market penet.	Market dev.	Product dev.	Divers.	Ab.	Main.
1									
2									
3									
4									
5									

The main risk components can be considered as follows.

1. Dramatic changes in the macro-environment. What are the possibilities of political, economic, social or technological factors changing in a dramatic way over the planning horizon? Forecasting trends will reduce the uncertainty but in volatile environments the risk element will be substantial.
2. Competitive advantage. What risks are there that the proposed action path will fail to gain competitive advantage?
3. Competitive reaction. What are the chances of the proposed action path producing an over-severe competitive reaction?
4. Failure of employees. Will the management/workforce be able to handle the proposed action path effectively, and what are the risks involved in the level of proposed achievement? Will the structure of the company adequately reflect the task requirement and will the skills and motivation of the workforce be sufficient to ensure its completion?
5. Shareholders/owners. What is the likelihood of the shareholders or owners reacting adversely to the proposed actions?
6. Time scale. What are the risks of the proposed actions failing to be completed within the available time scale? The way in which the various alternative action paths interact over time will be an important issue that can be explored with the use of decision trees.
7. Cannibalization. What are the risks of the proposed actions interfering with each other either within the company or inside the market?

Identifying the main action path and the fallback alternative

Once the risks have been identified, decisions can be made about the most effective path from the broad alternatives available. Once the preferred route has been established the second best action path can be identified as the fallback position, the path that should be considered if the initial direction of action fails.

Chapter 5

IMPLEMENTATION

FINALIZING THE MARKETING MIX

Certain marketing mix issues which relate to the chosen action path also require attention.

1. *Structure*. Does the current or proposed marketing mix structure meet the requirements of the action path – are new structures required?
2. *Staff*. Are there sufficient staff with an adequate level of skills to meet the line of proposed action? What are the requirements of the particular action plan?
3. *Systems*. How should staff be motivated, recruited and directed for the task in hand?
4. *Control systems*. Which areas of the external and internal environment need to be monitored to ensure that the plan is achieving its aims?
5. *Segmentation criteria*. Organizations will first have to determine the segment of the total market at which they are aiming to direct the marketing activity. The segmentation criteria will vary according to whether the market is based on a consumer product or service or an industrial product or service. They are those defined in Chapter 3, and repeated here.

For the consumer product/consumer service the most commonly used segmentation variables are:

- age
- sex
- location
- household size
- life-cycle stage
- socio-economic group
- life-style group

- religion
- culture

For the industrial product/industrial service the most commonly used segmentation variables are:

- size of industrial unit
- type of activity
- location
- type of technology utilized
- buying patterns
- price sensitivity

6. *Product/service.* The organization must next define the nature of the product or service that will effectively meet the demands of the particular segment. This includes issues of quality, size, range of products, packaging and guarantees. For the service company factors such as location, design and the way in which the service is carried out may also be important.

7. *Distribution.* How will the company reach the particular segment? This involves considering the different available distribution channels, stock levels, and physical distribution decisions such as method of transport and speed of delivery.

8. *Pricing.* Pricing levels will reflect the segmental/product/distribution decisions, the underlying cost structure of the company and the chosen action path.

9. *Promotion.* Promotional or communication decisions will involve evaluating both the available promotional channels (for example TV, radio, posters, personal selling, public relations) and total expenditure related to the segment/ product/distribution/pricing and action path requirements.

The outlined marketing mix proposal is open to successive revisions or optimizations because there will be a number of pay-offs – between price and promotion, between distribution methods and personnel, between packaging and price, and so on. For any particular problem the interactions between factors will be complex and not easily resolved without greater understanding of the market forces than the

Table 5.1   Grid for assessing elements of the marketing mix

	Product	Price	Place	Promotion	Packaging	Process	People	Physical
	+ Increase in							
Product								
Price								
Place								
Promotion								
Packaging								
Process								
People								
Physical								
– Decrease in								

case study normally allows. Considering increases or decreases in particular elements of the mix on a grid basis (Table 5.1) can give some indication about where the optimal point is likely to be.

Finalizing the marketing mix involves considering a large number of pay-offs, or possible alternatives to a certain proposed level of pricing, promotional investment or product change.

Some of the many pay-offs that exist are summarized next.

Group I: alternatives to changing the price of a product or service

Manufacturing factors

1. Reducing raw material consumption by:
   (a) redesign;
   (b) improving quality control;
   (c) reducing high-cost ingredients.
2. Reducing waste in the production process by:
   (a) improving quality of ingredients;
   (b) improving subcontractor performance;
   (c) improving maintenance;
   (d) improving operations (storage, handling etc.).
3. Improving manufacturing efficiency by:
   (a) investing in more cost-effective machinery;
   (b) improving factory layout.
4. Reducing overheads by:
   (a) subletting unused space;
   (b) reducing raw material stocks by implementing better ordering procedures;
   (c) minimizing overtime and maximizing factory staff performance;
   (d) introducing performance-related pay structures;
   (e) employing more part-time employees.
5. Improving purchasing procedures by:
   (a) widening the range of competitive quotes;
   (b) increasing order quantities;
   (c) changing financing methods.
6. Reducing losses by:
   (a) improving security;
   (b) improving stock control.

Possibilities to change the product impact on the pricing problem

1. Reduce or increase range.
2. Provide extended guarantee periods.
3. Increase or reduce credit.

Distribution factors

1. Reduce stockholdings.
2. Reorganize warehouse systems.
3. Change physical distribution methods.
4. Change the level of service offered – frequency of delivery, size of order.
5. Use new distribution channels.

Discounting system

1. Change discount structure.
2. Combine products across ranges to improve discount structures.

Salesforce

1. Sell more profitable products.
2. Sell to more profitable customers.
3. Train salesforce.
4. Redesign sales territories and workloads.

Promotion

1. Promote to improve customer loyalty.
2. Run short-term customer promotions.

Group II: alternatives to raising promotional expenditure

Product

1. Improve quality control.
2. Develop new uses of packaging material.
3. Redesign packaging.
4. Improve display ability.
5. Improve guarantees.

Public relations

Investigate ways of using public relations more effectively.

Salesforce

1. Increase numbers.
2. Introduce other salesforce methods, e.g. telephone sales.

3. Train and support salesforce more effectively.
4. Reorganize salesforce.

Distribution

1. Increase number of intermediaries.
2. Change pricing structure to improve motivation.

Promotion

1. Change timing and structure.
2. Change promotional method chosen.

Price

1. Reduce price.
2. Provide improved credit.

Group III: alternatives to changing the nature of the product

Manufacturing

1. Investigate improved manufacturing techniques.
2. Improve staff training.

Product

1. Redesign packaging.
2. Find new uses for packaging.
3. Improve quality control.
4. Change guarantee structure.
5. Improve display features.
6. Improve usage instructions.

Distribution

1. Develop new distribution channels.
2. Use more intermediaries.

Price

1. Reduce price.
2. Change price structure to encourage distribution.
3. Combine products with others.

Promotion

1. Increase promotion to encourage purchase.
2. Change promotional methods.

Salesforce

1. Improve training.
2. Change emphasis of activity.
3. Change targeted customers.
4. Improve service provided by salesforce.

Group IV: alternatives to increasing salesforce numbers

Promotion

1. Use more end-user-orientated promotional material.
2. Use more coupon/direct response material.
3. Provide improved point of sale/information brochures.

Distribution

1. Use more intermediaries.
2. Direct marketing.
3. Use third parties for specific sales tasks.

Personnel

1. Train.
2. Change recruitment policy.
3. Redefine jobs.
4. Use technology to make the salesforce more effective.

Order processing

1. Use telephone sales.
2. Use technology to speed up ordering.

Product

Provide more sales information on the product.

Price

Change pricing structure to concentrate on larger customers.

Creation of the budget

Once the various pay-offs have been considered, the final budget can be created reflecting the particular issues on which the action plan is based. Classically this will involve measures of:

(a) sales volume;
(b) sales value;
(c) fixed and variable costs;
(d) promotional expenditure.

The action plan

Each individual case will provide different amounts of information and it will be in some instances only that the time scale involved in the completion of each of the main activities will be available. In these cases it will be possible to determine:

(a) what actions need to be taken;
(b) a schedule of their priorities – that is, the order in which they will need to be completed;
(c) a timing schedule – when each action will need to be completed to achieve the final desired result.

A useful technique in these instances is the application of network and critical path analysis, defining the crucial series of steps that must be closely monitored to ensure that the time scale initially decided upon is adhered to.

Media planning

Within the agreed overall promotional strategy, the organization will then have to implement the promotional budget. This involves media planning – structuring the budget over time so that it effectively meets the demands of the promotional strategy.

There are various components involved in effective media planning.

1. Target audience and promotional channel. What is the target audience and how best can it be reached with the particular information demands of the product/ service?
2. Exposure requirements. How many times will the audience be required to receive the promotional message?
3. Frequency distribution. For each medium, advertising expenditure will be unevenly spread amongst the population, with heavy, light and moderate users.
4. Decay considerations. The way in which the advertising message will be forgotten over time.

5. Seasonality of sales. Sales achieved via advertising will be proportional to the general level of sales and therefore the underlying seasonality will be an important consideration in structuring advertising expenditure.
6. Seasonality of advertising cost. Advertising cost will also vary through the year, being less expensive during the summer months than the winter, and this will have an effect on the cost-effectiveness of the media schedule.

Chapter 6

PRESENTING AND WRITING UP THE MATERIAL

INTRODUCTION

For both reader and writer when they later come to review the material, the final document should provide a clear and logical series of steps leading to a definite recommendation for action. Too often is the analysis completed in extreme detail whereas the action plan is left untended and sketchy in outline. Each case varies in the amount of detail that can be provided in the action plan; in many a number of assumptions will have to be made as to profit margins, turnover figures and the like. As stated earlier, assumptions are a fundamental part of all planning processes and *provided both the writer and the reader are aware of what assumptions have been made*, they will create a framework which clarifies both the additional information that may be required and the degree of risk inherent in the decisions that are taken.

WHAT THEN IS THE FINAL FORMAT?

Though an approach based on the use of headings followed by notes is often mechanical and constricting, they provide a useful skeleton which can then be 'fleshed' out, and in examination conditions they will be all that time allows. The greater the use of graphics in the presentation, the clearer the format is likely to be: pie charts, bar charts, representations of product/market interactions and organograms to define personnel responsibility and development will all help in the final form of the presentation. The final format will obviously also depend on the exact use to which the case study is being put and the area which is being concentrated upon. The following structure is therefore but a particular suggestion for a review process that would be suitable for the creation of a marketing plan for a particular organization, and is not intended to be followed slavishly in every case.

I: Setting the scene

(a) Defining the market/company interaction

A brief introduction accurately defining the market in which the company operates and the products/services that it provides.

(b) Defining the operating unit/profit centre/product group

Different subdivisions of many companies will be subject to different external and internal forces. It will be important that the way the analysis has been carried out is defined at an initial stage.

II: The wider context

(a) The macro-environment

Included under this heading should be brief comment on the *important* elements of the external environment as they affect the particular case under consideration, together with analysis of major problems and opportunities.

1. Political.
2. Economic.
3. Social.
4. Technological.
5. Geographic.

(b) Competitive environment

A similar schedule of comments can be drawn up regarding the competitive environment with particular attention to the following issues.

1. Market (size, growth, share, capital investment).
2. Distribution structure (buyers, intermediaries, physical distribution issues).
3. Product (branding, packaging, speed of change).
4. Promotion (channels, level of expenditure).
5. Price (price sensitivity, demands of distribution channels).

   Other factors will be important in specific cases, e.g. location, design, personnel in the service sector.

(c) Resource environment

This will include comment on a number of issues.

1. The financial environment in which the firm operates.
2. The organizational strengths and weaknesses.

(d) Product/service resource

The analysis of area (d) should concentrate on the current strengths and weaknesses of the products and services supplied by the company and the options that exist for change. The use of relevant product analysis methods such as forecasting, BCG, GEC and other portfolio techniques may be relevant.

III: The future

What important elements of the environment are likely to change significantly over the planning horizon?

(a) Macro-environment.
(b) Competitive environment.
(c) Resource environment.

IV: Assumptions and market research

All case studies (and the majority of real-life problems in companies) will suffer from the fact that there is never enough information.

The analyst of the case will have to make the following decisions:

(a) What are the key assumptions that will have to be made – and then list them in order of importance.
(b) Whether there are one or more assumptions that are so important that research will need to be planned to fill in the relevant gaps, and when this research can be completed.

V: Objectives

Different cases will vary according to the problem, some being far more short-term than others. The important difference between short-term objectives and medium-/long-term issues is their specificity – short-term objectives should contain clear targets in terms of volumes, percentages and the like, which can be translated into budgetary goals in the implementation phase (Table 6.1).

Table 6.1 Budgetary objectives

	Short-term	Medium-term	Long-term
ROCE	%	%	%
Margin	%	%	%
Cash flow	+ or − £x		
Market sector/share	%	%	%
Distribution target	%	%	%
Product development	x new products	y	z
Personnel	numbers/wages	+ or −	+ or −
Shareholder/owner	e.p.s./dividend	+ or −	+ or −

VI: Main alternative action paths

Briefly outline the main options for achieving these objectives in broad terms by for example:

(a) concentrating on a particular market sector;
(b) expanding into new markets;
(c) changing organizational/production/distribution structure.

The risks of each option should be discussed, however briefly.

VII: Chosen action path and fall back position

The chosen action path should be the one that best meets the objectives; a fallback plan should be included in case the proposed plan does not succeed.

VIII: Implementation

The implementation proposals should include the details of how the company is actually to follow through the action plan in detail – the degree of detail depending on the nature of the case material, and the area of concentration required.

The main factors that will need to be considered are:

(a) the organization required to manage the implementation effectively;
(b) the staff necessary to implement the decisions;
(c) the control systems necessary to monitor progress;
(d) the consumer segment or the buyers that are the target market;
(e) the distribution channels by which this segment will be reached;
(f) the product/service/physical/process involved in servicing the particular segment that is chosen;

Table 6.2 Implementation proposals

	Short-term	Medium-term	Long-term
Segment			
Distribution channels			
Product			
Price			
Promotion			
Personnel			
Finance			

Table 6.3 Example 1: Broad budget

	Time period 1	2	3
Sales volume	+++	+++	+++
Price	...	...	...
Revenue	---	---	---
Gross margin	***	***	***
Distribution costs	,,,	,,,	,,,
Promotional costs	###	###	###
Net return	$$$	$$$	$$$
Other overheads	£££	£££	£££
Profit	&&&	&&&	&&&
Cash flow	xxx	xxx	xxx
Capital employed	!!!	!!!	!!!
ROCE	%	%	%

(g) the price that reflects the chosen segment, distribution channels, the product/service, and the volume/cost environment;
(h) the promotional method that is consistent with the requirements of the segment, the distribution channels, the product/service and the volume requirement;
(i) the financial requirements for the completion of the plan and where the finance will be obtained.

These issues will need to be considered in detail over the short term and in outline for the medium and long term (Table 6.2).

IX: Budgets and investment flow chart

Whether or not a detailed budget and expenditure plan is possible will depend on the information in the body of the case study. The case may demand either a build-up on an annual basis or, in the case of a detailed case based on media planning for example, a month by month assessment of volume sales and costs, together with a month by month investment activity plan for the company (Tables 6.3. and 6.4).

Table 6.4 Example 2: Detailed activity budget

Activity	1	2	3	4	5	6	7	8	9	10	11	12	Months
Woman		–		–		–		–		–		–	
House & Garden													
Sales promotion													
TV													
Radio													
Posters													
Total:													

FOREWORD TO THE CASES

The creator of the case study has to steer a fairly delicate course between a number of conflicting currents. The company providing the information is often justifiably unwilling to reveal information that may be of value to the competition, but it is those very details which are often of most value to the student.

How far the case study should go down the path of realism, by reporting conversations or meetings, is also a complicated issue; whether they in fact improve the understanding of the issues involved or merely serve to flesh out a topic is also a moot point.

Finally, the amount of background to provide in order that the case can be seen in context is also a difficult question.

The author has followed a number of clear guidelines in creating these cases.

First, where companies are identified with their real name, information pertaining to product costing, sales volume and consumer research has been altered – often significantly – so that operating confidentiality has been maintained. Where data sources are quoted the information is in the public domain and easily obtainable. Where the company name has been concealed or the context has been created, the student will need to be aware that through the merging of fact and fiction (or 'faction') a much more detailed analysis of operating costs, profits and investment can be made than would be possible in cases derived entirely from identified companies.

Second, the involvement of personalities has not been considered important for the particular type of case studies under consideration, and individual comment or interaction is avoided. In common with other case study approaches the material is not supposed to imply judgement or criticism of the actions taken.

Finally, each case contains an element of background material to enable the topic to be considered in context – this often introduces what may be considered a mechanistic approach, but one which it is essential to provide.

PART II
CASES

CONTENT OF THE CASES

Case	Sector	Strategy	Forecasting	Product issues	Pricing	Distribution	Promotion	Personnel	International	Small companies
1. Analysis										
Twydale	Consumer	•		•		•	•			
Sansui	Industrial	•	•			•		•	•	
AFI	Service	•		•			•	•		•
Airfix	Consumer	•		•	•			•	•	
Prestel	Service	•		•						
Technochem	Industrial	•	•	•		•		•	•	
Northmouth	Public							•		
Transit	Service	•			•			•		•
Club Med	Service	•		•	•	•	•		•	
Exton	Public		•		•					
2. Alternatives										
Nestlé	Consumer	•		•	•	•	•			
Doorlarm	Consumer			•	•	•	•			•
Hotel	Service			•		•				•
Gascofix	Industrial			•	•	•	•			•
Adnams	Consumer			•	•	•	•			
Benjamin's	Service			•	•				•	•
CupCo	Industrial	•		•	•	•				
Yamazka	Consumer			•	•	•		•	•	
Meon	Industrial			•	•	•		•		•
3. Implementation										
Barnet	Consumer	•	•	•	•	•	•		•	•
Zenith	Industrial		•	•				•		
Drive-in	Service		•	•	•		•		•	
Alonzo	Consumer			•	•	•	•			
Clara	Consumer			•	•	•	•			
Cascade	Consumer			•	•	•	•			•
Fantsis	Consumer			•	•	•	•			
Axe	Service			•	•	•	•	•		•

Case 1

TWYDALE

BACKGROUND

The marketing department at Twydale Turkeys, a market leader in turkey meat products, was reviewing company marketing strategy for the forthcoming five-year period. Twydale was part of the Bibby group at the time of writing – it has since become part of Hillsdown Holdings along with Buxted – one of the major food-processing companies in the UK with interests in animal feed, agricultural products, supermarket own brands and catering products. Having altered its management structure in the early 1980s, Bibby was attempting to improve the overall group profitability and looking for steady improvements in return on capital employed throughout the group.

By 1977 Twydale Turkeys – acquired by Bibby in 1969 – had expanded to occupy a purpose-built site at Driffield in Yorkshire. The company continued to breed and raise the vast majority of its own turkey products near the Driffield site, on company-owned farms. Every year some birds were bought in but these remained a minority. Part of the group philosophy was to maintain the tradition of low labour turnover and continued high employment levels: 550 people were currently employed by the company, which continued to achieve reasonable levels of profitability in what was a highly competitive industry.

THE MEAT MARKET

With the exception of poultry products, the meat market in the UK had declined over the previous six years. One reason for this continuing trend was the steady increase in the price of red meat. Although the EEC's Common Agricultural Policy (CAP) was partly responsible, nevertheless the price of beef had increased by 60 per

Table C1.1   Market shares of meat products by percentage

Sector	1979	1980	1981	1982	1983	1984
Beef and Veal	35	33	32	30	30	30
Lamb	11	12	11	12	12	11
Pork	20	20	20	21	20	20
Bacon/Ham	14	14	14	14	13	13
Poultry	21	21	22	23	24	25

cent over the five-year period while poultry had increased in price by only 8 per cent. Table C1.1 gives percentage shares for various products.

THE POULTRY MARKET

Consumption patterns in the total poultry market revealed that the percentage of chickens to turkeys and other poultry (ducks, geese) had remained more or less constant at 80:11:9; though there had been a slow trend away from chickens towards the consumption of ducks and geese. By 1984 the total consumption of turkeys was 94,378 tons or an estimated 25.8 million birds (Table C1.2). The market was estimated to be worth around £150 million at retail.

Two distinct market sectors can be identified for the turkey market.

1. Whole birds.
2. Further processed products.

These broad segments could be further subdivided into both fresh and frozen as in Table C1.2.

Demand for the entire range of turkey products has been affected by the changes among consumers.

1. An ageing population discovering that poultry products are easy to cook and digest. The percentage of the elderly in the population is expected to continue to rise well into the twenty-first century (Table C1.3).
2. Smaller family size (Table C1.4) affects the quantity of the product that is most often consumed; the emphasis being increasingly on the smaller products within the range.

Table C1.2   Tonnage consumed by sector of turkey market

	1979	1980	1981	1982	1983	1984
Whole fresh	21,347	19,425	19,786	19,299	21,026	22,129
Whole frozen	45,130	46,718	54,603	46,451	53,403	54,249
Further fresh	2,324	3,328	3,719	3,875	4,083	5,013
Further frozen	3,599	10,985	12,719	12,857	12,885	12,987

Table C1.3   UK Population age structure by percentage

	1983	2003
under 15	20	20
15–29	23	18
30–44	20	22
45–64	22	24
65+	15	16

Table C1.4   UK size of household 1984

	% of total households
1	25
2	32
3	16
4	18
5	6
6 oe more	3

3. The greatly increased percentage of women of working age in employment outside the home increased demand for convenience foods, especially in conjunction with the growth in ownership of microwave cookers.
4. Concern about healthy eating focused attention on substitutes for fat in diets, poultry being a prime example of low-fat meat.
5. Greater affluence and more sophisticated eating habits as a growing number of families travel overeseas.
6. The reluctance of consumers to buy products with additivies. High levels of water retention in frozen chickens and turkeys had become an important consumer issue by the mid-1980s.

The various market sectors show fairly distinct characteristics in terms of price, seasonality, and speed of change.

1. *Whole frozen.* This could be regarded as essentially a commodity market: product can be stored over long periods, being bought on price by the major retailers. Seasonality is reduced by the use of large cold-storage centres. Frozen turkey had been bought by the consumer at Christmas but is now also purchased during the year as an alternative to frozen chicken.
2. *Whole fresh.* Fresh turkeys posed a series of shelf storage problems which affect the manufacturing and pricing policies. Fresh whole turkey sales are highly seasonal with peaks in March–April and November, with far lower volumes in the summer. Because of the problems of production, fresh whole turkeys sell at a premium of 10–15p a pound over the frozen. Consumers clearly identified fresh turkeys as a product for a special occasion.
3. *Further frozen.* The further frozen market has many of the advantages of the

whole frozen sector, with the added benefit that the grade of turkey used in the manufacturing process can be far broader than that normally used for the provision of fresh or frozen whole turkeys; in other words the level of wastage is minimized. Part of the market is dominated by the boneless turkey roasts and other convenience foods supplied by Bernard Matthews; other further processed frozen items such as thighs, drumsticks and breasts are seen by the consumer as competing with chicken on price. Gradually the market for frozen oven-ready products is increasing, largely due to the steady growth in the home penetration of microwave cookers – owned by an estimated 25 per cent of UK households by the end of 1986, up from 11 per cent at the end of 1984. It is likely that microwave ownership will rise to 35 per cent by 1987, falling much into line with freezer ownership.

4. *Further fresh*. Further fresh processed products are the highest added-value products in the turkey sector. Though less seasonal than whole turkey products, shelf life is very limited and can be effectively supplied only to those outlets able to guarantee an uninterrupted chilled distribution system from manufacturer to final retail cabinet: 'the cold chain'. These further processed fresh products compete directly with similar chicken-based products: consumers being unable to separate clearly products such as turkey tandoori or chicken tandoori. Product life spans being fairly short, manufacturers must provide a continuing stream of new product concepts for the supermarkets.

Because of the high levels of investment required in turkey and chicken production it is unlikely that the supermarket groups would in the foreseeable future buy back into the production process as they had done in other sectors; with over-production the groups could already be demanding on price. Profit margins were in general terms better for the further processed and best for the further processed fresh products (Table C1.5). Each turkey manufacturer tended to have a different way of allocating the very large level of fixed overheads involved in turkey production, but approximate margins can be defined as in Table C1.6.

Table C1.5   Typical price per pound at retail for various turkey products

Whole frozen	70p
Whole fresh	90p
Further processed frozen	120p
Further processed fresh	160–180p

Table C1.6   Approximate profit margins

Whole frozen	20%
Whole fresh	35%
Further frozen	45%
Further fresh	60%

POLITICAL FACTORS AFFECTING THE TURKEY MARKET

The vast majority of turkeys consumed in the UK are produced at home. During the late 1970s, French government subsidies had helped the small French producers to compete in the English market but once these were withdrawn the much larger volume UK manufacturers were able to regain market share. As a corollary, UK turkey manufacturers find it very difficult to export to the EEC due to differing national hygiene and labelling regulations.

The CAP has a further effect on the total industry by its influence on the level of animal feed costs, which in the 1980s were running at around £110 per ton, £30 above the free market price. However, grain surpluses have had the effect of narrowing the differential between the two prices by the mid-1980s. The high cost of feedstuffs did, however, mean that UK turkey manufacturers could not effectively compete on the world market against the US manufacturers with their higher volumes and lower feed cost bases (particularly in an era of depressed agricultural prices).

LEGISLATION

All poultry manufacturers must comply with strict regulations on hygiene and storage, which have encouraged the development of a few major companies operating in the market. The EEC Poultry Hygiene Regulations require manufacturers to pay for regular veterinary inspection, which can be effectively amortized only across large volumes of production. Due to the risks of Salmonella infection, all poultry products have clearly defined shelf lives. For the deep frozen product this is fairly long but for the fresh product it can be of the order of three to four days, though shelf life for the complete turkey is normally ten days (Table C1.7).

Large manufacturers invested in automated production lines where hygiene problems can be monitored and minimized. The introduction of new techniques such as packing under inert gas or the introduction of irradiation techniques will require substantial investment.

Table C1.7 Storage viability of further processed/fresh turkey products

Product	Days of shelf life	Days at home
Stuffed breast joint	4	2
Turkey fillets	6	2
Thighs/fillets	6	2
Basted breasts	5	2
Turkey loaf	3	2

Table C1.8   The most important retail outlets for turkey products

Store group	Total grocery market share
Sainsbury's	12.5
Co-op	11.0
Tesco	12.0
Dee	11.0
Argyll	9.0
Asda	8.0

Table C1.9   Own brands

Store group	% own brand 1979	% own brand 1985
Marks & Spencer	100	100
Sainsbury's	35	57
Tesco	18	42
Dee	8	17
Asda	–	12

DISTRIBUTION

The vast majority of turkey products are sold through the main supermarket outlets in the UK, in contrast to the overall meat market where 48 per cent of product is still sold through butchers, underlining the importance of the frozen and further processed frozen product to the turkey market. The most important grocery outlets are in Table C1.8.

Table C1.8 ignores Marks and Spencer for specific grocery products. For poultry, Marks and Spencer can be considered a more important outlet than Sainsbury's, especially in the further processed sector of the market. One of the effects of the growing power of the retailers is in their demands for the production of own-label products; this had always been the philosophy of Marks and Spencer but during the late 1970s other store groups steadily expanded demand for own-label products (Table C1.9).

The growing power of the store groups is also affecting the speed at which new products have to prove themselves; Marks and Spencer will, for example, demand that a poultry product is withdrawn if it does not achieve a sale value of £20,000 nationally in the first week.

Some store groups require direct delivery to store, which can have a considerable effect on profitability of small volumes of fast-moving lines.

Finally, the introduction of bar coding in many of the supermarket groups as a means of improving stock control, speeding customer movement and identifying profitable lines means that suppliers must meet the packaging demands that this imposes, particularly difficult for suppliers providing products which vary slightly in weight.

Table C1.10   Major UK butcher chains

Company	Outlets
Dewhurst	1,500
Co-op	500
Matthews	200

Table C1.11   Market shares and major companies in the turkey market: market share by company and sector 1984

	Whole birds	Further processed
Buxted	19.1	6.7
Bernard Matthews	22.3	38.9
Swifts	11.7	10.0
Sun Valley	4.5	13.3
JP Woods	5.0	8.9
Twydale	12.7	10.0

Changes in Twydale market shares over five-year period

	1980	1981	1982	1983	1984
Whole birds	12.4	11.6	13.2	12.9	12.7
Further processed	–	–	6.6	8.8	10.0

Table C1.12   Media expenditure by company

Organization	1984 expenditure (£m)
Matthews	4.9
Turkey Federation	0.6
Swifts	0.2
Others (including Twydale)	0.1

There are also major butcher chains, though with slightly less total dominance within the market sector. The most important are in Table C1.10.

INDIVIDUAL COMPANIES

Table C1.11 gives the market shares of the major companies, and Table C1.12 detail of media expenditure.

Bernard Matthews

Market leader producing around 9 million turkeys per annum; concentrating on the production of frozen, whole birds and frozen further processed products, diversifying into both lamb and beef. Majority of product grown on Bernard Matthews farms. Matthews was starting to move into the dehydrated ready meal market which was currently dominated by Vesta (produced by Batchelors, a Unilever subsidiary). Matthews planned to compete on price with Vesta with a range of meals at around £1.10 for two.

Swifts

A subsidiary of the Beatrice Corporation of the United States. Produces around 3 million turkeys as well as substantially higher chicken production. Concentrates on the production of whole frozen birds, but also produces frozen thighs and turkey escalopes in the further processed sector.

Buxted

Buxted is one of the leading chicken producers in the UK and also produces around 3 million turkeys, and turkey pieces, concentrating on the frozen whole bird market. Recently Buxted had entered the frozen ready meal market with oven-ready chicken and chips, and was experimenting with a range of frozen convenience meals.

Sun Valley

Sun Valley produces a range of own-brand and branded fresh further processed products for major supermarket groups including Marks and Spencer and Tesco. Sun Valley produces both chicken and turkey further processed products such as tandoori, and chicken kiev. In late 1985 it introduced a range of frozen convenience meals including chicken curry, sweet and sour chicken and chicken provençal.

Other producers of further processed poultry

A number of chicken producers started to supply product to the large supermarket groups (Table C1.13). The largest of these was Padfields based in East Anglia, but recently the large Dalgety group began to test a range of products for the fresh further processed sector. It was estimated that the fresh further processed chicken market was around five times the size of that of turkey.

Table C1.13   Companies supplying further processed fresh turkey products to the major grocery retailers

Company	Tesco	Asda	Sainsbury's	Dee
Sun Valley	●	●		
Sovereign				●
Dalgety	●			
Padfield			●	
Buxted	●		●	●

Table C1.14   Twydale: percentage contribution to turnover

Whole birds: frozen oven ready	17%
fresh frozen	33%
standard frozen	17%
Further processed: fresh	33%

Table C1.15   Twydale 1984 product range

Whole turkeys
Standard frozen oven ready
'Country Baste' frozen oven ready
Fresh oven ready

Fresh further processed

Boneless turkey roast	Stuffed turkey breast
Butter basted boneless breast joint	Breast chops
Leg chops	Turkey and bacon loaf
Stuffed turkey parcels	Turkey fillet
Turkey breast slices	Boneless turkey thigh
Turkey drumsticks	Turkey wings
Turkey soup packs	Crown roast

Some manufacturers, in addition to Matthews, were experimenting with dehydrated convenience food as a means of entering the market – General Foods and Lockwoods both had products in this market sector and two of the supermarket groups, Asda and Tesco, were testing own-label products.

Twydale

Twydale produces a range of frozen and fresh whole birds which are branded, and supplies major retailers with own-label fresh further processed turkey products. It does not compete in the further processed frozen sector of the market. The 1984 percentage contribution to turnover is shown in Table C1.14 and the 1984 Twydale product range in Table C1.15.

Like other manufacturers of further fresh products, Twydale found that consumers' taste for products changed fairly rapidly, and though standard lines such as turkey drumsticks would continue to be popular the development of new lines in the ready meal sector would have to be continued at a fairly high level.

Distribution of Twydale products

Twydale relied heavily on the top twelve accounts for 80 per cent of its total revenue, with 50 per cent coming from the top three. This pattern had remained fairly unchanged over the past three years. In consequence the company relied very heavily on certain outlets for some items in the range (Table C1.16).

Table C1.16   Twydale products by retailer

Product	Retailer							
	M & S	Tesco	Sainsbury	Argyll	Co-op	Asda	Dee	Dewhurst
Boneless roast	+	+	+	+				
Stuffed breast	+		+	+				
Turkey and bacon	+							
Turkey fillets		+	+	+		+	+	
Drumsticks		+	+	+				
Fresh frozen	+							+
Standard frozen		S	S	S	S			

S = stocked seasonally

Table C1.17   Number of retail stores by outlet

Sainsbury's	278
Tesco	411
M & S	265
Dee	1,400
Argyll	1,060

Table C1.18   Average daily turkey product sale per supermarket by group

Sainsbury's	£153
Tesco	£130
M & S	£170
Dee	£65

(Rough estimates based on market shares, square footage of stores etc. Ignores seasonality.)

To meet the supermarket delivery schedules, Twydale has to maintain a large distribution system involving its own fleet of refrigerated lorries and outside contractors as well. The company also maintained vehicles to transport turkeys from farm to factory; a total of seventy-two company-owned vehicles. The costs of delivery always bedevilled the fresh turkey industry. Because of short shelf lives, a limited distribution chain was essential and this could add considerably to costs. Though transport cost varied to an extent with the size of vehicle the cost of delivering a full lorry load from the north to south of England was around £200, when wages, fuel and depreciation were included. Though there were a number of frozen food distributors in existence, none was totally suitable as an intermediary, partly because of their inappropriate plant (suited more to frozen than to fresh) but also as a result of their delivery cycles, which averaged three days – reasonable for frozen food but inappropriate for products such as fresh turkey with such a limited shelf life. For the national retailing groups, the large number of stores involved made distribution a complex issue (Table C1.17). Table C1.18 gives details of average group sales per outlet.

Case 2

SANSUI

INTRODUCTION

Sansui Ltd is one of the many companies that sprang up in the Far East to produce electronic circuitry for the massively expanding electronics market. From its factory outside Pusan, in South Korea, it had become a major supplier to companies in Japan, America and Europe, with a rapid rate of growth between 1981 and 1986 (Table C2.1).

Table C2.1   Sansui company progress ($ million)

	1963	1968	1971	1976	1981	1986
Sales	55	76	127	280	389	670
Gross profit	15	19	28	56	70	100

THE MARKET

The market for electronic components can be divided into *passive* or *active systems* each with different product, investment and customer requirements. A fundamental distinction existed between companies providing components for the final manufacturers (OEMs) and those acting on their own behalf in the market.

The passive market consists of a variety of product categories including:

Wires	Cables	Fuses
Resistors	Connectors	Switches
Capacitors		

This market is highly standardized and international, economies of scale and high volume production being crucial for success. As a result, the major multinational companies were taking increasing shares of a market which had stabilized in product design since the late 1970s. The world market continued to grow at a steady rate of around 15 per cent per annum in volume terms, though in value around 8 per cent indicating that the price of products continued to drop in real terms. Investment levels in manufacturing technology continued to rise, especially in some of the new product areas, such as optic fibres, which were becoming more important.

The active component market was much larger, consisting of:

(a) semiconductors;
(b) integrated circuits;
(c) microprocessors.

These active components were the backbone of two major industries.

1. Industrial electronics, active in the following areas:
   (a) telecommunications (telephone, telex, fascimile);
   (b) computers and peripheral units;
   (c) monitoring and measuring equipment;
   (d) office equipment (photocopiers);
   (e) design and manufacturing processes (CADCAM);
   (f) defence technology;
   (g) vehicles;
   (h) consumer goods manufacture, cars, washing machines, cookers (including microwave ovens).
2. Consumer electronics:
   (a) television;
   (b) video recorders;
   (c) audio equipment (tuners, amplifiers, compact disc players);
   (d) home computers/calculators;
   (e) watches and clocks;
   (f) radio.

The market for the component semiconductors falls into six segments.

1. Standard devices with exact definition of function dependent on external input. These are mass produced to service a wide range of basic computing and control devices. The characteristic of such a device is that it maintains a high level of flexibility while, on the other hand, not carrying out a single task with the highest degree of efficiency. An example would be the standard 64k 'chip' which was an integral part of many home computers.
2. Exclusive devices which perform general tasks but which are patented to provide a particular type of engineering expertise.
3. Specific devices that are an integral part of some particular device but are still largely dependent on external input for exact function.
4. Custom-built devices which provide a single exact function and are designed

solely for it. These contrast with the standard devices, being highly efficient at carrying out single functions but incapable of broad application.
5. Microprocessors. These can be mass produced but programmed for a range of specific functions.
6. Semi-custom devices. These contain a mixture of standard microprocessors and custom-built circuitry.

The integrated circuit market changed substantially between the late 1970s and early 1980s to become increasingly competitive. The prices of standard components continued to fall during the period; a cost reduction of over 100,000 times per function since the development of the industry. This led major manufacturers to concentrate more and more heavily on high levels of investment to lower the unit cost and hence remain competitive. As a result the degree of investment necessary to remain cost competitive in the volume market had risen steadily and the degree of concentration had grown as the market developed.

By 1982 fifteen manufacturers accounted for 55 per cent of total world production of standard circuitry, an increase of 10 per cent over the position in 1978. The main manufacturers were:

- Texas Instruments
- Motorola
- IBM
- Philips
- Hitachi
- Toshiba
- NEC

With the incredibly rapid pace of product development, the market was becoming extremely capital-intensive as manufacturers endeavoured to recoup large expenditures on R & D by high volume sales. Research and development investment was running at around 20 per cent of sales revenue by the mid-1980s as manufacturers attempted to achieve greater manufacturing efficiencies and chip reliability. The increasing sophistication of the chip technology was also pushing manufacturers into steadily higher investments in fundamental research as molecular circuitry and superconductor applications became more realistic.

Steadily increasing volumes and reducing prices led to a trade war, with several casualties; the eventual sale of Fairchild Semiconductor by Schlumberger after the loss of hundreds of millions of dollars was a particularly extreme example. Many of the companies involved in the sector were forced by the extreme price competitiveness of the market to dispose of product at or below cost. This led the Reagan administration to press for action on the trade imbalance between America and the Pacific Basin, primarily Japan.

Many of these manufacturers were vertically integrated in that they produced semiconductors entirely or almost entirely for their own operations. The specialist manufacturers of semiconductors were thus forced either to concentrate on volume production or specialize in the development of integrated circuits specifically designed for particular tasks. The development of specialized circuits demanded a high level of investment in research and development, a close relationship with the major companies requiring integrated circuits and a high degree of personnel expertise in the design of circuits and software.

The installation of circuity is, however, a labour-intensive activity, and as labour costs rose in the world markets and manufacturing sources the balance between production of the circuitry and the production of the circuit boards changed towards the concentration of production of circuits in the main industrialized countries and an increasing manufacture of circuit boards in low-cost economies, especially those of the Pacific Basin such as Taiwan, the Philippines, the People's Republic of China, Thailand, and – as a likely development of the 1990s – the Indian subcontinent. The share of this business was changing rapidly with Japan importing 90 per cent of its circuit board requirements by the mid-1980s up from 10 per cent in 1979.

THE CONSTITUENT MARKET SECTORS

Industrial

Design and manufacturing control

Specialist companies producing robots and microprocessor-operated machine tools were gaining steadily increasing shares of the world market. Because of the complexity of the control systems involved, the demand of these OEM manufacturers was for highly specialized custom-built circuitry. As a result they tended to establish close links with subcontractors who could meet the stringent requirements that were placed upon them.

The motor vehicle market

The vast world motor vehicle market increasingly used microprocessor systems to improve engine efficiency and vehicles. With the concentration of production among a smaller number of volume manufacturers, the demands were for more and more sophisticated custom-built devices manufactured in large quantities. Some of the manufacturers such as General Motors had purchased companies with expertise in the field of microprocessor design and had become vertically integrated.

World computer market

The computer market is complex, consisting as it does of a number of clearly defined sectors each of which has particular characteristics (Table C2.2).

Table C2.2   Sectors of the world computer market ($ billion)

Market sector	1982	1984	1986	1988 (projected)
Mainframe	12	12	15	18
Minicomputer	17	25	27	30
Personal computers	7	18	26	36

The *mainframe* market is dominated by IBM and a few other manufacturers, selling sophisticated equipment, with a unit price of over £1 million, to major companies. The key selling criterion in this sector of the market was a high degree of reliability and back-up together with substantial software expertise, the ability to design and help with the complex software required by companies buying mainframe computers.

The *minicomputer* market is supplied by companies with substantial expertise in computer systems design and software requirements with units costing from £75,000 to £375,000. The main companies operating in this market are Burroughs, UniSys, NCR and Honeywell, with well-established European and Japanese competition such as ICL, Thompson Bull, Siemens, Fujitsu and Hitachi. The key selling criterion in this area is largely software expertise in particular areas, though reliability remains important. Thus one finds companies with particular expertise in certain areas – ICL and NCR in retail systems, for example.

The *personal computer* market showed the most dramatic growth in the late 1970s, and by the late 1980s was expected to rival the mainframe and microcomputer markets in total size. As the market had become more and more oriented towards selling consumer as opposed to business product, a proliferation of manufacturers had entered it and the high street audio dealers became increasingly important as distribution outlets. Because the industry had largely standardized around the concept of IBM compatibility, vast libraries of software are available and the purchase decision tends to be made on processing power in relation to price, though the manufacturer's reliability record is important in achieving initial distribution. The market became highly volume oriented; manufacturers such as Olivetti and Compaq, which could achieve international sales, found the market profitable despite the extremely high pace of product development. Many of the other 400 or so manufacturers in the market use standard components put together by third parties mainly in the Far East. Indeed, both Sansui and one of its neighbouring firms were involved in this activity; the neighbour was one of the major submanufacturers for the Amstrad computer range. In contrast to the other market sectors, the personal computer market is very much a high street phenomenon, the bulk of the products being sold through the main multiple retail chains throughout Europe, North America and other markets. Though there are a large number of companies operating in the market only a few could be considered to have reasonable market shares and profitability, whereas among the others there was a high failure rate.

The *home computer* market was a very important sector of the market in the early 1980s with in-home penetration running at around 15 per cent. However, with the decrease in costs of the personal computer the barriers between the two sectors became blurred, and many manufacturers began to concentrate on units able to service both the games and home applications market.

The *computer peripherals* market – printers, modems, disc drives, memory units, monitors and the like – was originally an attractive market sector for the independent smaller companies as manufacturers did not include these as standard in their product range. With the reducing hardware costs most large OEM manufacturers are now offering an increasing range of peripheral devices as part of a 'packaged system'.

The office equipment market

There are three main subdivisions in the office equipment sector:

(a) telephones and other telecommunications equipment;
(b) photocopiers;
(c) typewriters/addressing machines.

The telephone and telecommunications market shows continuing year-on-year growth of around 15 per cent and is expected to continue at this rate until at least the mid-1990s. By 1985 the world telecommunications market was estimated to be worth around $75 billion.

In this vast market are a number of distinct market sectors. The most important by far is the contractor segment of large projects and complex installations, dominated by such large international companies with substantial financial resources as NTT, ATT, Siemens, and ITT.

The large systems market covers a host of products from the telephone exchange down to the small office intercom system. The wide range of components involved – from the very complex and large exchange systems down to the office units – has led to dominance by companies such as GEC, STC (which had originally been part of the ITT empire), Philips, and Mitsubishi.

The peripherals market – handsets, cellular telephones and the like – is serviced by a whole range of manufacturers with no clear market dominance. It is similar to the personal computer sector because the market is growing rapidly, with large percentages of the products manufactured overseas. In contrast to the other market sectors, serviced either direct by the companies themselves or a dealer network, the peripherals sector is serviced through the retail sector, and is becoming highly price sensitive. Cellular telephone systems, slowly being introduced throughout Western Europe and the United States, offer a further growth market for the suppliers of peripheral systems. Estimates suggest that this market would be worth around £200 million a year by the late 1980s.

The market for photocopiers has grown steadily over the years with a similar segmentation developing. Xerox continues its domination of the large photocopier market but large Japanese manufacturers like Minolta and Canon have larger and larger shares of the medium sized copier and the small office sector. Much of the success of the Japanese manufacturers lies in their ability to develop effective worldwide sales and dealer networks able to provide an effective level of sales back-up. With the reduction in price and size, the photocopier market continued to grow at around 19 per cent a year and was estimated to be worth around $3 billion worldwide by 1985.

The typewriter sector has, in contrast, been severely eroded by the steady reduction in the cost of computers and word processing packages. The Amstrad word processing system, for example, sold over 750,000 units between its launch in 1985 and the middle of 1987. As a result, the typewriter sector has become highly price competitive.

The domestic appliance market

There was a steady growth of microprocessor systems in domestic appliances. However, in common with many others the market was dominated by multinational manufacturers producing most of the world output:

- Whirlpool
- Electrolux
- Philips

Economies of scale and heavy promotional investment are particularly important in differentiating basically similar products. This was especially true in the expansion of the microwave oven market, where Samsung had to invest heavily to build up a respectable market share throughout Western Europe.

The defence sector

The companies operating in this sector tend to be vertically integrated, producing all the electronic components for the systems required. It is increasingly the preserve of large companies operating in a global market:

- Dassault
- British Aerospace
- Aerospatiale
- Lockheed
- United Technologies
- Hughes

Some of the more sophisticated mircropressors are bought from specialist manufacturers but, due to the security implications, these tend to be nationally based institutions.

The consumer sector

Television

The world television market is heavily concentrated into integrated manufacturers, with the top seven manufacturers producing nearly 60 per cent of the total world consumption:

- Matsushista
- Philips
- RCA
- Zenith
- Sanyo
- Sony
- Toshiba

Much of the circuit board construction is carried out in low labour-cost markets though some of the major Japanese concerns are now investing heavily in robot technology to bring that back in house as well. Forthcoming developments in flat-screen technology and satellite programming will further concentrate the market into the hands of those manufacturers able to provide a sufficiently high level of investment to meet rising consumer demands.

Watches and clocks

The watch market has a number of distinct segments. The premium sector of the market is dominated by Swiss products, especially after the introduction of the Swatch concept. The middle of the market is primarily a Japanese preserve with companies such as Seiko, Casio and Citizen having carved out international markets based on the use of integrated circuits to replace traditional clockwork mechanisms. During the 1980s their dominance was threatened by a growing number of companies assembling units in other areas of the Pacific Basin, Hong Kong and Taiwan especially, which meant that the market was – in common with other consumer sectors – facing a continuing downward pressure on price. Sansui had provided circuit boards for some of the Japanese companies but by the early 1980s these companies had become fully automated and the company was no longer established in the market.

The audio market

The audio market has changed dramatically since the early 1980s. The basic record changer, tape deck and amplifier had developed from tried and tested technology and is now assembled in low-cost centres throughout the Pacific Basin. The rapid penetration of both digital audio-tape systems and compact discs is likely to overturn a market serviced by a wide range of manufacturers selling on a mixture of price and performance. The introduction of these products appears likely to concentrate the market in the hands of a small number of manufacturers able to provide the sophisticated systems required. The market shares of companies such as Philips, Mitsubishi and Sony seem likely to rise as a result.

Radio

After a period of rapid growth during the 1960s the world radio market started to decline as television entered more and more homes. With the fairly unsophisticated design of the circuitry the assembly costs were the most important element in the production of standard radios, which still comprise 70 per cent of the world market. The assembly cost factor led to the Pacific Basin supplying more and more of the total world market.

A growing sector of the market, particularly in developed economies like the United States, is for higher quality and more powerful units which require greater attention to the external design and packaging.

The video sector

Ninety-five per cent of the world video demand is supplied by Japanese manufacturers exercising rigid control of the patents on the various systems involved. Growth is rapid with in-home penetration varying from country to country in Western Europe and North America; 8 per cent in Austria to 32 per cent in the UK. The pace of technological development – including rumoured hard disc replacement of the moving tape system – should ensure that the Japanese continue to maintain their control over the entire sector.

The security market

With the steadily increasing crime rate in the developed world the sale and installation of alarm systems is growing. Industry estimates put the entire world equipment market at around $4 billion, though with such a wide range of activity included under the 'security' heading it is difficult to separate out the various component elements.

Again, there are a series of fairly clear divisions within the broad market.

1. The corporate security sector, with a range of sophisticated camera and alarm systems.
2. The small business and installed home system market, with a more basic range of alarm units.
3. The free-standing alarm market sector.

Of these sectors the first two were handled by agents that dealt with all the installation and maintenance requirements. The free-standing alarm sector was

Table C2.3   Sansui: financial profit 1963–1986 ($ million)

	1963	1968	1971	1976	1981	1986
Sales	55	76	127	280	389	670
Gross profit	15	19	28	56	70	100
Passive systems	23	20	29	45	56	115
Circuit boards	15	33	28	38	52	94
Microchips	15	16	45	85	120	148
Telephones			2	15	30	60
Televisions			3	25	35	45
Radios			5	25	30	40
Computers				22	31	103
Alarm systems	2	7	15	25	35	65

Table C2.4   Gross contribution by product line (%)

	1963	1968	1971	1976	1981	1986
Passive systems	45	48	35	30	27	25
Circuit boards	46	40	33	35	38	32
Microchips	55	67	45	35	30	22
Telephones			15	27	45	48
Televisions			25	27	34	38
Radios			33	31	30	28
Computers			37	30	35	33
Alarm systems	28	32	35	37	38	37

sold through retail outlets and had become dominated by low-cost products manufactured in Hong Kong (and the PRC), Taiwan and the Philippines.

A PROFILE OF SANSUI

Originally Sansui had concentrated on the production of circuitry and passive components for television and record players but, during the late 1970s, it transferred the bulk of its production into circuit boards and microprocessors for the growing information technology business (Table C2.3).

On a division by division basis, the gross profit contributions varied considerably over the years, though each sector showed an overall trend. Sansui analysed each product line on the basis of gross profit contribution rather than net return as it did not allocate the fixed factory costs to particular product lines (Table C2.4).

EMPLOYMENT

Sansui's three divisions employed 13,000 people.

Manufacturing occupied the bulk of the workforce, 11,700. All employees were

Table C2.5   Turnover analysis by area (%)

	1971	1985
USA	77	55
Europe	17	26
Pacific Basin	6	19

Table C2.6   Consumer and trade advertising (£ million)

	1971	1976	1981	1985
Exhibition (total)	1.0	2.0	2.5	2.8
Consumer		0.5	1.0	1.5
Industrial	1.0	3.0	7.0	8.5

from the Pusan area; the majority (65 per cent) were women with secondary school education. Sansui followed the tradition of offering lifetime employment to all its staff, though because of its high level of female staff labour turnover was quite high and was running at 15 per cent during the 1980s. Male supervisory staff had all received secondary education, and college graduates were increasingly being hired to fill the supervisory and lower mangement roles. Senior production personnel had normally been with the company a number of years, and were sent on intermittent training courses to familiarize themselves with the changing technology. Factory costs had historically been low, with labour costs far below Japanese levels. In the 1980s wages had risen and the heavy investment the company carried out to improve the profitability of the manufacturing process substantially raised the overheads of the entire operation. Sansui had considered the possibility of starting to manufacture elsewhere in the Pacific Basin, and carried out a pilot project in the Philippines. However, relocation of assembly operations would mean giving up substantial tax concessions provided by the Korean government (see below).

The sales, marketing and finance department had a staff of 350 and five offices in the major markets. Two were in the United States, one on the West Coast, the other on the North Eastern seaboard. The third serviced the European market from its Frankfurt headquarters, the fourth and fifth serviced the growing Pacific Basin market, with one office in Osaka and another in Singapore. The geographical split of the business had changed over the years with a slow decrease in the importance of the United States – previously the cynosure of the company's operations (Table C2.5). The marketing team reported on a geographic basis and there were no product divisions.

Employees in sales and marketing were normally promoted from within the company and then sent on training courses in Korea, for which the company maintained a considerable budget. Overseas postings for personnel were of three to four years' duration.

The company invested heavily in international exhibitions to establish links with potential customers. Up to the early 1980s this was the sole promotional

Table C2.7   Economic market data 1985

	US	Jpn.	WG	Can.	UK	Fr.	It.	Neth.	Bel.	Aus.	Sp.	Sw.	Den.	Saud.
Population (mill.)	233	120	62	25	56	55	57	15	10	15	39	9	5	10
GNP per cap. ($000)	14	10	11	12	9	10	6	10	9	10	5	13	12	12
Growth (%)	3.5	5.5	3	3	2	3	3	2	3	3	4	4	4	4
Inflation (%)	3	2	1	3	4	4	7	5	4	6	9	3	3	2
Household (mill.)	105	28	25	10	20	20	18	5	3	5	9	4	2	2
Telephones/000 pop.	940	670	571	900	524	541	404	575	417	820	345	889	718	420
Multiple grocer (%)	65	35	65	65	60	75	25	67	74	55	15	45	55	35

investment apart from the high levels of sales staff prospecting for likely customers and generating sales.

During the 1980s Sansui increased its consumer and trade advertising, particularly in the Japanese and European markets (Table C2.6).

The research and development department employed around 500. The company began to recruit academic staff in the early 1980s in the attempt to break into higher added-value products. The expenditure on research and development had increased from a low figure in the mid-1970s and by 1985 was running at 10 per cent of turnover. The investment in the development of microchip manufacture had put a considerable drain on the company resources in the late 1970s and early 1980s. By then over £120 million had been invested in a manufacturing facility.

INDIVIDUAL MARKETS

Individual markets varied considerably as to their ease of access, size of consumer market and the presence of competitors. The basic economic data available on the main markets is given in Table C2.7.

EEC members tended to have standard tariffs on the import of electronic products, though the degree of in-home penetration of consumer electronics varied considerably from high levels in West Germany and the UK to lower levels in Italy. High tariff barriers made the Swedish, Swiss and Austrian markets difficult to penetrate. This was also true of markets in Spain, Greece and Portugal which, although members of the EEC, had yet to harmonize their tariffs with those of other Community members. Import restrictions into the US and Canadian markets were limited and the Australian market was accessible though with high tariff barriers.

United States

This was by far Sansui's most important market. It supplied approximately 200 companies with components ranging from passive items to completed circuit boards. The company supplied Montgomery Ward with own-label television sets, and had a developing radio and telephone business through approximately 800 outlets on the Eastern seaboard.

United Kingdom

Sansui supplied circuit boards and passive components to about seventeen customers in the UK. Sansui achieved 60 per cent of its total television sales by manufacturing sets for one of the large rental companies.

West Germany

Sansui supplied circuit boards to fifteen customers in West Germany. The company also sold radios and televisions through one of the main retail chains.

France

Sansui had the contract to manufacture all the terminals for one of the major French computer companies, Thompson Bull, a contract which made up 75 per cent of all its computer sales in 1985, the remainder coming from similar contracts with smaller American and European operations.

Japan

Sansui had become established as one of the main suppliers of circuit boards to two Japanese manufacturers of shop till equipment; 65 per cent of its business in Japan was derived from these two companies. Sansui also sold a line of personal alarms in the Japanese market, and supplied two international trading companies in Hong Kong that sold these products on to the United States and Europe.

Middle East

Sansui had quickly identified the Middle East as a target market for boosting consumer sales effectively. The sales in this area were included under the Pacific Basin sales, but by 1985 were running at around £20 million, with highly profitable Sansui telephones and alarm systems selling throughout the Gulf via a network of consumer distributors.

Other EEC

Sansui had developed industrial sales in other West European markets such as Belgium, the Netherlands and Italy, where it had for some time supplied components to the growing Olivetti corporation. In late 1985 Olivetti gave up using third party manufacture and Sansui faced the loss of a £20 million annual contract to supply both passive systems and circuit boards to the Italian market.

Table C2.8   Sansui balance sheet 1983–1985 ($ million)

	1983	1984	1985
Assets			
Current assets: Cash	15	8	10
Debtors	100	120	180
Inventories	100	150	200
Fixed assets: Plant and equipment	80	120	180
Liabilities			
Current liabilities: Creditors	140	120	130
Bank overdraft	100	150	370
Net assets	55	128	70

Balance sheet policy

Sansui policy had been to amortize all the research and development in the year in which it was spent. Heavy investment in capital projects and research and development had led to the reduction in net assets between 1984 and 1985. The balance sheet figures are summarized in Table C2.8.

SENIOR MANAGEMENT

The company was founded in 1955 by the current chairman and managing director, Boon Lon Yuen, who had trained in one of the many American bases in Korea on the assembly and maintenance of electronic systems. The other board members have all been with the company since the early 1960s – the finance, production and research directors. All were now in their sixties. Because of the high level of bank borrowings there were two additional non-executive directors appointed by the bank, which was closely involved in monitoring the business.

In common with many other Korean enterprises the majority of the capital requirements were provided by bank lending (mainly government-funded and controlled national banks) as the stock market, as a method of raising long-term capital, was underdeveloped in the Korean system.

Case 3

AFI INSURANCE

BACKGROUND

AFI, established by a small but highly profitable, cash-rich financial services group, was a company offering a range of financial services to the motor trade. These included:

(a) extended warranty cover for the car owner, acting as a broker for an established insurance scheme;
(b) finance facilities;
(c) incentive holiday packages for sales promotions.

The company could also arrange car rentals and reduced-price car purchase but these were not mainstream activities.

After two years of operation the company was still encountering problems and the board of directors were reviewing the future direction of the company.

THE MARKET

The car market had shown little growth over the five-year period 1980–85. Forecasts tended to suggest that the market would remain relatively flat even though the reduction in interest rates and relaxation of credit regulations might be expected to have a slight influence on the overall direction of the market. It was likely that the market would grow by around 1 per cent per annum to the end of the century (Table C3.1).

The reasons for the slow growth in the market were numerous. First, in contrast with many other consumer durables that had fallen in price throughout the 1970s and 1980s both in real and often in absolute terms, cars had continued slightly to

Table C3.1   Car market 1980–1990

Year	Sales (millions)	Growth (%)
1980	1.51	(17.8)
1981	1.48	(1.9)
1982	1.56	4.7
1983	1.79	15.2
1984	1.75	–
1985	1.78	–
1986	1.60	(10.0)
1987	1.70	6.3
1988	1.80	5.9
1989	1.75	(2.8)
1990	1.70	(2.9)

Table C3.2   Car prices compared with RPI

	1975	1985
RP Index	100	279
Average saloon	£1,300	£6,100

outpace inflation (Table C3.2). Second, the cost of motoring had continued to rise throughout the period. This was the result not only of rising fuel prices partly caused by the Arab oil price increase but, more important, of the substantial increase in taxation on petrol and the escalating insurance claims that led to steeper and steeper premiums.

Manufacturers were also producing more reliable cars; coupled with the reduction in the average household mileage this meant that the demand for new replacement cars would continue to be placed under pressure even though the MOT road test would reduce the number of older cars considered roadworthy.

Long-term changes in the population were also having an effect, with a rising percentage of the elderly in the population, who were far less likely to drive long distances.

Multiple household ownership of cars was as a result still the exception rather than the rule in the UK (Table C3.3), although it was the pattern in the United States.

The effects on manufacturers and dealers have been quite considerable. Over-production has led to intense price competition with manufacturers insisting on dealers moving the stock to ensure that new models can be introduced. This has meant that many dealers and manufacturers are losing money in the car market – British Leyland being an obvious example. The search for new profitable activities is therefore important for both manufacturer and dealer; particularly for the independent dealer who is not part of one of the large national chains, which are becoming steadily more important in the UK motor retail scene. By 1984 there were 15,000 retail car outlets of varying types in the UK market. Of these, 8,000 were franchised (tied to one or more companies or known as main dealers), the

Table C3.3 Penetration of motor cars into UK households (%)

	1980	1981	1982	1983	1984
One only	44	45	45	45	45
Two or more	15	15	16	16	16
Total % ownership	59	60	61	61	61

Table C3.4 Approximate number of dealerships held by main manufacturers

British Leyland	1,570
Ford	1,211
Peugeot/Talbot	800
General Motors	660
Nissan	425
Renault	380
Volkswagen/Audi (VAG)	380
Fiat	380

Table C3.5 The main dealer chains operating in the UK market

Company	No. of outlets
Kenning	103
Caffyns	40
Henleys	40
Mann Egerton	40
Dutton Forshaw	30

remaining 7,000 were non-franchised. The relationship of the dealer, purchaser and manufacturer was further complicated by the level of direct sales that existed. Major car rental companies such as Swan National bought direct from the manufacturer, as some major employers were also prepared to negotiate on a national basis direct with the car manufacturer (Tables C3.4 and C3.5).

There is, as might be expected, an enormous variation in the volume of cars sold by outlet, depending on the type of customer being serviced. The average sale per outlet of around 350 cars could as a result be extremely misleading. Continuing changes in the structure of the retail car market are expected over the late 1980s and 1990s. The concentration of an increasing market share amongst the major chains is expected as declining profit margins in an increasingly competitive car market suggest that over 50 per cent of existing dealerships will either close down or change ownership over a ten-year period. Moreover, the incursion of grocery multiples and other groups into car retailing – heralded by an unsuccessful experiment by Asda–MFI in the mid-1980s – might, in conjunction with the out-of-town retailing sites, lead to a radical shift in the market structure. The implication of such a move would be that servicing and service contracts would have to be carried out away from the point of sale, enabling the manufacturers to operate on lower retail margins.

THE CURRENT CAR BUYER

Broadly, four main divisions exist, each with distinct product and service requirements.

1. *Private buyers.* The private buyer is the most cost-conscious customer and has the lowest mileage. Service and warranty issues are not, in general, major factors in purchase decisions.
2. *Self-employed.* The self-employed sector concentrates on the functional aspects of car design and maintenance. Reliability and back-up are essential considerations for many of the self-employed, who have higher than average mileages to consider.
3. *The car fleet buyer,* for salesforces and other employees who travel considerable distances as part of their job. Because of the high degree of standardization of car and the large numbers involved, these fleet operators are generally able to maintain a pool of cars some of which are available as replacements for company personnel during accident repairs or general servicing.
4. *The company buyer,* purchasing either for employees' 'perks' or for senior management. This segment of the market is commonly served by contract hire companies, which contract to service the car and provide necessary back-up when problems occur.

By 1984, because of the favourable tax treatment of company cars, the business sector comprised 43 per cent of total sales. Changes in the tax treatment would inevitably affect this figure and taxation on company cars has increased in real terms since the early 1980s, and continued to rise in 1986/88.

The level of sales to the business sector tends to move in line with confidence in the economy, whereas sales to private individuals remain more or less stable, growing at a slow rate.

The different car buyers use distinct types of outlet for their purchases. The private and the self-employed buyer use the local dealer for their purchases; the fleet buyer negotiates either direct with the manufacturer or purchases from one of the major national chains; the contract hire companies mainly buy direct from the manufacturer.

COMPETITION TO AFI

Manufacturers

Many of the main manufacturers – Leyland (Supersure), Ford (Extracover), GM

(Mastercare), Peugeot (Talisman), VAG (Extended Cover) – have well-established extended warranty products which provide a range of spare parts and labour cover after the first year. The VAG insurance scheme, for example, offers two years' extra cover for 24,000 miles at around £110.

Led by the Japanese manufacturers, many companies are now beginning to incorporate three-year guarantees as standard, and it would appear that as components become more reliable, the extended warranty period will be steadily pushed back. Manufacturers' extended warranties tend to be limited and often complex from the customer's viewpoint – they cannot be arranged for second-hand cars, though cover was often transferable. The extended warranty market had continued to suffer from a history of poor reliability and suppliers concentrating on the 'small print' of the agreement, to reduce liabilities. Many of the warranty operators in other market sectors, notably home improvements and consumer durables, have gone out of business leaving the owner of the warranty with a worthless piece of paper. These problems caused a wide-scale suspicion of independent warranty schemes.

Increasingly, car manufacturers offered finance as a competitive edge – Nissan, for example, offering zero-rate finance, both Renault and Fiat offering similar packages with low deposit schemes. The reduction in the level of interest rates in the mid-1980s encouraged this trend.

Financial institutions

Historically the majority of private buyers used either building society finance (the famous 'mobile kitchen concept') or borrowed from a bank. During the 1970s and early 1980s a wide range of finance houses started to offer consumer finance designed for car and other customer purchases, Mercantile Credit and Lloyds Bowmaker being the main market leaders.

THE AFI PRODUCT RANGE

Gold Bond

The Gold Bond service offers insurance for periods of two to four years and from 24,000 to 60,000 miles on new vehicles, and either twelve months/20,000 miles or two years/24,000 miles on old vehicles. New car buyers are able to choose the level of cover that relates to the level of mileage envisaged. In addition to comprehensive mechanical and electrical cover Gold Bond offered:

(a) AA membership included;
(b) Europe-wide insurance;
(c) loss of earnings insurance;
(d) transferability with the car on future sale;

(e) minimal paperwork; AFI would authorize immediate repair work at the garage chosen by the customer without the form filling that was integral with the other schemes;

(f) car hire facilities while car out of operation.

The cost for Gold Bond varies from £122 for two years and 24,000 miles for the basic family saloon up to £703 for four years and 60,000 miles for the high-powered executive car. The cost of cover for a second-hand car with less than 50,000 miles travelled and four years old is £192 for twelve months and £269 for two years.

Average profit for each Gold Bond agreement is around £50 for AFI, which acts purely as the intermediary, all claims being settled by the insurance company.

Finance

Through associated finance houses AFI could supply a number of financial services:

(a) hire-purchase facilities;
(b) leasing services;
(c) credit protection insurance.

From the viewpoint of the dealer, AFI offers higher commission rates than the majority of the competition, and slightly lower overall finance charges.

As with Gold Bond, there is no fixed price for the finance package but each individual unit sold to a customer nets AFI around £75. The profit for the dealer is approximately the same although this varies according to the value of the package sold.

Flexibreaks

AFI sells a sales incentive package of five vouchers each providing free holiday accommodation in any one of 300 selected European hotels for two people for three nights. The market for such packages is considerable, but mainly concentrated outside the motor industry where companies do not employ large numbers of sales representatives – in contrast to national office equipment firms or consumer goods companies. The main competition for sales incentive vouchers comes from companies such as Bonusbonds, which services this wider market and allows the customer company to offer sales representatives the opportunity to purchase a range of products such as consumer durables in addition to accommodation. Many companies also preferred to run their own incentive schemes which they would organize either individually or via one of the eighty or so sales incentive companies operating in the UK. The profit to AFI of the Flexibreak package was estimated to be around £25 per sale.

AFI DISTRIBUTION AND PROMOTION POLICY

Initially it had been decided to distribute AFI products via car dealers who would act as intermediaries in selling to the end consumer. In early 1984 the company recruited six sales representatives, paid on a commission basis only, to cover the country geographically, together with a general manager with considerable experience of the motor trade.

Promotional techniques concentrated on the development of informative brochures and press releases to reduce consumer resistance to the wider spread of independent warranty schemes. Each customer subscribing to Gold Bond was provided with a membership card that allowed him or her direct access to the company, which was regarded as a fundamental part of AFI promotional policy.

COMPANY PROGRESS

By June 1985 all the salesforce had left the company, leaving the general manager and secretarial staff. Because of the shortfall in sales the loss the company was making had recently increased and it was estimated that this would increase to around £40,000 for the year, even though a contract with a specialist car importer to provide Gold Bond cover for all its vehicles had been achieved. This continued to provide the main income for the company as sales to other outlets were disappointing without sales representatives, and the necessity for the general manager, who had considerable experience in the motor insurance field, to carry out all customer contacts. The company's experience showed that where sales representatives had been successful the bulk of the income received was coming from Gold Bond; the other services had not achieved any significant level of turnover.

OVERHEADS

The company overheads were low, consisting just of the office costs, estimated at £45,000, and marketing costs which had run at £10,000 in the past year.

CLUB MÉDITERRANÉE

BACKGROUND

Club Méditerranée is one of the most successful international holiday camp companies. Founded in 1950 by a Frenchman, Gerard Blitz, the company is still run from Paris headquarters. By 1977 the Club provided holidays for well over 500,000 people (called *Gentils Membres* or GMs by the organization). Of these around 50 per cent are French, 18 per cent from North and Central America, and 27 per cent from other Western European countries.

By the late 1970s the arrival of the Mitterand government in France meant that the amount of money French holiday-makers could spend abroad was seriously reduced. This led the group to concentrate on building up the number of holidays taken by non-French nationals at Club Méditerranée centres. With certain exceptions this policy has proved highly successful (Table C4.1).

The development of Caribbean resorts for the North American market significantly changed the pattern of Club Méditerranée sales and profitability, which continued to grow at around 10 per cent per annum. Overall, the Club had been one of the growth companies in France and the shareholders remained content with the progress of the organization.

The success of the American venture had been due to various factors.

1. Concentration on a particular geographic and socio-economic market, especially the ABC1 East Coast urban dwellers.
2. Emphasizing the large number of sporting facilities available at the Caribbean Club Méditerranée centres.
3. Attracting a specific eighteen to twenty-eight age group.

Table C4.1   Country of origin of Club Méditerranée customers

Country	Numbers 1980/81	%	Numbers 1982/83	%
France	377,700	49	359,800	44.6
Belgium	40,000	5	39,000	5
Italy	45,000	6	43,000	5
Germany	35,000	4	31,000	4
Switzerland	22,000	3	21,000	3
UK	3,800	0.5	6,700	1
North America	136,300	18	176,000	22
Total	770,100		807,400	

THE DEVELOPING STRATEGY

Following upon its successful American venture, Club Méditerranée strategy continued to concentrate on markets with considerable untapped potential. Of these the UK supplied a likely source of growth. Based on gross domestic product comparisons, the market for Club Méditerranée holidays in the UK would be around two-thirds that of Germany – in the region of 26,000 holidays. Though the percentage of French speakers in the two populations is fairly similar, the fluency of the English population was reported to be steadily dropping, even with the increasing investment in language laboratories in schools.

The UK company was run by Club Méditerranée UK, a wholly owned subsidiary of the French parent. All major decisions on pricing were taken by head office in Paris as the UK was such a minor part of the overall operation. The UK office faced the task of improving the total number of holidays booked with Club Méditerranée from the current low base of around 10,000.

THE CLUB MÉDITERRANÉE APPROACH

The holiday camps are run by a staff of over 11,000 (called *Gentils Organisateurs* or GOs) in addition to over 1,100 sports instructors. The *Gentils Organisateurs* were largely recruited in France from the French student population; in the Caribbean they were recruited from the American market. The sports instructors were the main full-time members of the organization, remaining under contract for several years at a time. Each camp had a permanent staff of two or three that handled day-to-day administration.

By the mid-1980s the Club had one of the most far-flung international networks of any holiday company in the world, with around eighty resorts in twenty-four countries, having bases in the Caribbean, Mexico, Africa and the Pacific, in addition to all the Mediterranean countries. All resorts are based around two key elements of Méditerranée philosophy – informality and free access to a wide range of sporting activities.

Table C4.2　Club Méditerranée sporting facilities

Activity	No. of sites	No. of instructors	Equipment
Sailing	49	385	1,215 boats
Water skiing	20	112	100 boats
Aqualung diving	9	89	
Tennis	59	107	370 courts
Riding	16	57	520 horses
Skiing	19	300	

The first is achieved by insistence on sharing meal tables, group activities and youthful staff who encourage the vacationers to participate. All meals and wine are included in the holiday price; only drinks at the bar are extra, and these are paid for by beads which are universal currency in the village complexes. Sport is emphasized with the large number of instructors and the range of sporting activities possible at the Club Méditerranée sites (Table C4.2).

Most of the holiday camps in Mediterranean or tropical locations are huts accommodating four, built amongst trees leading down to the beach and restaurant area. Facilities in the huts are fairly basic, in line with the appeal of the Club Méditerranée of 'going back to nature'.

THE UK HOLIDAY MARKET

In 1986, 17.5 million holidays were taken by Britons abroad, an increase of around 20 per cent on 1984. Between 1970–1982 the number of overseas holidays taken by UK residents expanded steadily while holidays at home remained static. For example, in 1979 only 20 per cent of total holidays were taken overseas – by 1984 the figure had risen to 30 per cent and this trend was set to continue. More UK families were also taking two holidays abroad, with Christmas and Easter growing in popularity. The popularity of a skiing holiday for the young ABs had been a new feature of the 1980s.

Long-haul holidays were showing the most substantial growth, around 25 per cent per year, which had to an extent been fuelled by the lowering of the dollar against the pound, but the Far East was also becoming increasingly attractive as a centre for winter holidays.

The industry, however, faced a number of continuing problems.

1. A trend towards late booking. Historically tour operators could always rely on more than two-thirds of their business being forward booked in the early months of the year. Recently this percentage had started to drop and there had been a substantial increase in the number of late bookings, which were offered at a discount via Prestel which had become a major clearing house for holiday bookings.

2. Rising inflation in the main holiday resorts. A 13 per cent rate in Spain had continued to push up the cost of holidays; Greece also suffered from high inflation rates.
3. Highly competitive environment. The continuing battle between the two market leaders, Thomson and Intasun, for market dominance had resulted in a substantial number of smaller tour operators going out of business each year. This and certain well-publicized holiday cancellations in the aftermath of the Laker collapse helped establish a pattern of booking the standard package holiday through major operators.
4. Continuing market segmentation. The growth in the number of overseas holidays meant that there was an increasing demand for specialized holiday providers; adventure holidays (Encounter Overland), interest holidays (Swans Tours, for example, providing lecture tours of Ancient Europe), group holidays (Saga holidays, Club 18–30). The major tour companies were also adding specialized brochures to their established ones, an example being the introduction of the Thomson organization 'Freestyle' brochures. Throughout the industry, special interest holidays including study sessions were regarded as being more important.

    This segementation was underlined by the increasing variation of family size and structure, divided by the use of sagacity life-cycles which define stages of dependency (still at home but adult), pre-family (bachelor), family stages from worse off (−) with young children to better off (+) with older children and, finally, to the retired, post-child departure or late stage in family life (Table C4.3). This variety in family structure is also shown in the varying sizes of households (Table C4.4).

Table C4.3   Family life stages and socio-economic groups – percentage in each category

	ABC1	C2DE	ABC+	ABC1−	C2DE+	C2DE−
			(percentage of all adults)			
Dependent	6	10				
Pre-family	4	4				
Family			7	7	7	14
Late			5	10	6	20

Table C4.4   Family structure and household size

Household size	%
1	25
2	32
3	16
4	18
5 or more	9

Source: OPCS Monitor

Table C4.5   Socio-economic groups in the adult population

Social grade	Numbers of adults over 15 ('000)	Adult population (%)
A	1,349	3.1
B	6,123	13.9
C1	9,772	22.2
C2	12,540	28.4
D	7,919	18.0
E	6,398	14.5

5. There was a continuing trend towards higher advertising expenditure with the entire sector showing an increase from £45 million in 1979 to £93 million in 1984 (a substantial real increase over the 50 per cent increase in the retail price index over the same period).

6. A trend towards second holidays for the more affluent. More and more of the young, higher socio-economic group were taking second holidays, with a particular emphasis on winter sports as the second holiday of the year. This was particularly so with the ABs (Table C4.5).

The favourite destination by far was Spain, receiving more than a third of British tourists. Other favourite destinations were Italy, Greece and Yugoslavia.

THE PACKAGE HOLIDAY MARKET IN THE UK

The market is dominated by Thomson and Intasun, which between them provide 55 per cent of the total package holiday market. The result is that the holiday market is highly price competitive for the basic component of two weeks in the sun, generally in Spain. Table C4.6 breaks down British holidays taken in 1986, and Table C4.7 shows the most popular package holiday destinations.

Table C4.6   British holidays in 1986

	Taken in Britain	Taken abroad
Total	31.0 million	17.5 million
Package	14%	62%
Holiday began in May	9	9
June	14	14
July	21	17
August	25	14
September	12	14
Other	19	31
Travel by: Plane		70
Coach		27
Total expenditure (£m)	3,050	6,740
Average cost per person	£100	£370

Source: British Tourist Authority

Table C4.7   Packaged holiday destination

Holiday destination	Packaged holiday (%)
Spain	34
Portugal	4
Malta	6
Greece	9
Italy	5
France	12
Other Europe	5

STRUCTURE OF THE TRADE

Access to the market is through one of around 3,000 travel agents who book the vast majority of holidays (Table C4.8). There are a number of large groups within the travel trade (Table C4.9). W.H. Smith, which had a large retail travel agency presence in the early 1980s, has been pulling out of the market to concentrate on mainstream activities, and had only 20 outlets by the end of 1986.

With a large number of companies operating package holidays in the UK there is considerable competition for shelf space in the travel agents' outlets. Brochures that did not 'sell' were replaced with ones that did, so that while the market leaders Thomson and Intasun were automatically stocked, other companies had to fight for space.

One result is that the percentage of holidays booked direct slowly increased during the 1980s, particularly for the basic two-week package holidays in the main resorts. The main company, Tjaeborg, was slowly opening the market for other operators. Naturally, holiday operators booking direct save in a number of areas, including:

(a) travel agent's commission (around 14 per cent of gross price);

Table C4.8   Holiday bookings by outlet (%)

Travel agents	87
Direct	10
Other	3

Table C4.9   Outlets of major travel agency groups

Thomas Cook	430
Pickford	350
AT Mays	230
Lunn Poly	300
Co-op	200
Hogg Robinson	250
Exchange Travel	75
American Express	70

(b) the number of brochures produced (an increasingly expensive exercise as brochures would cost anything from £1.50, but for the larger operators there were impressive economies of scale).

The disadvantage was the holiday company would lack the specialized knowledge and sales ability of the local travel agent – important in selling up-market or 'special' holidays. In this sector, companies used sales representatives actively to push the travel agents to promote their particular brochure, organizing competitions for the most successful outlets.

THE CURRENT MÉDITERRANÉE OPERATION

Sales

UK sales of Club Méditerranée holidays grew steadily over the last five years but were still substantially below expectations (Table C4.10).

Sixty-eight per cent of holiday bookings were from London and the South East; only 25 per cent came through travel agents. Only about 10 per cent of travel agents kept the up-to-date Méditerranée brochure, though there was quite a high degree of trade awareness of the company.

Competition

Though no holiday group was directly comparable to Club Méditerranée, there were a number that operated in the same type of market sector; Club 18–30, Club Mark Warner, and Club Cantabrica. The price for a two-week holiday in Spain and the facilities offered are in Table C4.11.

Attitudes of current or potential consumers to a Club Méditerranée holiday

1. Advantages of a Club Méditerranée holiday:
   (a) relaxed and informal;
   (b) children can be 'organized';
   (c) sophisticated French atmosphere;
   (d) excellent sporting arrangements.
2. Complaints about Club Méditerranée:
   (a) staff did not speak English, and there was often no one available to deal with complaints from English-speaking guests; all sports tuition was in French;
   (b) often basic accommodation;
   (c) required to share with other people;
   (d) poor administration and facilities – no television, or pool tables in the bar.

Table C4.10 UK bookings of Club
Méditerranée holidays

Year	Bookings
1978/79	5,692
1979/80	6,476
1980/81	7,779
1981/82	8,178
1982/83	9,404
1983/84	9,707

Table C4.11 The competition to Club Méditerranée

Operator	Price (£ per person)	Accommodation	Meals	Sports facilities
Méditerranée	385	3 star	All	Free
Mark Warner	240	Basic	All	Free but limited
Club 18–30	200	Basic	HB	Extra
Cantabrica	150	V. basic	SC	Extra

(HB = half board, SC = self catering)

Table C4.12 Profile of Club Méditerranée clients

Number of people in group:
1   43%
2   33%
3   25%

Age of individuals booking Club Méditerranée holidays:
12–18   12%
18–25   25%
25–35   53%

Socio-economic group:
AB   67%
C1   21%
C2   12%

Method of transport:
Direct flight   65%
Own arrangement   20%
Via Paris   15%

Length of stay:
One week   40%
Two weeks   58%
Over two weeks   2%

Table C4.13   Attitude survey

On a scale of agreement between 1 and 5 (strongly disagree to strongly agree) the following pattern emerges for a series of issues.

Factor	Not visited Méditerranée	Visited
Value for money	1	4
Strong sexual element	5	2
Only for French speakers	4	2
Sports are voluntary	1	5
Good standard accommodation	3.5	3.5
Wide choice of destinations	3.5	3.5
Good value for families	1	4
Food is excellent	3.5	4.5
Sophisticated holiday	3.5	5

Table C4.14   Club Méditerranée advertising (£000)

	1982	1983	1984	1985
Sunday magazines	36	98	90	267
Channel 4 television			51	

There was a high degree of repeat purchase among those who had been on a Club Méditerranée holiday, with around 65 per cent of first time Club vacationers going for a second time. Table C4.12 gives a profile of the Club clients, and Table C4.13 the results of an attitude survey.

Advertising

Table C4.14 gives details of Club Méditerranée's advertising expenditure from 1982 to 1985.

Case 5

TRANSIT

INTRODUCTION

Transit was a limited liability company established in 1980 in the West Midlands. It was involved in four activities.

1. Vehicle repair – mainly of buses and lorries in the commercial and public sectors, and included a large amount of metal-bashing and repainting work.
2. Bus hire – mainly school buses hired to local authorities. Transit leased the vehicles on an annual basis and then hired out the buses to the local authorities, providing the necessary drivers and carrying out all the maintenance.
3. Manufacture and hire of buses specially adapted for disabled passengers – a service used by local authorities, homes for the elderly and charitable organizations for the elderly and infirm. The company owned two vans, which had been specially converted at the Transit works at a total cost of £40,000. In common with the bus hire operation the company hired out these special vehicles to the local authorities.
4. A garage – supplying petrol and providing servicing and MOTs for motor vehicles. The vast majority of the servicing work was carried out at the same time as vehicle repair. Of total mechanic time, only 10 per cent was spent on the bus hire or disabled vehicles as both were new and well maintained.

By late 1985, though the company had rapidly grown in turnover from around £50,000 in the first year to a current budgeted figure of £350,000, the level of borrowings continued to rise, and one of the major shareholders, the local authority, was worried about the viability of the operation. Tables C5.1 and C5.2 give sales figures for 1984 and 1985, and a monthly breakdown of the latter.

Table C5.1   Transit sales progress 1984/5

Sales (£)	1984	1985
Garage	78,000	75,000
Motor repair	125,000	180,000
Bus hire	55,000	65,000
Disabled vehicles	40,000	48,000

Table C5.2   Transit month by month sales analysis 1985

	1	2	3	4	5	6	7	8	9	10	11	12
Garage	6	6	6	6	7	7	7	6	6	6	6	6
Motor repair	10	10	8	8	20	26	20	22	22	10	8	16
Bus hire	5	5	5	5	5	5	5	5	5	5	5	5
Disabled vehicles	1	1	1	3	9	10	9	8	4	1	1	1

(Sales in £000 – some rounding adjustments.)

THE COMPANY MARKET

From its West Midlands site, Transit serviced a territory roughly 30 miles in radius. In this area there were twenty local authorities, each with its own school bus policy. Transit had contracts with three of the larger authorities and was negotiating with five others. Contracts were slow to obtain but once acquired would continue for a considerable period: of those currently held, one contract would run for four years, and two for two. Local authorities emphasized the need for reliability of the bus network, and Transit was well able to provide this. The pricing of the contracts did not appear to be too important, though Transit knew that each year the contracts were put out to tender and three of the local bus companies continued to pitch for the business. Once the contract was agreed with the local authority Transit was paid one-twelfth of the annual amount, monthly. With the move to privatize these services, Transit was fairly content with future prospects both within and outside the area, though this would have a number of administrative implications. Though there had been slight reductions in the number of children attending school in the area, the market for this service was likely to remain substantial for the foreseeable future.

In the same catchment area, there were around 250 bus and commercial vehicle operators. The size of the firms varied considerably from owner–drivers with one or two vehicles to firms with fleets of several hundred. Transit serviced the medium to small companies unable themselves to maintain a cost-effective service facility. Little of this work was on a regular basis as these companies had their vehicles serviced during slack periods. The average size fleet serviced by Transit was seven vehicles. The industry was characterized by a fairly high level of company failure; debts were paid only slowly and Transit faced continual problems with bad debts and slow payments, which reflected in their balance sheet (discussed later). The economy affected the amount of servicing that companies demanded. When times were good haulage operators bought new vehicles; when times were hard they tended to postpone non-essential maintenance. The recession in the Midlands continued to hit this business, especially in the level of prices that could be charged.

Though it had more sophisticated equipment than many others, Transit found that this particular market was very competitive as there were a large number of other garages offering similar services and, in addition – because of the high level of unemployment – there were a substantial number of freelance mechanics available to service vehicles on a company's own premises.

Different divisions of the same local authorities provided the main customers for the disabled vehicles. There were also a large number of private nursing and retirement homes throughout the area that from time to time required transport for occupants. In this last category there were an estimated 300 institutions that might occasionally take advantage of the Transit services. Transit was the only company offering a custom-built disabled bus service, with special arrangements for wheelchairs and the like. In contrast to the school bus business the company had been unable to develop any permanent contractual relationships with the local authorities or other institutions. Hiring of the disabled buses tended to be *ad hoc*. In common with the rest of the country the Midlands had a growing elderly population, which indeed had first encouraged the company to enter this specific market.

Payment proved a problem in this sector, though it was common to experience some delays in payment in other areas of the company's operations as well.

For Transit, promotional activity was limited. Fred Smith, Transit's managing director, handled the negotiations for the bus contracts personally and the company obtained its repair work through the Yellow Pages. Every six months Transit sent out to all institutions a reminder about the disabled bus concept.

The garage operated as one of many in the area providing fuel and MOT inspection facilities.

COMPANY OVERHEADS

There were two sites operated by Transit.

The workshop

This also included the head office and was based in large, newly constructed premises of some 3,000 square feet, rented at £6 per square foot. The workshop was used by Transit for its manufacturing operations as well as for garaging the fleet of hire buses. Staffing here was as follows:

(a) eight mechanics, each earning £7,000 p.a.;

(b) one mechanic, skilled in sheet metal work and at modifying vehicles for
     disabled passengers, earning £8,500 p.a.;
(c) two secretarial/administration staff, each earning £4,500 p.a.

All staff were paid on a flat piece-work basis though there were additional
payments for overtime and weekend working, which was often necessary for
vehicle repair.

There was a very high workforce turnover; despite being in an area of high
unemployment, the average mechanic stayed with the company for only six
months, in contrast to the secretarial and administrative staff, who had been with
the company from the start.

Other overhead costs included the following:

(a) heating and lighting for the workshop amounted to £2,000 p.a.;
(b) workshop rates cost £2,000 p.a.

There were a variety of other miscellaneous costs, totalling £10,000 per annum.
These included the telephone, post, and accountancy and selling costs.

A substantial and rising overhead was the finance charges on the amount the
company was currently borrowing. It was likely that in 1985 total outgoings (loan
plus capital repayment) would be of the order of £25,000. By the end of 1984 the
company had reached the ceiling on its borrowing allowed by the local branch of
one of the clearing banks.

The garage

The garage was on a single site five miles from the workshop, owned by Transit on
a 99-year lease, for which it had paid £30,000 in 1982. It had been bought as a
diversification from the original core business as it was thought at the time that it
would provide a steady cash flow to help iron out some of the variations that the
company had experienced during the early years.

Commercial property values had fallen during the early 1980s and it was
unlikely that the company would be able to realize a similar figure in the current
environment. There were three other garages nearby, two of which had recently
refurbished forecourts. Both of these belonged to national chains and could offer
substantial discounts on petrol sales, selling 4-star petrol at 5p below the price
Transit could achieve. The recession had continued to reduce the average annual
motoring mileage and this had had the effect of lowering total petrol sales in the
area.

There were two full-time employees at the garage:

(a) one mechanic on a salary of £7,000 p.a.;
(b) one petrol pump attendant, paid £3,000 p.a.;
(c) occasional part-time staff cost around £1,500 p.a. each.

Table C5.3   Transit balance sheet 1984

Assets		£
Fixed assets:	Plant	45,000
	Leasehold property	32,000
Current assets:	Stock and work-in-progress	45,000
	Debtors	95,000
	Cash	5,000
Liabilities	Creditors	55,000
	Bank loan	113,000
Net assets		54,000
Financed by:		
Paid-up share capital		54,000

Table C5.4   Transit cost of activities

Cost of sales (£)	1984	1985
Garage	55,000	54,000
Motor repair	80,000	115,000
Bus hire	30,000	34,000
Disabled vehicles	20,000	25,000

Garage rates cost £850 a year. Other overhead costs such as heating, lighting and the telephone cost £1,200 per annum.

FIXED ASSETS/EQUIPMENT

The company did not have a large amount of fixed assets, but there were a number of substantial items, including:

(a) metal-working machinery costing £20,000;
(b) two buses for the disabled, costing £20,000 each;
(c) miscellaneous equipment with an estimated value of £1,500.

Table C5.3 shows the 1984 balance sheet.

The cost of sales figure (Table C5.4) included all the material costs relating to the specific activity – petrol for the garage, oil and spare parts for the repair activities, the hire costs of the buses from the manufacturers and the wages of the drivers. It did not include the overhead cost of the labour or the fixed costs of the buildings Transit operated from.

MANAGEMENT

Transit's founder and major shareholder was Fred Smith. He had been in the transport business for some twenty years in a company run by his father which had gone bankrupt, and had mortgaged his house for £35,000 to start the company. Fred Smith received an annual salary of £15,000 from Transit.

His brother Dave Smith was a non-executive director receiving £5,000 a year from Transit as well as holding 25 per cent of the company's shares, since he had put up the remaining £10,000 required to start the company.

The Borough of Drotwick owned 20 per cent of the Transit shares as part of its policy of encouraging local employment in a depressed area. It had provided additional finance during the early part of 1982 so that the company could move from its original site under some railway arches to a purpose-built workshop in the local trading estate and take on five additional staff.

Case 6

EXTON COMMUNITY CENTRE

INTRODUCTION

Exton Community Centre was built as part of the redevelopment of Exton, one of the suburbs of Birmingham. The town's population was around 20,000. Like many other towns in the Midlands, Exton suffered from a high level of unemployment in the 1980s. Local rates had risen to 18 per cent with the closure of the major printing and packaging works that had been one of the main employers in the town. The rising number of elderly in the area was also a cause for concern, though the proportion of the over-sixties in the population was not exceptional and merely reflected the national average.

THE COMMUNITY CENTRE

The Community Centre was a purpose-built brick building in the centre of the town not far from the public library and the two main supermarkets. It had two large function halls and six smaller meeting rooms; in the reception area there was a coffee lounge.

The Centre was a non-profit making association. There was a board of trustees appointed by the local council that provided the main proportion of the funding; the remainder was received from functions organized by the Centre and from letting rooms to particular interest groups. Under the terms of reference from the local authority, the Centre was obliged to offer space to all interest groups of a non-political nature. It could not make space available to anyone on a permanent basis under the terms of the charter and moves to try to establish the Citizens' Advice Bureau in the Centre had been refused because of this stipulation.

The following groups currently meet regularly at the Community Centre.

- Exton History and Archaeology Group
- Exton Natural History Society
- Exton Painting Group
- Exton Chess Club
- Exton Bridge Club
- Exton Horticultural Society
- Exton Flower Arranging Group
- Exton Anglo-European Group
- Exton Dressmaking Group
- Exton HelpLine Group
- Exton Divorced Circle
- Exton Youth Club

Most of these groups met weekly for two hours of an evening, though the Youth Club was far more active, meeting three evenings a week for three hours. The membership paid for the hire of the rooms from their subscriptions.

Some groups were excluded under council guidelines. The Exton Film Club and the Exton Dramatic Society were excluded on the grounds of programme content; the Exton Gilbert and Sullivan Society and the Exton Operatic Society on grounds of noise.

The function rooms were used every weekend for a craft market, which had proved a continually popular event. Occasionally in the evenings particular groups such as the British Legion held dances; attempts to run regular events for a wide range of the town's population by offering such events as singles evenings or youth discos had always been failures, and with the cost of the licence extension and extra staffing had always led to a loss of between £100 and £250. The reason for this failure was that there were two discos in the town that held dances every night of the week (except Sundays) and had developed programmes for specific interest groups in the community. There were also many more complaints to the police about noise and disorderly conduct arising from evening events organized at the Centre.

The charges the Centre could levy were agreed with the local council, at £3 per hour for the small meeting rooms and £15 per hour for the function rooms. Every year the management committee negotiated with the freelance group that worked the coffee bar; the revenue the Centre received from this source had risen steadily to a projected £3,000 in 1987. This was substantially in excess of what the Centre had achieved when it ran the coffee bar itself.

Because the Centre was open long hours the staffing costs were high, even though most staff worked part time. The Centre did not pay rent or rates as it was sited on council property. With the current hours and the need for supervision it was very unlikely that the staffing costs could be substantially reduced.

The reduction in rate support from central government meant that the local council had to reduce funding for a number of activities such as the library and the

Table C6.1   Funds statement (£)

	1985	1986	1987 (projected)
Income: Local authority	20,000	21,000	21,000
Functions	12,000	13,000	13,500
Expenditure			
Wages	19,000	21,000	23,500
Heating/lighting	3,000	3,700	4,200
Publicity	2,000	2,500	3,000
Telephone	1,000	1,200	1,500
Insurance	500	700	800
Breakages etc.	300	300	300
Maintenance	4,000	4,500	5,500
Cleaning	2,000	2,200	2,300
Total	31,800	36,100	41,100
Surplus (deficit)	200	(2,100)	(6,600)

Citizens' Advice Bureau. The council had decided to continue to hold the grant to the Community Centre at the same level in absolute terms for the year 1987 (which meant a drop in real terms of around 5 per cent in the funding the Centre received).

To break even the trustees of the Centre realized that they would have to raise hourly room rates by around 50 per cent. Initial response from many of the groups involved was that they would actively seek accommodation elsewhere and most were likely to find places in nearby church halls; a loss of 50 per cent of the groups regularly using the Centre was anticipated.

Table C6.1 shows funds statements for the Centre for the last three years.

Case 7

PRESTEL

BACKGROUND

Originally conceived as a mass medium to popularize computerized information, Prestel was the world's first public viewdata system and was launched by the Post Office in 1979. A concerted campaign by government, television manufacturers, semiconductor producers, broadcasters and retailers publicizing both the sets and broadcast service helped to stimulate public awareness and interest in the new service.

Prestel has its origins in concern about cost-effectiveness and efficiency. While working on a computer register of hotel vacancies in the late 1960s, its inventor found that most of the cost of that system was absorbed in the high labour costs and overheads in the central bureau which operated it. Sam Fedida felt that it would be more efficient if the customer was able to gain access to the information in the computer without the need for office clerk intermediaries. After joining the Post Office in 1970, the research engineer began experimenting by putting texts on to viewphone – a system allowing callers to see whom they were speaking to – and from there to adapting the ubiquitous television set. At this time British Telecom was a public sector company and the government was encouraging the development of new technology throughout the sector. British Telecom, however, was and continued to be a provider of telecommunications equipment and could be considered a hardware provider. Very little of the resources available within the company went on the development of software, of which the Prestel concept was essentially a part. By 1985, investment in non-mainline activities was only around £10 million per annum in a corporation with a £4 billion turnover. The main thrust of the Post Office (and, following privatization, British Telecom) had been to concentrate on the provision of a profitable telephone network. The main investment thrust following privatization had been to concentrate on reducing manpower by investing in new capital equipment.

THE VIDEOTEXT AND VIEWDATA MARKET

Videotext needs to be clearly separated from viewdata. Videotext transfers computer-stored information to a modified television set. Two kinds of videotext are in use in the UK: broadcast videotext and viewdata. Broadcast videotext, known as teletext in Britain, supplies information via the television, using spare capacity on existing television channels, and is available from the BBC as Ceefax and from the IBA as Oracle. Both these services cater for the general public, providing a wide variety of up-to-date information in over 1,000 pages, including general, financial, sports and news information. Both provide relatively inexpensive ways of transmitting computer-based information to the public although the speed of the service is slow and the graphics and text on screen are crude by both television and computing standards.

In contrast, viewdata systems like Prestel convert the domestic television set into a terminal displaying words and graphics. The television set is linked by telephone to a central computer which stores hundreds of pages of information.

Prestel has the advantage of being interactive – teletext being a read-only service. Viewdata users can both receive information and send instructions to the main computer to answer questions, order shopping or use their bank account, for example. Teletext is essentially free after the initial outlay of £50–100 for a modified television set. In addition to the cost of modifying their sets, Prestel users must pay a subscription fee, local telephone charges, time charges and any others levied by the companies supplying the information.

Pilot studies carried out to determine interest in Prestel revealed that 60 per cent of businesses interviewed would be interested in using it were it to become available. Only 20 per cent of householders interviewed were interested.

FOREIGN VIEWDATA

Internationally, Prestel has two major rivals: Teletel and Telidon.

Teletel is the French viewdata system, which has enjoyed a huge amount of government support. One experiment supplied French homes and offices with Minitel terminals to replace telephone directories in the expectation that once a population of terminals had been created, information providers would be able to sell other services to users. The French government has also used the system to communicate with businesses, for example for filling in forms, with the intention of installing viewdata wherever it was likely to be cost-effective in streamlining government and reducing paperwork.

Telidon, the Canadian viewdata system, has two technical advantages over Prestel: graphics – drawn geometrically instead of using an alphamosaic pattern – are better but require terminals with large memories as well as accurate data transmission. Telidon also separates the information storage from the communications and display terminals so avoiding the problem of rapid technical developments making data unusable. Telidon is expensive: Canadians currently pay more

Table C7.1 Breakdown of worldwide videotext techniques

Standard	'000s	%
British	2,260.0	98.2
French	30.0	1.3
Canadian	5.8	0.3
Others	4.2	0.2
Total	2,300.0	100.0

Source: UK Videotext Industry Association

than £850 for a terminal and the low user base means that it does not supply a great deal of information. Recently the Canadians have joined forces with the Japanese in the hope of reviving Telidon and providing a joint world standard for viewdata.

In April 1983 there were 2.3 million videotext terminals throughout the world. One million were in the UK, which dominates world markets. This apparent dominance is, however, almost entirely due to the large number of Oracle and Ceefax users; the UK market share of viewdata services being 60 per cent (Table C7.1).

THE DEVELOPMENT OF PRESTEL

The system

A frame (24 rows of 40 character positions) is a screenful of information displayed on a Prestel terminal. A page is a basic unit of Prestel information, which is most often a sequence of a few successive frames.

End pages contain the actual hard facts.

Routing pages guide the user to the end page, each one giving a menu of up to ten choices. Having to work through these pages to the hard facts at the end can be time-consuming.

The telephone user can gain access to Prestel in a number of ways.

1. Through a television adaptor costing about £260 plus VAT.
2. Through a microcomputer adaptor, with prices ranging from £100 (by the mid-1980s) down to around £60 for the Sinclair Spectrum Adaptor to £300 for the IBM PC Adaptor.
3. Through a dedicated terminal, for the office user, available from manufacturers like Sony and Philips, on lease or purchase.

Each user is provided with the necessary access keyboard or keypad. A printer can be attached to the system for those likely to require hard copies. By pressing a single button on the keypad, the user telephones the nearest Prestel computer; each user is registered on at least two computers.

GATEWAY

The Gateway system was introduced in 1982 in an attempt to alter Prestel radically so as to make it more economically viable. Rather than trying to supply information itself, it was felt that Prestel could supply a network which would link users to computerized information systems.

By means of a suitable password, Gateway gives the Prestel terminal user access to third party computers. For the cost of a local telephone call, desk-top access to data stored in computers anywhere in the country can be gained. The service makes possible telebanking and teleshopping. In January 1985 there were seventeen Prestel Gateways in operation.

THE INFORMATION PROVIDERS

Data supplied by the information provider, through a specially designed terminal, is transmitted to the nearest updating centre and thence to the appropriate information retrieval centre containing the database. For many information providers Prestel's interactivity is its greatest advantage: for airlines it means that travellers can book their own flights direct instead of via the travel agent; manufacturers can sell direct to the consumer. Although the majority of pages are free, some information providers levy an access charge – price is indicated on the top line of each page.

Some of the larger information providers, like the London and South East Library Region (LASER), are umbrella organizations acting for those who wish to use Prestel for advertising but find the costs too high. These lease a frame, or half a frame, at very competitive rates, and bear the cost of updating and maintaining the system. In the year ending 31 March 1985, there were thirty-one organizations purchasing space from LASER for community and local information, or library information.

The total number of Prestel information providers had stabilized at 160 by 1985, following financial problems among some of the smaller contributors and a number of withdrawals from the system by organizations like W.H. Smith and Eastern Counties Newspapers Ltd. The emergence of umbrella information providers has meant, however, that in reality the number of organizations and individuals contributing to the service is probably in excess of 500.

CLOSED USER GROUPS

Prestel can provide information to selected groups of users, or closed user groups. This means that only users nominated by the owner of the frames have access to the information, thereby allowing those who use it to create their own private viewdata systems without the costs and problems of running it themselves. Organizations involved include Micronet 800, the microcomputing club, and Farmlink.

This service has potential for those listing classified information such as wholesale and commodity prices and trade information. The closed user group facility also makes it possible for any department of a company to send information to another quickly and relatively cheaply, especially as staff do not need any specialist skills to operate the system.

PRESTEL'S ORIGINAL OBJECTIVES

British Telecom initially invested more than £50 million in Prestel.

The strategy outlined for Prestel was:

(a) to generate profits;
(b) to establish Prestel as a standard viewdata system in as much of the world as possible;
(c) to provide a good value for money service;
(d) to get customers to use their telephones in the evening when the network has massive over-capacity.

Prestel broke even for the first time in 1985, after losses of £30 million in the first two years of operation. Table C7.2 compares Prestel use in 1980 and 1985.

Prestel had been established as a separately accounted profit centre in the Post Office and it had to set its prices at a level which would cover its identifiable costs and earn an adequate return on the capital it employed. No account was taken of the revenue British Telecom gets from telephone calls to Prestel, as it was felt that

Table C7.2   Prestel use in the UK

	1980	1985
Frames in use	160,000	337,000
Subscribers	10,000	62,000
Total accesses/year	20 million	379 million
Average weekly accesses:		
– per subscriber	40	118
– per frame	2	22
Prestel usage by type (estimated)		
Travel	50%	65%
Database usage	22%	15%
Mail transfer	6%	10%
Misc. (Yellow pages etc.)	12%	10%
Market shares by value (estimated)		
Teletext	75%	55%
Prestel	10%	8%
Other databases	15%	37%
Total value	£50 million	£180 million

this revenue was needed to expand the telephone system and that a cross-subsidy would have enabled Prestel to compete unfairly with private viewdata services.

With the privatization of Telecom in 1983, the first national competition, Mercury, was granted a licence by the regulatory body, the Office of Telecommunications (Oftel). By the end of 1986 Mercury was still not offering a truly national service but had already made headway with a number of business users in the main cities. Early on Mercury announced its intention of providing a similar service to Prestel. With potentially lower access costs (Mercury charges for long-distance calls are substantially cheaper than BT) the proposed service would become increasingly competitive. By the end of 1986 this service was under test and is likely to be available to Mercury subscribers during 1987 or 1988.

The British market was further complicated by the fact that in 1986 Telecom introduced a directly competitive service to Prestel; Hotline to compete with Mercury in the business sector.

PROGRESS

Both the teletext and viewdata operators had foreseen that the availability of specially converted television sets would be an important motivating factor in determining the eventual demand for the service.

The production target of 50,000 sets for the 1979 Prestel launch had to be reduced to 20,000 and, as a result, some of those information providers who would have participated in the scheme decided to pull out in view of the uncertainties. Despite the fact that there were few sets available the Post Office went ahead with a £750,000 advertising campaign designed to attract domestic users.

Table C7.3   Teletext receivers in use in the UK (millions)

1983		1984	1985
January	November	June	January
0.8	1.4	2.2	2.4

Source: Viewdata Industry Association

Table C7.4   Prestel receivers in use in the UK ('000s)

1983	1984		1985	
January	January	November	January	November
22	35	50	52	62

Source: Prestel

NB: The November 1985 figure conceals the fact that some users have a single registration but more than one terminal. Of these users the majority were business operators, though there had recently been an increase in the amount of home use due to the installation of business terminals at home following the increased level of home working.

Initially teletext was expensive, but the cost of receivers dropped by more than 60 per cent since 1979 and many new television sets have teletext built in. The figure of 2.4 million teletext receivers for January 1985 represented 12 per cent of all UK households.

Uptake was by people from socio-economic groups A and B, but the base has subsequently broadened.

A strategic relaunch of Oracle took place in November 1983 and the service claims to have a daily audience of 2 million with the ability to reach 3.5 million per week. Oracle's advertising revenue has doubled and it is expected to reach £50 million by 1990, most of which will be profit. By then the service will have achieved up to 85 per cent penetration of UK households with an installation base of 12 million sets (Tables C7.3 and C7.4).

OTHER COMPETITION: THE GROWING SPECIALIST DATABASES

During the 1980s there has been a rapid growth of dedicated databases specializing in particular aspects of industry. The speed of expansion has been marked in a number of areas.

1. Financial services (Datastream, Extel, Reuters, *Financial Times*).
2. Research and development (Lockheed, AMA).

Though there is often a degree of overlap with viewdata (for example Citiservice operates on Prestel), the main developmental thrust has been towards establishing individual accounts with the major institutions. Mercury was expected to provide a substantial amount of the cable connections for these developing networks.

The potential database market

The database market is among large institutions and specialized professional agencis providing specific services to a wide range of small institutions. There are some exceptions to this rule – for example travel agents (in excess of 3,000 outlets) required immediate access to travel booking data, and farms employing few individuals also required some on-line information (Table C7.5).

COSTS OF PRESTEL

The 1985 costs of the various options available under the Prestel system and of some examples are estimated in Tables C7.6 to C7.10.

Table C7.5　Potential database market

Size of employment unit	Number of units
1	115,000
2	129,000
3–4	185,000
5–10	258,000
11–24	163,000
25–49	70,000
50–99	33,000
100–199	17,000
200–499	10,000
500–999	3,100
1,000–1,999	1,100
2,000–4,999	417
5,000+	64
Specialists (by approximate number of practices)	
Accountants	5,000
Solicitors	8,000
Architects	1,200
Stockbrokers etc.	800
Consultants (misc.)	3,000
Tertiary higher education	250
Secondary schools	10,000

Source: Department of Trade

Table C7.6　Prestel: cost of standard access for domestic and business user

	Domestic user	Business
Standing charge (quarterly)	£6.50	£18
Time charge:		
Mon.–Fri. 8 a.m.–6 p.m.	0.6p per minute	
Saturday 8 a.m.–6 p.m.	0.6p per minute	
All other times	free	
Local telephone call		
Information provider levy		

NB: Telephone charges are included on the quarterly telephone bill, not on the Prestel bill which is issued separately.

Table C7.7　Likely company costs of Prestel when using more than standard information screens an average of 30 minutes a day (£)

Standing charge at £18 per quarter	72.0
Time charges	453.6
Frame charges	197.6
Telex charges	10.0
Citiservice subscription	90.0
Phone charges	302.4
Total including VAT	1,125.6

Table C7.8   Likely domestic costs of Prestel when using other than
standard service an average of 30 minutes a day (£)

Micronet 800 subscription at £16 per quarter	64.00
Time charges	112.68
Frame charges	98.80
Club 403 subscription at £6 per quarter	24.00
Phone charges	164.66
Toal	464.14

Table C7.9   Prestel services: some business examples

Facility	Information providers	Closed user groups	Costs	Competitors
Citiservice	Stock Exchange, brokers, banks, financial institutions	Yes – but some pages available to all users	level 1 – free level 2 – £18/qtr. level 3 – £90/qtr.	Topic Bulletin Datastream
Agricultural Service	Farmlink	Yes	£40/qtr.	ICI Grapevine ICI Agviser
Telex			100 words: 50p (UK) £1 (Europe) £2 (N. Am.) £3 other	Conventional telex machines
Mailbox				Telecom Gold Istels' Comet
Travel/hotel bookings	Numerous travel agents, travel companies, hotels			Travel agents, credit card booking services
Micro-computing	Micronet 800 'Busnet'	Yes – but some pages available to all users	£16/qtr.	
Closed user groups Private viewdata			£320 p.a.	In-company private viewdata systems

Table C7.10   Prestel services: some domestic user examples

Facility	Information providers	Closed user groups	Costs	Competitors
News, sport and general information				Ceefax, Oracle other media
Consumer advice				Which?
Teleshopping	Littlewoods Shop TV	No		Mail order catalogues
	Club 403	Yes	£6/qtr.	
Home banking	Nottingham Building Society	Yes	None if balance £1,200 or more; less – charge £2 per month	Other banks Home banking schemes
	Bank of Scotland	Yes	£50/qtr. includes Prestel subscription	
Micro-computing	Micronet 800	Yes – but some pages free to all users	£16/qtr. including Prestel subscription	Communique Comp-u-net
Mailbox				Telecom Gold Istels' Comet
Travel/hotel bookings	Travel agents, travel companies, hotels			Travel agents
Citiservice	Stock Exchange, banks, financial institutions	Yes – but some pages available to all users	level 1 – free level 2 – £18/qtr.	*Financial Times*

HOTLINE

Hotline is a more recent British Telecom business information service giving subscribers instant access to a wide range of expanding data sources. It covers European markets and company data, together with the latest business news from some of the world's leading business publications (Table C7.11). A typical search on Hotline will take only ten minutes. Telecom is acting as an intermediary for the relevant database (essentially an information wholesaler). The quoted charges exclude the costs of the telephone line (Table C7.12).

Table C7.11   Information available on Hotline

News:
  Wall Street Journal
  Marketing Week
  Daily Telegraph, Business Section

Company information:
  Company Information Database
  Global Analysis System: Company news monitor
  Marketing Week: Advertising agency list

Market information:
  Euromonitor: Market directions and surveys
  Euromonitor: Market indicators, sizes, volumes and values
  Euromonitor: Market parameters, trends and retail facts
  Saatchi & Saatchi: European advertising and media information
  Saatchi & Saatchi: Worldwide advertising and media information
  China Express Newsletter: business news on China
  China Contracts: Opportunities to tender in China
  Peat Marwick Grants: Finance for new projects in UK
  Global Analysis Systems: Daily risk monitor
  Global Analysis Systems: Country risk analysis
  Global Analysis Systems: Statistics and ratings monitor

Telecommunications and information technology:
  Cambridge: *Telecoms and Technology News*, 1982–1986
  IEE INSPEC Files: Sections B, C and D
  Cable and Satellite Express

Table C7.12   Hotline price list

Single user ID and password	£1,000 – includes 10 hours' search time
3 user IDs and passwords	£3,000 – includes 40 hours' search time
10 user IDs and passwords	£10,000 – includes 150 hours' search time

Usage beyond free hours is charged at the rate for the individual database, per connect hour:

News files	£60
ICC	£120
GAS – Company risk	£90
Midirect	£120
Eurofile	£60
Eurofacts	£60
Grants	£60
GAS – Daily risk monitor	£70
GAS – Country risk monitor	£90
GAS – Statistics and ratings	£120
Euromedia	£60
UK Media	£60
Worldmedia	£60
Chinex	£60
Chinapro	£75
Cambridge	£70
Cable & Satellite Europe	£60
Cable & Satellite Express	£60
Inspec	£95
Telescope	£120
Dow Jones Files	£60
Dow Jones Disclosures II	£75
Consultancy	£75

Case 8

NORTHMOUTH HOSPITAL GROUP

INTRODUCTION

Charles Davies is the recently appointed general manager of the Northmouth Hospital Group I. Recruited at a salary of £30,000 per annum he has joined the hospital group from a job as a senior marketing controller for Ranks Hovis McDougall. Now he is attempting to define a long-range plan for the hospital group.

THE GROUP

Northmouth Hospital Group I is one of the three hospital groups servicing the town of Northmouth and the surrounding area, which is one of the suburban areas on the south coast of England and has a population of 420,000. The three hospital groups together report to the Ravenmark District Health Authority, one of the 200 authorities in the UK, which in its turn reports to one of the fourteen regional health authorities, the Wessex Regional Health Authority, which is directly responsible to the Department of Health and Social Security.

Northmouth I has three hospitals.

Ravenmark Central with 600 beds – the maximum size permissible by government for a district general hospital – is one of the most modern in the UK, having been completed in the early 1980s, with the capacity to treat all general cases in the area, including outpatients, cardiac cases, casualty and emergencies, and some maternity cases.

The other two hospitals are more specialized. Northcliff Orthopaedic Hospital, built in the 1940s on a barrack room plan to house war wounded, has 205 orthopaedic beds.

Mansion Hospital, an old Victorian hospital in the centre of Northmouth, was converted after the completion of Ravenmark Central to provide 225 beds for elderly long-stay patients, including an open ward for the mentally disturbed.

In total Northmouth I employs (when fully staffed) 980 nurses, 150 doctors (including 25 consultants), 872 ancillary staff divided amongst various duties and an administrative staff of 142 (including admissions and secretarial staff) which report to the general manager.

MANAGEMENT STRUCTURE

The management committee of the group is made up of the general manager, the three managers of the individual hospitals, the three senior consultants (currently the senior consultants for geriatrics, cardiology and orthopaedics), the senior nursing officer, and two union representatives.

The post of general manager has been recently created and was advertised both within and outside the Health Service. Among the 105 applicants for the post were two of the senior consultants now on the management committee, two of the three current hospital managers and the senior nursing officer. Recent practice was for the general manager to be appointed from outside the Health Service, but to leave and to be shortly replaced by an internal appointee. One of the consultants, Adam Markinoff, pioneered the development of new orthopaedic surgery in Northmouth and has for many years been trying to create a special orthopaedic surgery unit at the hospital.

The general manager is responsible for the efficient and cost-effective 'administration' of the hospital group. It is a well-established precedent in the context of the history of the NHS, whichever government is in power, that administrators cannot interfere with 'clinical' decisions involving the occupancy of beds in the wards and the priority assigned to cases on the hospital waiting lists. This lack of authority also extends to the level of nursing staff regarded as necessary to staff wards, and the type and frequency of cleaning and catering activity. The general manager also has limited authority in determining how hospital beds should be utilized in general terms as there are national guidelines relating to bed numbers for specific types of complaint. However, DHSS guidelines on any issue relating to the NHS have always tended to be hedged with qualifications, such as 'local priorities will naturally be affected by a range of factors – demographic, social and practical – peculiar to individual areas'. But administrators are responsible for hospital admission logistics and are therefore in the direct firing line for queue-jumping complaints.

The management committee reports to the district health authority on a regular basis. The area health authority consists of part-time unpaid officials together with representatives from the local authorities. For the Northmouth Hospital Group the amount of involvement is minimal, local authorities preferring to focus their attention on the next tier up – the regional health authority. The same cannot be said of the community health council, the local 'consumer' advisory panel, which contains representatives from local interest groups who have been campaigning for a substantial reduction in the waiting lists for non-urgent orthopaedic and abdominal surgery. Several members of the CHC, one a member of the Family Planning Association and a nurse from the Northmouth Health Centre, are especially concerned about issues affecting women's health and about the inadequate laboratory support for 'Pap' smear tests for cervical cancer in Northmouth.

The CHC can only make recommendations and complaints about the level of local service; the area health boards can make small discretionary payments as can the regional health authorities. However, it tends to be inevitable that members of these bodies are linked to health care provision in other ways. They can, and do, actively lobby members of other NHS committees – if not already represented on them – to ensure that account is taken of their views. Frequently such lobbying is on an informal basis. Failing this there are always the local MP and the press.

The majority of the budget is determined at a national level – there are national agreements on pay and conditions for all the main groups employed in the hospitals. Under the government funding regulations hospitals are restricted to a clearly defined cash budget for the year, which must be spent in the year of provision. Breaking the cash limits is not acceptable and individual hospitals must find savings within their areas of operation.

Manning levels are also determined nationally by the DHSS for each particular category of hospital and patient. However, it again falls to the hospital administrators to implement budgets and police manning levels, the impact of which is obviously felt locally, not nationally: the hospital may close wards and not fill posts as a response to budget requirements.

GOVERNMENT AND HEALTH CARE

The 1982 reorganization of the NHS was the third in fifteen years. Set up in 1948, the NHS was designed, as Aneurin Bevan told the House of Commons, to 'divorce the ability to get the best health care from the ability to pay and to provide the people of Great Britain, no matter where they may be, with same level of service'. One of the founding principles of the NHS was that preventive and curative medicine are fundamentally and immutably linked and that attention should be paid to both sides of the equation. Bevan also rejected proposals for funding the NHS through insurance contributions and every subsequent government has adhered to the principle that funding should come from centrally allocated general taxation.

The complexity of the 1948 undertaking has since proved to be a continual problem. In 1948 the original estimate for the cost of the NHS was £148 million, but the out-turn was £225 million. Expenditure committed to the NHS exploded during the high inflation periods of the late 1960s and 1970s, but in real terms expenditure continued to rise by 3 per cent per annum over the forty-year period since its inception. The Conservative government of 1979 followed the previous administrations by attempting to improve management efficiency (previous efficiency campaigns were carried out in the early 1950s, the mid-1960s and the late 1970s), but expenditure continued to rise inexorably. Though all administrations have been aware of the problem there has been little effective measurement of either the cost-effectiveness of health care (reducing the time that individuals stay in hospital or the speed at which operations are performed) or measuring the quality of health care provided, which was often seen as entirely contradictory to cost-effective management as it implied longer stays in beds and extended periods of care to meet the needs of individual patients.

During the late 1970s and early there was a slow shift from capital expenditure to current. With the Conservative government's reduction in the increase of NHS expenditure to 1.9 per cent in real terms, the transfer of resources from capital to current expenditure continued apace.

THE TRENDS IN HOSPITAL CARE

Hospital records of all activities involving Northmouth I identify major trends. In almost all cases the demands on the hospital services are increasing. Of particular concern are orthopaedic care, with the introduction of plastic hip-joints, renal dialysis, a steady increase in the use of outpatients departments due to a growing amount of referral work from local health centres, and steady advances in medical techniques leading to a greater and greater use of neo-natal and cardiac services.

Tables C8.1 and C8.2 give details of changes in the main areas of Northmouth hospital care.

Table C8.1   Trends in hospital care in Northmouth I

	1980/1	1986/7
Outpatients	188	212
Emergencies	61	82
Physiotherapy	173	172
Bed admissions	27	34
Operations:		
General	5	6
Orthopaedic	3	4.5
Ear, nose and throat	2	2
Cardiovascular	–	1
Urology	2	2
Other	4	6

(All figures in thousands.)

Table C8.2   Percentage bed occupancy in Northmouth I

	1984	1985	1986
Ravenmark	92	96	98
Northmouth Orthopaedic	97	97	97
Mansion	98	97	94

THE WAITING LIST

Though Northmouth is favoured in the number of staff and the modern facilities that exist in the main hospital, waiting lists for certain types of operation have grown steadily over the past three years. The waiting lists are, in the case of the Northmouth Group, a function of hospital bed occupancy; it does not suffer from the problems of other hospital groups working with antiquated and limited operating facilities (Table C8.3).

Waiting lists throughout the country have risen, though the situation is worst in the North East and Northern Ireland. For Northmouth the waiting lists for general surgery are spread broadly across age groups, whereas cardiovascular waiting lists are mainly made up of younger people; in contrast 90 per cent of demand of orthopaedic operations is from those over fifty-five. Many of the rises in waiting lists in other sectors are due to a shortage of appropriate equipment. A dialysis machine which can treat six patients costs around £20,000; the increase in cardiovascular cases is due to a shortage of intensive care facilities, which could be installed at the cost of £15,000 a bed and which would lead to an improved throughput of around fifteen patients per year.

Bed occupancy levels continue to rise throughout the three hospitals but because of their differing roles comparisons are superficial. Patients in the main hospital now leave hospital after an average of 3.9 days (as against 5.6. in 1982), in the orthopaedic unit 27 days (35) and the Mansion Hospital 67 (82).

THE HOSPITAL BUDGET

The total budget for the hospital group for 1986 was just under £30 million (overspent by around £1.5 million), and expenditure for the financial year 1987 was planned at £32,650,000. Inflation is expected to be around 4 per cent for the next two years, and income is expected to continue to rise at around 6 per cent per annum.

COMPONENTS OF THE BUDGET

As might be expected the wages bill makes up the bulk of the total expenditure in the hospital group, around 70 per cent of total expenditure (Table C8.4).

Table C8.3   The Northmouth I waiting list

	1985	1986	1987
General	2,500	2,800	3,200
Orthopaedic	1,000	1,300	1,400
Ear, nose and throat	400	425	410
Cardiovascular	100	150	180
Urology	50	300	350
Other	1,880	2,100	2,400

Table C8.4   Northmouth Hospital Group expenditure

	£000
Wages	
Nurses	8,103
Doctors	2,620
Administrators	1,500
Ancillary	3,100
Technicians/physiotherapists	5,250
Material costs	
Drugs	1,870
Other chemicals	2,350
Catering/cleaning/heating	1,520
Administrative costs	820
Buildings:	
Maintenance	800
Capital improvements	300
Equipment:	
Replacement	2,250
Additional equipment	1,100

Nurses

Though Northmouth is more fortunate than most hospital groups in maintaining the level of nursing staff, there are high levels of labour turnover. Turnover has increased from 15 per cent in 1982 to 28 per cent in 1986/87, and the hospital is becoming slowly more and more under-staffed, being around 5 per cent under complement by 1986/7. While the current full-time pay scales are from £6,000 for junior nurses and from £8,000 to £10,000 for sisters, the hospital has from time to time to employ agency nursing staff at triple the rates of pay for full-time staff. It was hoped that the situation would improve, as there had been several increases in pay levels over the past five years but the promotion structure does not recognize the acquisition of special skills, which fact has been increasingly discussed as a major area of concern. The annual increase in the annual wages bill has run at around 7.7 per cent over the past three years. Nurses' wages have increased by 30 per cent in real terms over the past five years, and this trend is likely to continue.

Ancillary workers

NHS ancillary workers are among the lowest paid in the country. Pay rates vary from £80 to £105 for a full week, though there is a substantial part-time element. Wages over the past three years have slightly outstripped official inflation with settlements ranging between 4.5 per cent and 5.5 per cent. The workforce is supported by a strong and active local trade union branch, who are pressing for substantial increases in the wage levels with a 25 per cent wage rise currently being demanded. By the end of 1986 there was talk of industrial action. Ancillary labour can be reduced only after lengthy consultations with the unions and then only if there are clear areas of manpower reduction caused by changed working practices.

Doctors

The hospital medical staff ranged from junior housemen to senior consultants with salaries ranging from £12,000 to £25,000 per annum. Because of its location the hospital has never had problems in achieving a high level of staffing, and has a low rate of medical staff turnover. Salaries have risen by 5 per cent per annum over the last five years. Promotion within the hospital system has been perceived to be a problem and the NHS recently moved to increase the number of consultancy posts throughout the main hospital network.

Technical workers

The 'other' worker category covers a wide range of skills within the hospital. Laboratory technicians, X-ray operatives, dieticians, physiotherapists and pharmacists are included under this umbrella heading, all on various rates of pay and having widely differing degrees of responsibility. Wage levels and employment in this sector have steadily grown in response to the rapidly changing technical demands of hospital work; the annual figure has been expanding at around 8 per cent.

Drugs

Drugs expenditure has steadily increased in real terms over the five-year period partly as a reflection of the new products available but also because of the increasing use of the hospital facilities by the local health centres. The DHSS's encouragement of the introduction of generic drugs to replace some of the branded products previously prescribed together with the introduction of prescription charges have slowed the real growth in drug costs from 8 to 6 per cent per annum. The hospital administrator cannot interfere with the clinical decisions of the doctors for drug prescriptions.

Medical equipment

The medical equipment budget is continually overspent. This is a result of the spiralling costs of equipment replacement and the demands for more sophisticated diagnostic machinery to carry out a wider range of tasks. The hospital is at present unable to consider the purchase of items such as a body scanner which would cost in the region of £800,000. The cost of replacing current and ageing equipment is typically leading to a need for the equipment budget to be increased at a rate of 10–12 per cent per annum.

Within the NHS there was a pilot project to computerize numerous hospital activities including much of the diagnosis and analysis; the admissions and bed management system; and the operation planning and control. The early results suggested that the introduction of such equipment into Northmouth would reduce operating costs by around £200,000 per annum and reduce staff in three areas:

(a) ten doctors;
(b) twenty-five technicians;
(c) twenty administrative staff.

The costs of full computerization would be in the region of £350,000 for the three hospitals.

Building maintenance and reconstruction

Large sums of money continually need to be spent to maintain the ageing fabric of the Orthopaedic Hospital, the weather-boarded buildings of which have long passed their planned effective design life of ten years. The Mansion Hospital also suffers from leaking roofs and decaying brickwork. Both of these require substantial and continuing sums to be spent on kitchens, laboratories, lifts and heating systems.

There have been a number of architects' reports on the Orthopaedic Hospital suggesting that a ground level redevelopment could be carried out on a piecemeal basis, creating buildings for thirty patients at a time. Current costs for such units are £2.5 million.

Another project that has often been suggested is to build a swimming pool for the physiotherapy department and the orthopaedic unit, a facility a number of other hospitals have found very effective in reducing hospital bed time and returning injured patients to the community. The probable cost of this is in the region of £500,000 though, in common with other past capital projects, there would be cost over-runs.

The lifts in the Mansion Hospital are continually breaking down and an internal report suggested that they should be replaced at a cost of £45,000.

The new ambulances in service caused substantial problems with the narrow road access at all three hospitals. Remedial work to improve mobility would cost £300,000.

Catering, cleaning and other services

Catering, cleaning and heating levels are laid down in national guidelines. Each patient must, for example, receive a minimum of five hot drinks per day; dietary controls are strictly monitored. Heating and cleaning are clinically determined but attempts at high levels of hygiene are part of the hospital regime. The current structure of the catering service is that each of the three hospitals purchases and cooks food individually for its particular patients. Cleaning and laundry services are carried out in the main Ravenmark laundry. The regional health authority recently put the cleaning contract out for tender as a reaction to the government pressure for privatization, and this was won by the current workforce at a saving of £70,000 per annum.

There was a proposal from a consultant that the catering of the hospital could be centralized by introducing a unit which would prepare meals in advance, freeze them and deliver them for on-the-ward heating by microwave oven. The redesign of the catering service would involve capital expenditure of around £120,000 but would allow a reduction in staffing of around forty ancillary workers.

Heating costs are largely dependent on the nature of the building. The main Ravenmark Hospital, with double glazing and efficient insulation, has a substantially lower heating bill than either the Orthopaedic Hospital or Mansion. All three hospitals use different fuels, which further complicates the picture. The Orthopaedic Hospital uses electricity, Ravenmark uses gas for all heating and cooking, while Mansion converted to oil in the mid-1960s and the costs of reconverting have steadily risen to over £75,000.

Private care

The main Northmouth Hospital was designed so that one of the wings, currently containing fifty beds, could be converted into a private ward with thirty individual rooms. These beds could achieve a very high occupancy rate (estimates suggested that this would be above 90 per cent) and would be charged to patients at the rate of £150 per day, in addition to providing revenue for operating theatres and the X-ray department. Davies has put forward a proposal to make more effective use of the beds.

The representatives of NUPE and COHSE reminded him that their members are bound by a standing order not to provide services for private patients. Most of the hospital ancillary staff belong to one or other of these two unions. The chief nursing officer takes the view that private patients have become socially unacceptable in NHS hospitals and that this is a major reason why the fifty private beds have been so little used in the past. As a nurse, she has always had doubts about measuring health care by bed occupancy rates. In her experience it means the quality of health care suffers and this was no less true of the pay beds. Obviously the higher the turnover, the more money consultants would get out of the private beds. Although

Table C8.5   Number of kidney disease patients under
dialysis or transplant by million population

UK	62.0'
Switzerland	136.1
Denmark	132.4
France	102.2
West Germany	87.7
Sweden	85.4

people paid for them to jump queues, they did not necessarily get better health care and that is why most NHS nurses were unhappy to look after private patients. If Davies were to bring in nurses and ancillary workers from private agencies the cost of an NHS pay bed could not compete with that in the nearby private Nuffield Hospital.

The consultants on the management committee wanted to know whether Davies had particular consultants in mind. The majority of consultants in Northmouth I are full-time, salaried employees of the NHS and so would not be interested in the proposal. Reviving the emotive issue of pay beds would not be good PR in a community that was giving a lot of its attention to hospital waiting lists.

EXPERIENCE IN OTHER COUNTRIES

The trend in the majority of the European countries has been to invest steadily in capital equipment to reduce the labour content of health care. Thus the typical nursing ratio in West Germany is 3.5 to every 1,000 of the population; in France the figure is 4.0 compared with 8 in the UK.

This emphasis on capital investment has meant that many services in Europe are at a higher level of provision (Table C8.5).

Case 9

TECHNOCHEM

INTRODUCTION

The Technochem Inc. board was reviewing the performance of the company's European operations, which still lagged significantly behind the rest of the group in such key performance criteria as total sales, market share and profitability.

Technochem, with headquarters in downtown Burbank, California, was founded at the turn of the century by a colourful ex-rodeo showman, Max Klei, who had identified the growing need for both diagnostic equipment and high-grade reagents in the developing manufacturing sector of the East Coast. The move to California took place during the Second World War with the tremendous growth in electronics manufacture in nearby states and the demands of the Manhattan project in New Mexico with which Technochem had been closely involved.

The company grew throughout the 1960s and 1970s by concentrating on areas of specialization and by a judicious mix of manufacturing in-house and buying in components. Historically, the company had concentrated on the United States for the bulk of its business though the overseas expansion of American manufacturing activity had led to a rapid growth of demand for Technochem products from the overseas subsidiaries of American companies.

By the early 1980s the senior management of the company were more aware of the need to develop some form of strategy towards overseas expansion as the world market was increasingly dominated by a small number of large companies with integrated production and supply facilities, which would eventually be able to out-perform companies such as Technochem.

The company operated in three sectors by 1984. Each was regarded as an independent profit centre with its own management and sales teams within the United States though there was a degree of overlap in some small overseas markets.

TECHNOCHEM STRUCTURE

The *Electronics Division* produced laboratory diagnostic equipment primarily for the education sector, a second most important sector being both industrial and government research laboratories. The product range was currently assembled at the company plant at La Jolla, California, using semi-skilled labour from south of the Mexican border. Worldwide the market was increasingly competitive, particularly on product/technical quality, and to a certain extent on price, though this was less of a worry in the majority of markets. Because most sales were to research type institutions the competitive advantage of fast delivery times was minimal.

The *Reagents Division* manufactured a range of basic industrial materials such as alcohols, aldehydes, and ketones used in a variety of organic syntheses. Recently the company had become more and more involved in the manufacture of pure energy sources for the rapidly expanding bio-technology sector. By 1984 two sophisticated integrated manufacturing sites, both costing around $200 million, were producing the range of company products, one on the West Coast not far from the Electronics Division plant and the other near the coast in Virginia. The reagents market was highly price competitive throughout the world because it was in the main perceived as a range of commodity products. In general it was very demanding on delivery schedules, as many of the major buyers in the world manufacturing sector had moved over to Japanese just-in-time material ordering patterns.

The *Resins Division* had initially formed part of the Reagents Division but now traded separately. It was involved in the manufacture of the increasingly complex resin products required by the manufacturers of composit materials such as glass and carbon fibre. The initial plant purchased by Technochem and then extensively modified and extended was on the outskirts of Chicago, from where the company serviced its entire US and European operations. In contrast to the Reagents Division, where the manufacturing plants were operating slightly below capacity, the Chicago plant was already at breaking point due to the rapid growth of sales, even though continual improvements and modifications kept the operation running. Company executives were in the process of deciding where to locate a new $150 million plant. Resins were tailor-made for particular applications; Technochem worked closely in conjunction with the OEM design teams to determine the loads and stresses that would be involved in a particular application. Because of the specificity of the product, the market was not price sensitive, but very concerned about the reliability of delivery schedules because of the expensive manufacturing processes involving the resins.

The company had concentrated on two markets: the USA, where Technochem was particularly strong on the Western seaboard; and Europe. Over the seven-year period both sales and profit had grown at a more rapid rate in Europe than in the United States, and at current rates of progress the European activities would be providing the bulk of company profits within the next three years. The worrying feature was that the European operations still yielded lower levels of gross margin.

Table C9.1   Company sales ($ million)

	1978	1979	1980	1981	1982	1983	1984
Total sales	450	520	630	800	890	1,190	1,300
Total profit	32	56	80	100	130	170	200
Division (sales)							
Electronics	250	260	280	290	300	310	320
Reagents	160	190	250	290	310	450	520
Resins	40	70	100	220	280	430	460
Division (profit)							
Electronics	21	26	32	30	35	60	65
Reagents	10	15	20	26	30	42	49
Resins	1	11	28	44	65	68	86

Table C9.2   Sales by market ($ million)

	1978	1979	1980	1981	1982	1983	1984
Total sales	450	520	630	800	890	1,190	1,300
US	360	380	420	450	480	550	640
Europe	90	140	210	350	410	640	660
Total profit	32	56	80	100	130	170	200
US	27	45	50	67	88	97	115
Europe	5	11	30	33	42	73	85

This was partly a result of the competitive environment in Europe but mainly due to high distribution costs in the electronics and reagent businesses (Tables C9.1 and C9.2).

In Europe during the mid-1970s Technochem was split into the three divisions of the parent company, each acting as a profit centre within the organization though there was a degree of overlap in manufacturing.

PRODUCTS AND MARKETS

Electronics Division

The Electronics Division concentrated on the design and final assembly of diagnostic equipment for manufacturing industry, and research laboratories. Its main products were oscilloscopes, fluoroscopes and chromatographs. They were assembled in Arizona, from components made to the company's design by a range of sub-manufacturers both within the United States and, increasingly, from overseas. During the early 1980s Technochem began to develop a range of products for the hospital sector, dialysis machines and portable X-ray equipment being most important.

The use of sub-manufacturers allowed Technochem continually to upgrade its products at negligible cost. Technochem was at a competitive disadvantage in a situation where the integrated companies could gain economies of scale from the manufacture of the components and the finished products.

The market environment was changing rapidly as the major manufacturers in the sector invested heavily to produce new sophisticated multi-function measuring equipment. The level of investment the competition envisaged necessary for the new generation of equipment was around $200 million, including the creation of an integrated manufacturing plant.

For Technochem the production process of the three main types of equipment could be separated into the preparation of the circuit boards, the production of the outer casing, and the final assembly, which involved the addition of various other sub-components such as screens and leads. The circuit boards were currently bought from the best suppliers within the Pacific Basin and imported into the United States; both the assembly and the production of the outer casing were in-house. Technochem had considered having the entire production subcontracted overseas, and although this would decrease the cost per unit by around $5, it would tend to reduce the advantages of the current manufacturing process, that could easily make slight modifications to products for specific overseas markets.

The costs involved in the production process for the main product lines sold through each sector are shown in Table C9.3. Included in the cost of the circuit board was the $2 duty payable on import into the United States; freight for such a small, high-value item was relatively negligible.

The freight cost between the United States and mainland Europe averaged $3 per unit. The company tried to ship container-load quantities to each of its main European markets, shipments to smaller markets being grouped with other American products. Because of the large volume of shipping between the United States and continental Europe the speed of delivery was generally good; a delivery period of four weeks from date of order could generally be maintained though this varied with product type and the availability of shipping to small markets.

The cost of shipment to the various European markets varied slightly, but the overall average was around $2 per unit; duties, however, varied considerably (Table C9.4).

Import duties for components as opposed to finished goods varied slightly from market to market. There were exceptions to this general rule; component import into the UK was significantly higher at 25 per cent than for finished goods, whereas the duty on the import of components into Austria was 5 per cent lower.

Table C9.3 Electronics Division production costs ($)

	Circuit board	Outer casing	Assembly
Oscilloscope	25	12	15
Fluoroscope	30	10	25
Chromatograph	68	12	40

Table C9.4   Duty and transport costs within Europe – Electronics Division

	Average trade price ($)	Import duty (%)	Cost of internal distribution ($)
Austria	130	15	3.0
Belgium	110	8	1.5
Switzerland	180	35	1.5
UK	100	8	2.5
West Germany	180	8	2.0
Italy	120	8	1.5
France	140	8	3.0
Scandinavia	190	27	2.0
Iberia	85	32	4.0
Greece	90	25	4.0

NB: Greece though in the EEC had yet to harmonize duties on the import of electronics components.

Table C9.5   Technochem annual country review – Electronics Division

Country	Market size ($ million)	Sales ($ million)	Average margin (%)	Relative market price (average: 100)
Austria	28	4	40	125
Belgium	35	6	55	112
Switzerland	27	3	45	160
UK	110	26	37	98
West Germany	150	34	42	102
Italy	115	22	32	88
France	130	18	28	85
Scandinavia	45	7	45	132
Iberia	25	5	23	145
Greece	18	2	22	176

Technochem carried out a review of each of its major markets every year to determine future marketing tactics. Table C9.5 reports the most recent.

The Electronics Division in Europe did not handle any of the hospital range, which accounted for over 30 per cent of total world divisional turnover. As a result, the European contribution to total turnover was more limited than for the other two divisions.

Each of the main European operations varied since each had grown up as an independent unit when Technochem had set up new subsidiary companies, appointed agents or had bought distributors in other markets. The law relating to agency termination varied throughout Europe and would also be subject to individual court rulings. One of the main competitors to Technochem in the reagents sector had carried out a realignment of its distribution structure, and had on average ended up paying compensation of three years' market revenue to each of the dismissed local company representatives.

Austria

The Austrian market was serviced by a distributor based in the Austrian capital Vienna. The distributor – with a salesforce of five and two qualified service engineers – supplied local services for Technochem products, which were used by around 350 customers throughout Austria. Stock with an average value of $200,000 was held in the Vienna warehouse.

Belgium

The Belgian market was serviced by a commission agent, which was one of the first companies to handle Technochem products overseas. It employed seven sales representatives and serviced approximately 400 customers throughout Belgium and Luxembourg. A major problem for Technochem in the Belgian market was that the agent found the level of service support difficult to maintain. Another difficulty was that the lack of stock held in the market led to orders taking more than three months to meet, a slowness of response that could be offset only by the competitiveness of the pricing policy the company followed.

Switzerland

The Swiss market was also serviced by a local commission agent, with three sales representatives servicing 200 clients. The Swiss market was relatively large because of the large number of research laboratories established there. However, the market demanded sophisticated products and a large amount of technical back-up and Technochem was slowly losing market share as a result. The Swiss agent held stock to an average value of $300,000.

United Kingdom

In the UK Technochem had bought, in 1972, an industrial wholesaler specializing in the distribution of analytical equipment. The company now employed twenty-five staff and a salesforce of ten, calling on around 600 customers. Holding stock included all the major lines (on average $600,000 in value) and full service back-up throughout the country.

West Germany

In West Germany Technochem used the same distribution arrangements as the Reagents Division, with a salesforce of twenty (shared across the product lines) calling on around 300 industrial customers. The company held stock to the average value of $250,000 but found it difficult to provide a full service and technical back-up, generally relying on third parties to carry out the necessary technical work.

Italy

In Italy, Technochem had one of the most successful distributors throughout Europe. The company also distributed technical glassware to industrial customers. It had followed a policy of maintaining only small stocks of the Technochem range but paying the premium for air-freighting the product in from the United States when required. This meant that it could keep the level of stocks down to around $50,000, while being prepared to pay the extra $10–15 per unit for air freight charges. The distributor was able to provide a full technical service to customers in the industrial north, while using third parties south of Rome.

France

In France, the Electronics Division operated through a wholly owned local subsidiary with a staff of twenty-eight, and was able to provide a full technical service throughout the French market, calling on approximately 1,100 customers. The sales subsidiary held stock of around $400,000.

Scandinavia

The Scandinavian market was serviced by a commission agent with five sales representatives calling on around 450 major customers throughout the market. Both market sales and share had been declining due to the inability of the commission agent to provide customers with the high level of service demanded, and to the slow delivery of equipment – which often took three months to arrive.

Iberia/Greece

Both the Iberian and Greek markets were serviced via distributors. The Iberian market was supplied by a company with headquarters in Madrid, calling on around 250 customers in Portugal and Spain, with a salesforce of five. The company had been unable to provide effective service back-up, losing market share as a result. A similar process was occurring in Greece, where Technochem was badly under-represented with only fifty long-term customers. Both distributors carried small stocks of around $100,000 in value.

Reagents Division

The Reagents Division in Europe had developed differently from Electronics. The management team saw themselves as operating in the chemical industry and had concentrated on the problems of moving bulk material within the European land mass. The market was increasingly dominated by the industry majors – Hoechst and Bayer in Germany, ICI in the UK, Montesidon in Italy and Rhône Poulenc in

Table C9.6 Duty and transport costs within Europe – Reagents Division

	Av. trade price/ton ($)	Duty (%)	Cost of internal distribution ($)
Austria	880	3	45
Belgium	760	3	30
Switzerland	900	15	27
UK	740	3	35
West Germany	800	3	30
Italy	880	8	25
France	720	3	42
Scandinavia	900	12	38

France. Over-capacity in all markets meant that the sector was highly price competitive with the inevitable effects on profit margins.

Duty costs were significantly lower than for the Electronics Division but the group faced much higher costs of transport from the United States and internal distribution within the European market. The average costs of transport by sea from the United States worked out at $40 a ton of product. Transport costs within Europe were also extremely high, with most of the product being moved by road. Because of the high freight costs, Technochem tried always to ship by bulk carrier. This requirement and the problems of manufacture of a wide product range meant that the delivery time from receipt of order would be in the region of eight to ten weeks; this required the European distributors to carry higher stocks than the Electronics Division (Table C9.6).

In contrast to the Electronics Division, there were only three operating units in Europe – in France, Italy and West Germany. The French company serviced the markets of France, UK, Belgium, Spain, Portugal and Switzerland; the German company Germany, Austria, the Netherlands and Scandinavia; the Italian company Italy and Greece.

The best-established company in the distribution network in Europe was in France. This was a wholly owned subsidiary of the parent company, Technochem. It employed a sales staff of forty-five and maintained substantial stocks of speciality products (around $10 million) at the Le Havre warehouse and headquarters. From there the product was transported by truck to the 1,200 customers.

In Germany, Technochem had established a joint venture with one of the smaller German manfacturing companies to distribute products of both the Electronics Division (only in the German market) and Reagents Division. The twenty-strong salesforce called on the main 350 customers in the market. The company held a large stock valued at around $5 million in its warehouse near Frankfurt.

The Italian company was far the smallest of the three European operations. Technochem had appointed a distributor in 1975 to handle this market. This company held stocks of all the main product lines, valued at around $500,000, and called on 120 major customers in the north with a salesforce of five.

Table C9.7   Annual market share estimate – Reagents Division

Country	Market size ($ million)	Sales ($ million)	Average margin (%)	Relative market price (average: 100)
Austria	350	22	15	95
Belgium	280	18	12	90
Switzerland	180	24	16	110
UK	600	49	18	102
West Germany	780	82	22	110
Italy	380	15	14	102
France	550	34	18	95
Scandinavia	295	22	20	110

Like the Electronics Division, the Reagents Division produced an annual market share estimate for all the major European markets (Table C9.7).

Resins Division

As a new and specialized product sector the Resins Division had followed a separate course from the other two divisions. It had established a single company subsidiary located in Brussels to service the entire European market. Within each country there was a sales office but all the European technical staff were based in Brussels and would travel from there to hold discussions with individual client companies.

Because of the high margins in the sector, the company held $15 million reserve stocks of all customer product ranges in the Brussels headquarters, even though the majority of product was air-freighted from the Chicago factory to individual customers. The resulting freight costs were high, but relatively low as a proportion of the total value of the product – the average cost per kilo from the United States was $2, because of extremely favourable rates the company had negotiated with several of the transatlantic carriers. As a high proportion of product was air-freighted to national airports direct from the United States internal distribution costs were negligible, but when product was shipped from the Brussels warehouse by road they tended to be high by contrast. The use of air transport enabled Technochem Europe to meet the demanding supply requirements of the major customers.

As the market was growing rapidly and there was a general lack of production capacity able to supply the highly complex resin material to individual customers' specifications, prices were high and margins and satisfactory throughout Europe (Tables C9.8 and C9.9).

Table C9.8   Duty and transport costs within Europe – Resins Division

	Average price/kilo ($)	Import duty (%)	Cost of internal distribution ($)
Austria	34	2	2.0
Belgium	32	2	–
Switzerland	40	10	2.0
UK	36	2	3.5
West Germany	40	2	3.5
Italy	42	2	3.5
France	38	6	4.0
Scandinavia	52	5	3.0
Iberia	55	12	5.0
Greece	45	15	3.0

Table C9.9   Annual market share estimate – Resins Division

Country	Market size ($ million)	Sales ($ million)	Average margin (%)	Relative market price (average: 100)
Austria	230	45	65	130
Belgium	300	70	55	102
Switzerland	130	30	56	140
UK	200	25	45	120
West Germany	380	45	45	115
Italy	260	22	48	135
France	330	27	34	98
Scandinavia	270	3	45	120
Iberia	120	–	–	–
Greece	95	–	–	–

MANAGEMENT

The three Technochem divisions were organized in a similar fashion.

The main board

The main board of the company, located at its headquarters in Burbank, comprised the six executive officers:

- William Dougall, Chief Executive
- Michael Zabronski, Finance Director
- Daniel Cohen, Communications Director
- Toby Anderson, Head of Electronics Division
- Simon Parker, Head of Reagents Divison
- Michael Giorgiou, Head of Resins Division.

The operating divisional structure

Reporting to the divisional heads at divisional headquarters, each of which was based in the United States, were subsidiary boards consisting of:

(a) production director;
(b) research director;
(c) finance director;
(d) sales and marketing director.

Within each department, each director had two regionally based teams, one for the United States and the other for Europe.

Case 10

AIRFIX

INTRODUCTION

Towards the end of 1979, a board meeting was held at the company headquarters of the Airfix group, one of the most famous British toy companies. The company had reached the upper limits of its bank borrowing and faced the imminent arrival of the receivers.

Airfix was a limited company with 26 million shares, of which the Norwich Union held 6.34 per cent and the M & G Group around 5 per cent. Institutions were believed to hold around 60 per cent of the total equity. In the early 1970s the shares had been valued at over 150 pence, but were now trading at around 15. Earnings per share of 12.4p in 1976 had slumped to 4.1p in 1979; a positive cash flow of £5 million in 1976 had been replaced by a negative cash flow of £4 million in 1978/79 (Table C10.1).

The board of directors

The Chairman, R. Ehrmann, had been with the company since 1950, and held just over one million shares.

The Managing Director, and Group Director of the Plastics Division, was D. Sinigaglia, who had been with the group since 1963. He held 45,000 shares.

A new finance director and operations director were being appointed.

There were two non-executive directors.

Senior management

Most of the senior management of the group were of fairly recent appointment as the group had always experienced a high management turnover. Each company

Table C10.1
Parent company balance sheet
As at 31st March, 1979. Airfix Industries Limited.

	£'000	1979 £'000	£'000	1978 £'000
Fixed Assets		4,021		3,523
Investments in Subsidiaries		5,207		5,032
Amounts due from Subsidiaries (Note 1)		6,737		6,301
		15,965		14,856
Deferred Asset				
Advance Corporation Tax Recoverable		610		1,180
Current Assets				
Trade Investment	–		70	
Quoted Investment	84		5	
Debtors and Sundries	579		245	
	663		320	
Current Liabilities				
Sundry Creditors	528		373	
Taxation	255		255	
Dividends	595		518	
	1,378		1,146	
Net Current Assets		(715)		(826)
Net Assets Employed		15,860		15,210
Bank Accounts		3,216		2,715
		12,644		12,495
Deferred Liabilities				
Mortgage	524		550	
Deferred Taxation Account	–		110	
		524		660
		12,120		11,835
Capital and Reserves				
Share Capital		5,194		5,194
Share Premium		439		439
Capital Reserve		800		800
Loan Stock 1992/97		733		845
Revenue Reserves		4,954		4,557
		12,120		11,835

R.R.M. Ehrmann, D.R. Sinigaglia, Directors

Note 1.
Included in this account is £483,000 (Nil) due from Meccano Ltd. This amount is not repayable on demand and is subordinated to the claim of all other creditors of Meccano Ltd. Airfix Industries Ltd. has also agreed to provide, subject to periodic review, such further financial support as may be necessary for Meccano Ltd. to maintain operations.

Comparative financial statement

	1978/79 £'000	1977/78 £'000	1976/77 £'000	1975/76 £'000	1974/75 £'000
Turnover	43,205	38,865	39,399	33,660	24,452
Earnings					
Net Trading Surplus	5,012	5,545	6,669	5,979	4,297
Benefit of Government Grants	82	101	114	95	89
	5,094	5,646	6,783	6,074	4,386
Depreciation	2,280	2,081	1,875	1,644	1,207
*Group Profit before Interest and Taxation	2,314	3,565	4,908	4,430	3,179
Interest	1,294	877	874	990	576
Group Profit before Taxation and Minority Interest	1,520	2,688	4,034	3,440	2,603
Taxation	409	(301)	(1,712)	1,635	1,293
Minority Interest	59	259	419	275	–
Net Profit after Taxation and Minority Interest	1,052	2,730	5,327	1,530	1,310
Extraordinary Items	41	(513)	191	–	–
Net Profit after Taxation, Minority Interest and Extraordinary Items	1,093	2,217	5,518	1,530	1,310
Appropriations					
Distributed in Dividends	951	837	750	353	344
Retained Profits	142	1,380	4,768	1,177	966
	1,093	2,217	5,518	1,530	1,310
Net Assets Employed					
Fixed Assets, Moulds and Tools	12,975	11,604	10,096	8,384	6,655
Net Current Assets including ACT recoverable	17,570	15,538	12,095	10,197	8,804
Minority Interest of Outside Shareholders	(1,121)	(1,062)	(696)	(491)	–
	29,424	26,080	21,495	18,090	15,459
Attributable to Shareholders of Airfix Industries Limited					
Representing:					
Capital	18,208	18,178	16,836	10,113	9,019
Long Term Liabilities	561	1,189	2,222	4,528	3,279
Bank Balances	10,655	6,713	2,437	3,449	3,161
	29,424	26,080	21,495	18,090	15,459
Net Assets per Share	67.3p	66.7p	61.4p	43.1p	38.5p
*Return on Net Assets Employed	9.6%	13.7%	22.8%	24.5%	20.6%
*Return on Turnover	6.5%	9.2%	12.5%	13.2%	13.0%

Comparative financial statement (contd.)

	1978/79 £'000	1977/78 £'000	1976/77 £'000	1975/76 £'000	1974/75 £'000
Earnings per Share	†4.1p	4.6p	7.6p	7.6p	6.5p
Gross Dividend per Share	5.32p	4.84p	4.40p	4.40p	4.24p
Standard rate of Corporation Tax	52%	52%	52%	52%	52%

†In line with the current practice of accounting for deferred taxation, earnings per share have been computed on profits after the net tax charge. In previous years deferred taxation adjustments were excluded.

In 1977/78 and 1976/77 deferred tax adjustments of £1,540,000 and £3,500,000 respectively were made, but it is considered that to adjust earnings per share to take these two sums into account would be misleading. No adjustment is required in respect of the Subscription warrants issued in April, 1972.

Consolidated balance sheet
As at 31st March, 1979, Airfix Industries Limited and Subsidiary Companies

	Note	£'000	1979 £'000	£'000	1978 £'000
Fixed Assets	1		8,914		8,364
Moulds and Tools	1		4,061		3,240
			12,975		11,604
Deferred Asset					
Advance Corporation Tax Recoverable	2		805		1,375
Current Assets					
Trade Investment		–		89	
Quoted Investment	3	84		5	
Stock and Work-in-Progress	4	16,442		14,863	
Debtors		10,452		8,441	
Total			26,978		23,398
Current Liabilities					
Creditors		9,316		8,104	
Taxation		302		613	
Dividends		595		518	
Total			10,213		9,235
Net Current Assets			16,765		14,163
Net Assets Employed			30,545		27,142
Bank Accounts	5		10,655		6,713
			19,890		20,429
Deferred Liabilities					
Mortgages	6	524		552	
Deferred Taxation Account	7	37		637	
		—	561	—	1,189
			19,329		19,240

Consolidated balance sheet (contd.)

	Note	£'000	1979 £'000	£'000	1978 £'000
Capital and Reserves					
Share Capital	8		5,194		5,194
Share Premium			439		439
Capital Reserve			800		800
Loan Stock	9		733		845
Revenue Reserves			11,042		10,900
Minority Interest			1,121		1,062
Capital Employed			19,329		19,240

R.R.M. Ehrmann, D.R. Sinigaglia, Directors

Notes on the accounts

2   Advance Corporation Tax

	£'000
Balance at 1st April, 1978	1,375
Paid and Payable for the year	430
	1,805
Less: Provision for irrecoverable ACT	1,000
Balance at 31st March, 1979	805

3   Quoted Investments

	£'000
Investment at cost	84
Market value at 31st March, 1979	90

4   Stock and Work in Progress
Stocks are analysed as follows:

	1979 £'000	1978 £'000
Finished Goods	10,612	9,669
Work in Progress	1,624	1,622
Raw Materials and other	4,206	3,572
	16,442	14,863

5   Bank Accounts
Bank Accounts are analysed as follows:

	£'000	£'000
Overdrafts	5,459	5,871
Borrowings repayable within 12 months	3,466	1,426
Borrowings repayable within 1 and 3 years	887	1,290
Borrowings repayable within 3 and 5 years	2,170	–
	11,982	8,587
Balances in Hand	(1,327)	(1,874)
	10,655	6,713

The Parent Company has guaranteed borrowings of subsidiaries totalling £8,766,000 (£5,609,000).

6 Mortgages	Principal £'000	Interest Rate
These are secured on certain of the Freehold and Leasehold Land and Buildings. Repayable:		
– by 20 annual instalments	497	8½%
– in 1986 on the maturity of insurance policies. Total premiums paid to date are £33,381 at the rate of £2,640 p.a.	27	8½%
	524	

7 Deferred Taxation Account	£'000
Balance at 1st April, 1978	637
Less: Amount released to Profit & Loss Account	600
Balance at 31st March, 1979	37

Source and application of funds
For the Year ended 31st March, 1979. Airfix Industries Limited and Subsidiary Companies

Source of Funds	£'000	1979 £'000	£'000	1978 £'000
Profit before tax, extraordinary items and minority interest		1,520		2,688
Extraordinary Profits/(Losses)		41		(963)
		1,561		1,725
Adjustment for Non-monetary items				
Depreciation	2,280		2,081	
Exchange Adjustment	134		(131)	
Trade Investment Adjustment	–		48	
		2,414		1,998
Total Generated from Operations		3,975		3,723
Funds from Other Sources				
Reduction in Quoted Investments	–		17	
			–	17
		3,975		3,740
Application of Funds				
Redemption of Loan Stock	112		38	
Dividends Paid	874		783	
Tax Paid	750		581	
Purchase of Fixed Assets (net)	3,785		3,458	
Reduction of Mortgages	28		33	
Quoted Investments	79		–	
Reduction/(Increase) in Minority Interest	–		(107)	
		5,628		4,786

	(1,653)		(1,046)
Increase/Decrease in Working Capital			
Stocks	(1,579)	(2,548)	
Debtors	(1,922)	(622)	
Creditors	1,212	(60)	
		(2,289)		(3,230)
Movement in Net Liquid Funds being the net (increase) in bank overdraft and cash		(3,942)		(4,276)

Notes on the accounts

11 Interest

	1979 £'000	1978 £'000
Bank overdraft and finance facilities	1,239	800
Loans, repayable after 5 years	43	58
Loan stock	56	64
Total interest paid	1,338	922
Less interest received	44	45
Net	1,294	877

12 Taxation

	£'000	£'000
Attributable to Group – UK	(40)	995
– Overseas	(2)	203
Attributable to Minority Interest Overseas	51	41
	9	1,239
Provision for irrecoverable ACT	1,000	–
Deferred Taxation adjustment	(600)	(1,540)
	409	(301)

13 Extraordinary Items

	£'000	£'000
Net Profit on Redemption of Loan Stock	41	14
Less: Non-Recurring Costs	–	(977)
Attributable Taxation	–	450
	41	(513)

14 Dividends per Share

	Gross	Net	£'000	Gross	Net	£'000
Interim Dividend	2.0476p	1.3719p	356	1.8615p	1.2286p	319
Proposed Final Dividend	3.2730p	2.2911p	595	2.9754p	1.9935p	518
Total For The Year	5.3206p	3.6630p	951	4.8369p	3.2221p	837

15 Earnings Per Share
The calculation is based on the Group Profit after Taxation and minority interest of

£1,052,000 (£1,190,000). No adjustment is required in respect of the Subscription Warrants.

---

16   Capital Commitments
31st March, 1979 £1,050,000 (£519,000).
Authorised by not contracted for £1,664,000 (£2,815,000).

---

17   Meccano Ltd.
As stated in the note on Airfix Industries Ltd.'s Balance Sheet it has undertaken, subject to periodic review, to continue to provide such financial support as may be required for Meccano Ltd. to maintain its operations. Accordingly the accounts of Meccano Ltd. have been drawn up and consolidated on a going concern basis.

---

operated extremely independently and there was little central co-ordination of management systems or recruitment.

Other workforce

At the main Airfix factory at Wandsworth the remainder of the workforce had been with the company eight years or more. The salesforce of twenty-five, with a national accounts team of three, had also been with the company an average of five years or more.

BACKGROUND TO THE TOY INDUSTRY

At the end of the war the British toy industry was a dominant force in a number of market sectors which it had pioneered. Internationally known British brand names included:

(a) Pedigree dolls;
(b) Triang wheeled toys;
(c) Meccano construction kits;
(d) Hornby clockwork trains;
(e) Dinky, Matchbox and Corgi die-cast models;
(f) Spears and Waddingtons board games.

The toy industry differed from other consumer goods product sectors in a number of important respects. First, it was a highly seasonal industry with 70 per cent of sales during the Christmas period. Historically orders for the year-end would be placed at the major industry exhibitions – Nuremberg, Paris, London and, more recently, Tokyo – which took place during January and February. Although these exhibitions remained very important to the toy manufacturers, during the 1970s buyers began to place their orders towards the year-end, thereby increasing the manufacturers' problems of product development.

Second, toys are a fashion industry: tastes change rapidly, and repeat purchase levels are very low. This has always meant that the toy industry faces high

Table C10.2 Source of toy purchase ideas	
Children	55%
Television	30%
Newspaper	8%
Store displays	7%

development costs coupled with the need to repay this investment over a very short period, implying the need for high margins, and making toy companies particularly sensitive to changes in volume.

Third, the market has always had two fairly distinct components: the impulse buy and the planned purchase; in other words there is a distinct price point existing in the market which divides the two market sectors.

Fourth, adults may do the majority of the buying but the initiative for the purchase lies with the children (Table C10.2).

Fifth, distribution initially relied heavily on specialist outlets of which there were an estimated 12,000 in the 1950s. This changed as the market developed, but these specialist outlets remain an important market factor.

Sixth, the application of technology has been very important to the toy industry both in controlling costs and in the industry's absolutely essential new product development.

Finally, the market was becoming more and more international, with major companies becoming established. Of these the largest was Mattel, based in the United States.

AIRFIX: THE EARLY DAYS

New technology in the toy industry was largely responsible for the development and early success of the Airfix group. Founded in 1950 in the top room of a printer's workshop in Wandsworth, the company successfully applied the new science of plastic injection moulding to the production of a range of model kits (initially aeroplanes, from which the group name was derived). The early product range comprised small construction kits – purchased as pocket-money items – sold through specialist retailers appointed as Airfix stockists and a few department stores, particularly Woolworths, which gave Airfix considerable shelf space in return for higher levels of discount.

The limited range sold extremely well and, with the low distribution and promotional costs, the return on investment remained consistently high in the early 1960s at over 70 per cent. Table C10.3 gives Airfix's market share at this time.

In the early 1960s Airfix began to develop overseas sales as other companies, notably Revell in the United States and Heller in France, began to become established. Exports soon accounted for around 40 per cent of kit sales and substantially more of the profitablility.

Table C10.3   Construction kit market shares.

	1962	1963	1964	1965
Kit market (estimated: £m)	12	14	18	20
Airfix share (%)	60	55	52	50

Table C10.4   Airfix production

Series	Machine size (tons)	Start-up cost (£)	Units/hr
1–3	50	30	30
5–8	120	100	20
9–13	200	200	10
14–18	350	300	5

Airfix continued to invest in the development of the kit range, with an increasing number of moulds, dividing its range into a number of 'series' that retailed at standard prices for each series. By the 1970s, there were twenty series, with a total of 550 moulds in store, not all of which were in production.

Each series had a different variable cost of production and required a slightly different production process, with the higher series requiring increasing levels of pressure in the injection moulding process. Series 1 and 2 required only 50 tons of pressure; series 14 and above, often in the region of 350 tons. Setting up the production runs was therefore considerably more expensive for the higher series.

Whereas the smaller machines had a fairly rapid production rate, the larger machines could produce only a limited number of models during a production cycle and this was a further factor in complicating the production process (Table C10.4).

As the product range increased so did the types of machinery needed to produce it, and in the early 1960s Airfix moved to larger premises in the Wandsworth area, while establishing a distribution centre in south-east London near Charlton. This production remained unaltered throughout the 1960s and 1970s except for a continuing introduction of new machines. There was no production line and products were largely packed at the machine.

AIRFIX: INTO THE SECOND DECADE

As the kit market developed, Airfix faced competition from Matchbox, Revell and other foreign kit manufacturers, who were starting to erode its profit margins (Table C10.5). In response, Airfix expanded its range of toy products.

1. The Weebles (a range of pre-school plastic figures).
2. The Eagles (a range of small plastic play figures).
3. New Artist (a range of painting products).
4. Super Toys (a range of battery-powered products).

Table C10.5 Airfix sales/prices 1963–1965 (doz. units)

Product	1963 Sales (doz. units)	1963 Price (p.)	1964 Sales (doz. units)	1964 Price (p.)	1965 Sales (doz. units)	1965 Price (p.)
Spitfire (Airfix)	20,000	20	15,000	22	12,000	24
FW 190 (Matchbox)	5,000	18	6,500	18	8,000	20
Mustang (Revell)	3,000	19	5,000	18	7,000	18

In addition to this expanded product range, Airfix substantially expanded the UK salesforce to meet the growing competition in the market. Promotional expenditure throughout the 1960s was limited to trade magazines and exhibition appearances.

Certain members of the main board felt that the expanding home market for all kinds of plastics offered a rare opportunity. They argued that the expertise developed by the Airfix group in the production of plastic kits could be transferred to the home plastics market, which had grown to around £20 million by the late 1960s.

During the mid and late 1960s the company invested in:

1. Airfix Plastics, producing a range of household plastic containers under the Crayonne brand, and based at Sunbury on Thames.
2. Declon Foam Plastics, producing expanded foam products (balls, sponges), based at Dunstable in Bedfordshire.
3. South Wales Plastics, producing industrial plastic components, based at Aberdare in South Wales.

It was not until the mid-1970s that the plastics part of the group became profitable. It had faced continual quality control problems and had failed to achieve the public acceptability of quality household items in heavy duty plastic.

With the collapse of the Lines Brothers Group in the late 1960s, Airfix acquired the Meccano and Triang Pedigree companies, one based in Liverpool with 900 employees and the other in Merthyr Tydfil in Wales, with a workforce of 200. The Meccano and Dinky ranges were largely hand-produced, with Meccano competing against Lego and Dinky, which retailed at around £1.50 per unit against Far Eastern products and competition from both Matchbox and Corgi retailing at £0.40 (Table C10.6).

Table C10.6 Comparable Meccano and Lego pricing

Product	Consumer price (£) 'Starter' pack	Consumer price (£) 'Advanced'
Meccano	3.00	10.00
Lego	0.50	4.50

AIRFIX IN THE 1970S

During the 1970s the markets in which Airfix operated altered radically, for a number of reasons.

1. The recession. The entire toy market, especially the luxury high-priced items, were faced with a steadily deepening recession and rapidly rising price inflation.
2. Decreasing interest in kit construction products. The success toy of the 1970s for the boys' market was Action Man produced by Palitoy. This and ranges of characters from successful TV series eroded market demand for kit products. Simplicity of kit production was seen as increasingly important, with competing products such as Matchbox and Revell introducing coloured, easily assembled kit items, which could often be snapped together rather than glued.
3. Increasing cost of plastic. The steadily rising cost of raw materials in the 1970s, due to the oil price rises from 1973, reduced the ability of the market to produce cheap pocket-money items.
4. Increased competition. Far Eastern manufacturers were making steadily greater inroads into the toy market particularly in the die-cast and plastic toy sectors, where low-cost production was effectively destroying British toy manufacturers.

   The number of manufacturers of construction kits had significantly expanded – there were twenty-six in Japan alone, which had the world's largest construction kit market. It was not until 1978 that Airfix formalized the export function by the creation of an export department; there was no contact with either the Meccano group or other areas of the company with overseas sales. Table C10.7 shows Airfix's share of various export markets.
5. Increased automation in the production process. What had initially been a hand manufacturing process was increasingly being replaced by assembly line techniques. Competitors were investing in computer-aided tool-cutting processes, and conveyor belt methods of moving products from the production point to the final packing area. The costs for Airfix to re-equip its factory to a similar standard were an estimated £1.5 million, and the result would be to

Table C10.7   The size of world kit markets and Airfix share 1978

Country	Market size (£ million)	Airfix share (%)
Australia	1.5	30
Japan	60.0	–
USA	40.0	2
France	5.0	15
Germany	20.0	10
Italy	2.0	10

halve the mould production costs, a possible reduction of thirty to forty in the labour force and a substantial reduction in the variable production costs.

6. Changing tastes. Children were increasingly looking for topical items, such as jets and spacecraft.

7. Developing electronics sector. The introduction of hand-held games was becoming a major sector of the industry.

8. Declining birth rate. The falling number of births was affecting the entire toy market, particularly in the demand for pre-school items, though items such as construction sets and kits were facing similar declines in demand.

9. Changing distribution patterns. During the late 1960s and early 1970s the multiple chains became important outlets for toys at the expense of the specialist toy outlets, which were halved in number from 12,000 to 6,000.

10. Changing promotion methods. The development of commercial television had been used by major toy groups such as Milton Bradley and Palitoy to expand demand significantly at the peak Christmas period (Table C10.8).

11. Changing presentation methods. Presentation and packaging of toy items had become steadily more important, with high quality shrinkwrapping and well-designed cartons essential for the majority of toy products. Matchbox kits had a plastic window included in the pack so that consumers were better able to see the product. The Airfix packaging was seen as increasingly outdated.

12. Increasing costs of plastic moulds. The costs of new moulds had risen considerably since the 1960s. New mould manufacturing methods including

Table C10.8   Comparative advertising expenditure 1976

Company	£ million
Milton Bradley	0.75
Palitoy	0.65
Lego	0.60
Airfix	0.10

Table C10.9   The toy market in 1976

Market sector	Size (£ million)	Growth	Competition
Dolls	28	Nil	Far East, Mattel (Barbie)
Soft toys	15	Some	Far East
Wheeled toys	39	Nil	Far East
Kits	30	Negative	Europe, USA, Far East
Die-cast	60	Nil	Far East, Europe
Plastic toys	120	Nil	Europe, Far East
Board games	30	Some	Europe, USA
Pre-school	40	Nil	Europe
Electric trains	15	Nil	Europe
Toy sportsgoods	12	Some	Far East

computer-aided cutting had been pioneered in the Far East in order to reduce cost, but other companies were using low labour-cost countries, particularly Portugal, for their mould production.

13. Anti-war movement. The growth of the anti-war movement, particularly in countries such as Scandinavia where toy guns and any toy product with illustrations of gunfire were banned, was affecting the sale of aircraft products in particular.

Table C10.9 summarizes the toy market in 1976.
The Airfix group responded to the market changes in a number of ways.

1. By introducing a range of space figures from the Far East, the Micronauts.
2. By investing in the development of products in the space market and others with a wider educational appeal, such as wildlife, and products appealing to the hobbyist, the adult modeller who made up around 10 per cent of the total kit market.

   Of the 75p trade price of the series 2 models (Table C10.10), raw materials would typically account for 22p, though Airfix included a high mould depreciation charge on each kit produced to attempt to recoup the heavy expenditure on moulds.
3. By importing a range of sports equipment from the Far East.
4. By the development of a range of high quality electric trains, initially produced in the Far East, called Great Model Railways.
5. By investing in the development of more sophisticated battery-powered toys including a programmable car and controllable hovercraft, requiring substantial funding for the development of moulds and microprocessors. One of these, a model hovercraft, had a mould which cost over £100,000.
6. By purchasing a scale racing car company, Model Road Racing Cars in Bournemouth.
7. By buying its distributors in both West Germany and the United States, Plasty and Ava International, with production plants at Mannheim and Waco in Texas.
8. By further diversifying into footwear with the creation of Airfix Footwear, based at Harworth in Nottinghamshire, and an importing company Tal Impex, based at the Charlton distribution site.
9. By investing in the development of a factory for household plastics in the United States in New Jersey.
10. By selling the Triang Pedigree factory in South Wales.
11. By developing interests in packaging, via Airfix Packaging Development based in Surrey.
12. By forming a design company, Benchmark, based in London.
13. By buying a half share in a doll-manufacturing company based in Singapore.

Table C10.10 The pricing structure for the various Airfix series (£)

Series	Retail price	Trade
1	0.60	0.45
2	1.00	0.75
3	1.60	1.20
4	2.20	1.65
5	3.50	2.50
6	4.00	3.00
7	4.50	3.10
8	5.50	3.70
9	7.50	6.00
10	8.50	7.00
12–14	10.50	8.50
18	16.00	12.00
20	20.00	16.00

Table C10.11 Some key features of the Airfix Group

	1971	1972	1973	1974	1975	1976	1977	1978	1979
Sales £ million	11	14	17	24	33	39	38	43	42
Gross profit £ million	2	3	3	4	6	7	4	5	3
%	18	21	18	16	18	18	10	11	7
Bank interest £ million	0.2	0.2	0.2	0.5	1	2	2	3	3
ROCE	30	50	28	25	25	22	15	11	6
Stock £ million	2	2	5	9	11	12	16	18	20
Stock turn	5	7	3	3	3	3	2	2	2
Debtors £ million	2	2	3	4	5	8	9	10	11
Debtor length (days)	70	40	55	60	50	80	90	90	100

Individual divisions	1975	1976	1977	1978	1979
Sales: £ million					
Toys	17	25	28	26	27
Plastics	4	4	7	8	11
Shoes	4	4	4	4	4
Profit: £ million					
Toys	2	3	3	0.2	0
Plastics	0.1	0.2	0.6	0.8	1
Shoes etc.	0.1	0.1	(0.1)	(0.2)	(1)

Table C10.12 Estimated stock, profit and staff

Area	Staff	Sales £ million	Profit £ million	Stock £ million	Plant value £ million
Kits/pre-school	900	16	3	8	4
Trains	30	2	(1)	2	–
Meccano	700	4	(2)	4	1
Misc. (Micronauts etc.)	50	2	0	3	0
General plastics	400	12	1	1	0
Shoes etc.	150	3	(1)	1	0

THE DECLINING FORTUNES

Some of the key features of the Airfix group development are summarized in Table C10.11. Table C10.12 supplies a rough breakdown of the stock, profit and staff employed.

APPENDIX: AIRFIX PRODUCTS

Product	Introduced	Mould cost (£)	Average sales 1965/70 (units)	Sales 1976	Sales 1977
Series 1					
Spitfire	1957 and 1962	2,000	23,000	15,000	11,000
Messerschmitt	1963	2,500	18,000	11,000	8,000
Hawker Typhoon	1964	2,750	14,000	10,500	9,500
Bristol Bulldog	1958	1,850	11,500	6,500	5,500
Bristol Fighter	1956	1,750	13,000	8,500	7,500
BAC Provost	1966	3,500	17,000	11,000	9,000
YAK 9-D	1962	2,300	10,500	7,500	6,500
Gnat	1970	6,700	16,000	12,000	10,000
ME 262	1960	2,200	12,000	6,000	5,000
Cessna	1964	2,800	9,500	5,000	3,000
Kittyhawk	1961	2,500	16,000	8,000	5,000
Northrop F5A	1974	9,000	–	19,000	15,000
Westland Scout	1973	8,500	–	12,000	10,400
Gazelle	1969	6,500	11,000	8,000	7,500
HMS Victory	1959	2,000	8,000	7,800	8,000
HMS Shannon	1961	2,800	7,000	6,500	7,000
Golden Hind	1957	1,800	6,700	5,800	6,000
Campbelltown	1956	1,500	3,000	2,000	1,500
Panther tank	1965	3,700	9,000	1,500	1,500
Churchill tank	1964	3,500	8,000	5,000	4,000
Series 2					
JU 88	1956	3,500	8,000	6,000	5,500
Hellcat	1954	3,000	9,000	5,000	4,500
Fokker Wolf	1957	4,000	9,000	3,000	4,500
Mustang	1964	5,600	11,000	8,000	7,500
Mosquito	1968	9,000	15,000	7,000	5,500
Drakken	1972	11,000	–	12,000	11,000
Whirlwind	1968	7,500	7,000	6,500	5,800
Hurricane	1958	3,500	6,500	5,500	5,000
F80C	1955	3,500	12,000	9,000	5,500
Lightning	1964	6,500	11,000	8,000	6,500
Harrier	1975	13,000	–	18,000	17,000
F104G	1968	8,000	8,000	6,000	7,000
F86D Sabre	1960	4,500	5,500	4,500	4,000
Leopard tank	1966	5,500	3,000	2,700	3,000
Crusader tank	1957	3,000	2,000	1,800	1,700
Chieftain tank	1968	6,500	9,000	7,000	7,000
Panzer IV	1959	4,000	5,000	5,000	4,500
Angel Interceptor	1968	5,000	3,000	2,700	2,500

Product	Introduced	Mould cost (£)	Average sales 1965/70 (units)	Sales 1976	1977
Series 3					
Buccaneer	1964	8,000	11,000	5,000	4,000
Sea King	1968	14,000	9,000	7,000	7,000
Lynx	1969	13,000	7,000	6,000	6,000
Hudson	1959	5,500	3,000	2,000	2,000
Stuka	1958	5,000	5,500	3,500	3,000
Mig 23	1975	20,000	–	15,000	11,000
Jaguar	1972	15,000	–	17,000	15,000
Hawk	1974	15,000	–	12,000	11,000
Puma	1968	11,000	7,000	5,000	3,500
Lynx	1972	13,000	–	7,000	5,500
HMS Devonshire	1964	7,500	4,000	3,000	3,000
HMS Suffolk	1965	8,000	3,500	2,000	1,800
HMS Fearless	1968	9,000	4,500	3,500	3,500
Lunar Module	1972	12,000	–	1,500	1,700
Series 4					
Wellington	1962	9,000	3,000	2,500	2,500
Mitchell	1959	8,000	4,500	4,000	4,500
Dornier	1963	9,500	4,000	3,500	4,000
Hurricane	1966	11,000	4,500	4,000	4,000
Heinkel	1964	9,000	3,500	3,000	3,400
Tornado	1974	25,000	–	17,000	15,000
Phantom	1972	17,000	–	12,000	11,000
F-111	1973	22,000	–	19,000	13,000
Mirage	1970	15,000	–	10,000	9,000
Boeing 707	1968	9,000	2,000	2,000	1,500
HMS Hood	1954	3,000	1,300	1,200	1,300
Bismarck	1956	4,000	1,800	1,500	1,500
HMS Ark Royal	1960	6,000	3,500	2,300	2,300
Graf Spee	1955	3,000	1,500	1,000	900
Scharnhorst	1956	3,500	1,200	900	800
HMS Iron Duke	1952	3,000	1,100	700	600
Series 5					
Halifax	1956	5,000	4,000	2,000	1,800
Tomcat	1973	28,000	–	13,000	15,000
Heinkel	1962	10,000	5,000	4,000	4,000
Boeing B17	1964	12,000	6,000	5,500	3,500
Catalina	1960	8,000	4,000	3,500	3,000
Viking	1969	16,000	8,000	7,000	6,500
Prinz Eugen	1966	12,000	4,000	4,000	3,500
Moskva	1970	17,000	–	5,000	5,000
Vosper MTB	1963	10,000	4,500	3,500	3,500
Rescue launch	1959	7,000	3,500	3,000	3,000
Orion spaceship	1975	15,000	–	3,000	2,000
Tyrannosaurus	1976	8,000	–	–	4,000
Stegosaurus	1977	8,000	–	–	2,500
Brontosaurus	1976	7,500	–	2,500	1,800
Robin	1975	6,500	–	3,500	3,500
Kingfisher	1977	6,500	–	–	3,200

Product	Introduced	Mould cost (£)	Average sales 1965/70 (units)	Sales 1976	Sales 1977
Series 6					
Sunderland	1968	20,000	3,000	1,800	1,600
Stirling	1964	15,000	2,500	1,500	1,400
Airbus	1975	25,000	–	1,600	1,700
Concorde	1975	30,000	–	2,200	2,500
DC 10	1973	26,000	–	2,800	2,700
Tristar	1975	22,000	–	2,100	2,100
Queen Elizabeth	1966	31,000	2,800	1,800	1,800
SS Norway	1969	26,000	2,700	2,600	2,200
Series 7					
Mosquito	1975	45,000	–	2,600	2,200
Superfortress	1968	34,000	3,200	3,300	3,000
Starcruiser	1974	30,000	–	4,500	4,000
HMS Endeavour	1972	42,000	–	3,500	3,500
Series 8					
Lancaster	1976	60,000	–	–	5,000
Boeing 747	1975	48,000	–	2,500	2,500
HMS Revenge	1968	36,000	3,500	3,000	3,000
Crusader III	1972	50,000	–	1,500	1,200
Grant tank	1972	50,000	–	1,200	1,100
Series 9					
Hercules	1974	55,000	–	3,800	4,000
HMS Victory	1968	45,000	3,400	2,500	2,700
HMS Prince	1966	42,000	3,500	2,500	2,500
HMS Royal Sovereign	1970	48,000	3,000	3,000	3,000
Wasa	1972	60,000	–	5,000	4,000
Series 10					
E Boat	1967	47,000	4,500	4,700	5,000
Forrestal	1974	70,000	–	6,000	8,000
Moonraker	1975	80,000	–	–	12,000
Series 12					
ME 109A	1972	55,000	–	3,500	2,500
Spitfire	1972	55,000	–	3,000	3,000
Series 14					
Mustang	1973	65,000	–	3,500	2,500
Hurricane	1973	65,000	–	2,500	2,700
Series 18					
Harrier	1976	85,000	–	4,000	3,000
Stuka	1974	70,000	–	2,500	2,700
Fokker Wolf	1977	100,000	–	–	3,500
Series 20					
Bentley	1970	65,000	–	1,500	1,500

Case 11

WESTERN HOTEL

BACKGROUND

The Western Hotel is one of several located in the small town of Beachmouth in Devon. Beachmouth has a population of 10,000 and, historically, relied on tourism for the majority of its income. With communications improving following the extension of the M5, and the support of the nearby Exeter University, a large industrial park had been created bringing substantial employment to the area; with major companies producing computers, videos, laboratory and medical diagnostic equipment. As a result of this development Beachmouth was locally gaining the nickname 'Techmouth'.

The decline of traditional industries like fishing and agriculture meant that unemployment remained a chronic problem throughout the South West. Though it fared reasonably well in the national averages, with around 13 per cent of the population unemployed in 1985, the figure hid a considerable level of seasonal employment and part-time working. The level of unemployment for the unskilled was significantly higher than the national average. The development of the business park had provided significant local employment opportunities for school leavers and local college graduates but had done little to reduce unemployment rates in the thirty to fifty age group.

In addition to a good road network which connected it with both the South East and the Midlands, Beachmouth was serviced via Exeter with reasonable bus and train connections, though the rail track did have a tendency to wash away in the winter storms.

With the opening of the business park the pattern of visitors to Beachmouth had changed. Although still a popular tourist resort, with wide sandy beaches and donkey rides for the summer visitor looking for a quiet, family summer holiday, the amount of business traffic had significantly increased. This included head office executives visiting the local plants and more and more sales representatives, with whom the town was becoming popular as a base for the entire South West, as both road access and parking were far easier than in the majority of competing locations.

Some hotels, the newly built Holiday Inn especially, could take advantage of this new trend to improve their profit margins substantially. But the tourist hotels had achieved respectable occupancy rates by offering discounts of up to 40 per cent off list price for long-stay (weekly) residents. Business hotels did not face this problem.

A third trend which affected both Beachmouth and the entire South West was the increasing number of the elderly retiring to the area. Both Devon and Cornwall County Councils had commissioned surveys, which showed that the trend towards retirement homes and flats was rapidly increasing and would eventually put the entire social services under severe pressure.

THE TOURIST ENVIRONMENT

Beachmouth's main tourist attraction was the mile-and-a-half-long sandy beach sloping gradually and safely out to a relatively unpolluted sea. At one end was the small pier, changed over the last three years into an amusement arcade and restaurant.

Nearby resorts offered additional facilities. At Paignton (10 miles distance) there was a water-sports complex; Newton Abbot (5 miles) offered pony trekking in the Dartmoor National Park, and two large golf courses; Exeter (8 miles) was the main shopping and accommodation centre, with a large indoor swimming pool and two golf courses. Cornwall had always proved more popular with the offshore fishermen though there was a growing centre at Paignton, and others in the north of Devon.

THE TOURIST INDUSTRY

Tourist traffic to Beachmouth had changed since the early 1970s. Then, two-week 'long stay' holidays had been the norm. With the steady decrease in real costs of overseas package holiday, growing numbers were taking their holiday in Spain or Greece rather than the classic two weeks at the English seaside.

Beachmouth, like the other resorts in the area, experienced a significant shift towards the short-term visitor taking a break in addition to a holiday. These short-break holidays differed in several respects from the traditional family holiday in length and in what the customer expected. This was shown clearly in *ad hoc* research the local chamber of commerce carried out from time to time (Tables C11.1 and C11.2).

Table C11.1   Findings of chamber of commerce survey

	1981	1984
Tourist visitors	200,000	180,000
Days spent	2.3	2.1
Average spend (£)	110	85
Business visitors	15,000	22,000
Days spent	1	1.2
Average spend (£)	65	80
Socio-economic (%)		
A/B	55	
C1/C2	30	
D/E	15	
Age profile (%)		
under 10	3	
10–20	15	
20–35	25	
35–55	42	
55+	15	
Family size (%)		
1	17	
2	41	
3–4	33	
4+	9	

Table C11.2   Tourist perceptions of Beachmouth facilities

Factor	Age group				Socio-economic	
	10–20	20–35	35–55	55+	ABC1	C2DE
Quiet	7	3	2	1	2	6
Bathing	2	6	6	6	5	3
Food	3	5	8	7	6	4
Activities	3	7	4	3	4	5
Attractive	3	3	2	2	3	3
Price	5	5	4	4	4	5

(From 1 to 9: 1 favourable and 9 unfavourable.)

THE LONG-TERM RESIDENT

Local planners evaluating change in the long-term residential population relied on information, commissioned by the County Council, extrapolating an approximation of the population structure of Beachmouth. Because there was a tendency for the retired to concentrate in seaside towns rather than the countryside this meant that the percentage in Beachmouth was likely to be considerably higher than the countrywide average (Table C11.3).

Table C11.3 Beachmouth age structure

Age category	1979 (%)	1990 (projected) (%)
up to 10	8	6
10–20	15	12
20–35	28	27
35–55	25	24
55+	24	31

What the statistics could not reveal was the age structure of the population moving into the area and its net impact on the age structure of the Beachmouth population as a whole. However, on comparison with national figures it would appear that around 60 to 120 people reaching or past retirement age were moving into Beachmouth every year. Throughout the county it should be noted that there was a slow population growth as more people moved from the Midlands and the North into the South West, leading to an overall population increase of 1.25 per cent per annum.

The increase in Beachmouth's population had put pressure on property prices, which rose, fuelled by the retiring affluent. Demand was, however, restricted to small town houses and what flats were available. Several of the larger seafront houses had been converted, and two new developments were under way to construct purpose-built units. Prices ranged from £40–60,000, depending on size and location.

In addition to changes in property ownership there was a slow increase in the number of nursing homes or their equivalents throughout the South West. For many years there had been two in Beachmouth and both were now fully occupied, charging around £70 a week to each of their sixty residents.

THE COMPETITION

Beachmouth's hotels and guest houses varied considerably in standard, clientele and cost (Tables C11.4 and C11.5). The more expensive hotels attracted conference and business traffic, which had also given a substantial boost to the main guest houses in the town. None of the hotels in Beachmouth could be considered 'luxury' category – the nearest was in Torquay (15 miles away).

OCCUPANCY

The local tourist information office monitored occupancy rates over the year, and kept records which gave a rough indication of percentage occupancy both by time of year and also time of week. These records also gave an estimate of the average percentage occupancy over the past years, though there were slight discrepancies between the two figures (Tables C11.6 and C11.7).

Table C11.4   Beachmouth hotels by grading and facilities (double room or equivalent)

Hotel	Category	Rooms	Price per day (£)	Restaurant	Other facilities
Seaview	***	34	35	Yes	Conference room
Holiday Inn	***	60	45	Yes	Conference room/pool
Grand	***	55	40	Yes	Ballroom/conference room
Horizon	***	45	42	Yes	Swimming pool
Beachmouth	**	25	26	No	None
Langridge	*	20	18	No	None
Exeter	*	18	19	No	None
Western	*	20	18	No	Large grounds
Guest houses					
Kittiwake		15	15	No	None
Tides		12	14	No	None
Sonara		14	16	No	None

Table C11.5   Beachmouth: low-cost holiday accommodation

Name	Beds	Price per person (week)
Sandy Valley	160	£35
Palm	180	£37

Table C11.6   Average occupancy by year (percentage)

Hotel	1982	1983	1984	1985	1986
Seaview	45	42	46	46	47
Holiday Inn	–	65	76	78	84
Grand	55	60	65	68	74
Horizon	52	55	58	58	60
Beachmouth	48	45	44	47	43
Langridge	40	38	45	44	43
Exeter	47	45	42	40	39
Western	43	39	37	35	35
Kittiwake	55	56	60	66	72
Tides	60	58	54	60	65
Sonara	70	75	80	78	78

RESTAURANTS

A number of restaurants and cafés in the town were open at least part of the year in addition to those run by the hotels. Hotel prices for an evening meal averaged £8.50 per head including wine (considerably higher in the Holiday Inn, which catered mainly for the business trade and had little tourist traffic), though many residents stayed on inclusive half or full board terms and few outsiders ate in the hotel

Table C11.7   Average occupancy by month (percentage)

Hotel	1	2	3	4	5	6	7	8	9	10	11	12
Seaview	30	22	29	44	67	89	92	98	72	45	30	20
Holiday Inn	55	55	78	88	90	90	90	96	90	94	67	72
Grand	45	43	42	67	78	94	94	98	82	55	50	32
Horizon	40	40	39	55	58	78	82	80	66	55	48	46
Beachmouth	31	23	21	31	52	72	85	86	82	52	41	23
Langridge	21	22	32	34	54	67	82	84	78	48	50	55
Exeter	18	19	22	35	50	70	72	75	56	21	16	–
Western	16	15	17	21	38	65	77	78	51	32	13	12
Kittiwake	66	65	64	67	73	84	92	90	70	66	52	–
Tides	51	52	53	56	67	88	86	92	76	60	43	32
Sonara	77	76	66	67	90	92	94	94	76	68	65	–

Table C11.8   Beachmouth: specialist restaurants

Outlet	Tables	Cost/head (inc. wine) (£)	Open	Food
Fisherman	15	15	March–October	Seafood
Com Esta	12	12	March–October	Pizza
Maharani	10	9	All year	Indian
Wong Yu	12	11	All year	Chinese

restaurants. The food served in all the hotel restaurants could be summarized as 'traditional English'.

The 'specialist' restaurants in the town are in Table C11.8.

None of the eating places in Beachmouth was mentioned in any national guide book. The nearest restaurants included were at Brixham (12 miles), at Exeter and Tiverton (15 miles). The area was well served with fast-food outlets and other types of restaurants, particularly in Exeter and Torquay (12 miles). Margins in the restaurant business were extremely good in season; the average gross profit (excluding wage costs) on a meal costing £15 was around £11.

On the seafront were four pubs, which served lunch; one of these, the Jolly Sailor, was listed in the guides for the quality of its beer and food. Other cafés serving basic burgers and chips opened solely for the tourist season and closed at the end of October.

Though Beachmouth was primarily a quiet resort for the older holiday-maker, there was one night club called Barnacles, and many of the pubs to the north of the town, away from the seafront, had live music – primarily during the summer season.

PROMOTION

The hotels and tourist facilities in Beachmouth all subscribed to the local tourist board, which placed some advertising in the weekend press to promote the resort.

Some of the larger hotels also advertised separately, especially for out of season bookings and to expand their conference trade.

The most important promotional channel for much of the itinerant trade was the various guides, either national or regional. These had various production dates and lead times, but in general it would take a hotel six months to change designation, and what with the slow change-over of guide usage (not everyone, for example, used the most up-to-date guide), it would be two years before the change in status or facilities was universally recognized.

THE HOTEL

The Western Hotel had been built in the early 1920s on a three-acre site overlooking the harbour. Over the years it had slipped from being one of Beachmouth's premier hotels – largely as a result of damage caused during the war when it had been requisitioned as a staff headquarters for the Free French forces. In 1948 Captain Charles Adamson bought it on his retirement from the Navy, and his family had run it ever since. In 1985 Charles Adamson died and the hotel passed to his two sons, John and Michael, in equal shares. John, the elder, had worked at running the hotel since leaving school, whereas Michael remained an extremely junior partner in a firm of Exeter estate agents. John's wife, Frances, also worked in the hotel as receptionist cum breakfast cook.

Originally, the hotel had two wings built out from the central dining room/bar area and had a total of forty rooms. One wing had been demolished as a result of an over-exuberant party in 1942 involving one tank and two amphibious assault vehicles. The damage caused had also extended to the originally extensive kitchens, which had been only partly repaired.

By 1985 the hotel had been reduced to twenty bedrooms, half with bathrooms, and a restaurant serving breakfasts only.

The old design of the building made the Western Hotel expensive to maintain, heat and clean, and the large grounds required a full-time gardener for proper maintenance. As a result the overheads were higher than those of many other Beachmouth hotels (Table C11.9).

The staff currently employed were:

Table C11.9 Western Hotel overheads

Item	£
Rates	5,000
Heating and lighting	12,000
Wages (2)	9,000
Telephone and insurance	1,000
Repairs and maintenance	4,000
Promotion (brochures/advertising/tourist board contribution)	3,000
Bank loan	10,000

1. Dan Bowman, gardener, fifty-five years old. Had lived and worked at the Western Hotel all his life. Widower living on the premises.
2. Brenda Scutcheon, nineteen, parlourmaid and waitress. Recent addition to the Western Hotel staff after YTS traineeship.

The hotel had been valued for probate at £250,000, partly as a going concern but mainly to reflect the land values the hotel represented. Although the Adamson brothers had received some tax relief on the transfer of a family business, the tax levied had led to a slight increase in the level of bank borrowings which had slowly risen over the years as the hotel had become less and less profitable. By 1985, they stood at around £50,000.

The position of the elder brother John was further complicated by the fact that Michael, the younger, had received an offer to go into a larger firm provided that capital of around £100,000 was made available within the next six months. It was obvious that the hotel was no longer viable as a means of providing income for a growing family, and some action would need to be taken to generate capital.

A number of options were open to the family to solve their financial problems.

1. To raise a further substantial loan on the property. The bank had indicated its willingness to lend up to 60 per cent of the total value of the property, which could release up to an additional £100,000 (over and above the current bank loan).
2. To sell the hotel (this would probably take some time at the likely asking price of £250,000).
3. To sell a half-acre site, with planning permission to build ten to twelve apartments, to a developer for around £100,000. It was likely that the council would give permission at the north end of the hotel, which was opposite a major development. This was, however, the maximum level of redevelopment that the council would consider, higher density development would not be possible. Planning permission normally took a substantial length of time in Beachmouth, especially when there was a question of increased provision for either holiday or retirement accommodation. This was because there was increasing resistance within the council to further developments of this nature. It was likely that such planning permission would take around six months to come through.
4. To find outside finance. The ability to find finance outside the banks was likely to be limited.

UPGRADING THE HOTEL – OPTIONS

Provided that sufficient capital could be obtained there were a number of possibilities for securing improved profitability and long-term return. These included:

1. Upgrade the current bedrooms to reach three-star level. This was estimated to cost £90,000 and to take six months for completion, with half the bedrooms out of action at any one time.

Upgrading the hotel to three-star status would mean that extra staff would have to be employed to run the bar, provide a basic meals service and provide night-time reception, which together with other increased expenditure was thought likely to raise the annual overhead by around £20,000. Though the occupancy rate at the Western Hotel would certainly increase it was slightly out of town and in a quiet location and this might have an adverse effect on the eventual occupancy rates.

1. Rebuild the old wing to provide twenty-five new bedrooms, with attached car parking. This would cost approximately £120,000 but would not interfere with the current hotel activity. With additional bedrooms overheads would rise substantially, and it was estimated that the extra cost would be £30,000 per annum.

3. Convert the current hotel to an old people's home, which would cost around £15,000. This would not involve any increase in overheads, and would not interfere greatly with the current hotel activity.

4. Rebuild the restaurant and kitchens at a cost of £45,000 to serve premium meals costing around £15 per head. It was thought likely that an eighty-chair restaurant was feasible. Frances's brother, a sous-chief in a Rouen hotel, could be employed, but essential additional staff would raise overheads by £35,000 per annum. The reconstruction of the restaurant would not interfere with the current activities of the hotel.

5. It would also be possible to redesign the hotel grounds to include a nine-hole golf course. This would cost approximately £25,000 and take six months to complete. It would leave the hotel with only a small garden.

Case 12

NESTLÉ

BACKGROUND

Nestlé, the major Swiss multinational food company, has substantial food interests in the UK, including Carnation, Crosse & Blackwell, Chambourcy and Findus, in addition to being market leader in instant coffee with Nescafé Gold Blend and other varieties.

One of the world's major snack food manufacturers, Nestlé has always faced substantial competition in the UK market from Unilever (Batchelors, Birds Eye), CPC (Knorr), Heinz, the Imperial Group (Golden Wonder) – taken over in 1986 by Hanson Trust – and Nabisco (KP, Ritz), all with established market-leading snack food products. Product development had been a crucial factor in the success of these companies in the snack food market and Nestlé is no exception, with a worldwide search for new products and product sectors. With the purchase of Carnation Foods of the United States, Nestlé had fulfilled the first part of a global strategy to be one of the major world food manufacturers.

Like other Swiss companies, Nestlé has a series of worldwide subsidiaries but has a restricted percentage of equity that can be held outside Switzerland. This to an extent reduces its capacity to borrow extensively on the world money markets and means that much of the expansion has to be financed from retained earnings. This has resulted in the company concentrating on high margin products and seeking to establish dominant market positions wherever possible.

The main markets in which Nestlé is established and their importance to the company are summarized in Table C12.1.

The main subsidiary companies in the UK operate as separate profit centres with specific responsibilities.

1. Nescafé – coffee.

Table C12.1   Nestlé main markets

Market	Value (£ million)	Growth	Share	Market profitability
Coffee	430	Small	High	Good
Condensed milk	41	Negative	High	Excellent
Pet food	663	Nil	Small	Reasonable
Dried milk products	71	Moderate	High	Excellent
Soups	210	Nil	Medium	Poor
Sauces	102	Small	Medium	Good
Frozen food	2,200	High	Medium	Good
Tinned vegetables	450	Nil	Medium	Poor
Yoghourt	165	Moderate	High	Good

(Market share estimates and market profitability from trade sources.)

2. Carnation – condensed milk/pet food.
3. Crosse & Blackwell – soups, sauces, tinned vegetables.
4. Findus – frozen food.
5. Chambourcy – yoghourt.

As with many companies the economies of scale in food production have affected the way Nestlé operates in the UK market, with the concentration of production in a limited number of sites.

In the EEC, Nestlé has well-established operations in all markets and substantial expertise in the snack and chocolate markets. Diversification into one of these sectors was considered an important strategic development for Nestlé in the UK market.

THE UK SNACK MARKET

Demand for snack products has increased steadily in the industrialized world, and the UK has followed the pattern since the late 1960s. The factors influencing this trend are:

(a) the increasing number of women at work;
(b) decreasing family sizes;
(c) ageing population demanding smaller meal quantities;
(d) increasing affluence;
(e) consumer durables speeding both cooking (microwaves) and food preparation (freezers);
(f) new healthy eating awareness among consumers, resulting in a reduction in the amount eaten: replacing a heavy midday meal with something less calorific to improve health.

Available snack products can be divided into two groups:

(a) 'nibbles' – eaten between meals;
(b) meal substitutes – such as Vesta, cuppa soup, pork pies, sausages, bacon, sandwiches, omelettes, cheese and crackers, take-away food, beans, spaghetti and the like on toast, and pot snacks which are usually eaten in winter when a hot snack is thought to be appropriate.

Consumer attitudes

'My little girl likes all sorts of rubbish. She helps herself to cereal and crisps. They prefer snacky things to prepared dinners.' (Female, aged between thirty-five and fourty-four, northern, current user.)

Research shows that 'nibbles' are eaten mainly as a result of boredom, but also as meal replacement and during tea and coffee breaks. Interesting snacks can be symbolic, representing the 'calm before the storm', or comforting, as in a warming bowl of soup.

The impact of technology has considerably broadened the scope of snack manufacturers and the type of product that they can offer, and companies invested heavily to produce new styles of product. By the 1980s a number of broad market divisions could be identified together with the consumer attitudes relating to each sector (Table C12.2).

Table C12.2   Snack market segmentation and consumer attitudes

Group	Attitudes	Occasions
'Nibbles'		
Crisps	In-between meals	Any time
Sweet biscuits	Unhealthy	With tea/coffee
Chocolates		
Light meal		
Savoury biscuits	Not too heavy	Evening
Pâté		
Cheese spread		
Meal replacement		
Vesta meals	Artificial	Winter
Pot noodles	Quick	Not for family
Savoury rice		
'Healthy'		
Yoghourt	Healthy	Meal addition
Wheatgerm-based products		Summer
Children fillers		
Soup	Cheap	Winter
Spaghetti	Standby meal	
Beans	Substantial	

Table C12.3   Snack market sectors

Sector	Growth	Major features
Crisps	Small	Expanding varieties
Chocolate	Nil	Expanding varieties
Savoury biscuits	Moderate	'Healthy eating'
Meal replacement	Moderate	'Exotic'
Healthy eating	High	Expanding varieties
Children fillers	Nil	Expanding varieties

Competition in the snack market

There were a few major manufacturers in each of the main market sectors. Mars, Cadbury and Rowntree Mackintosh dominated the chocolate market; Nabisco, Imperial Foods and United Biscuits the crisp and savoury biscuit sectors; Unilever and Imperial dominated the meal replacement market. Crosse & Blackwell were well established in the children filler market with soups and baked beans, but faced strong competition from Heinz. Findus frozen food gave Nestlé a presence in the most rapidly growing sector of the market, meal replacement.

The entire snack market had become more 'fashion' conscious; products gained rapid acceptance before being replaced by other, new introductions. Different market sectors were reacting in varying degrees to this fashion trend (Table C12.3).

Distribution and the snack market

The concentration of retailing power in the UK affected new product development among manufacturers in various ways. As the pace of product introduction increased, retailers (Sainsbury's, Tesco, Asda, Argyll and Dee) expected new products to show them a profit within a shorter and shorter time span. They were, in consequence, demanding:

(a) a high level of advertising expenditure to support new products;
(b) a high level of initial consumer offtake – otherwise the product would be delisted.

The length of time allowed for products to establish themselves had been reduced from an average of six to three months. However, major companies like Nestlé, Unilever and Nabisco had well-established contacts with the major retailing chains and were normally successful in achieving high levels of initial distribution. The development of distributors' or retailers' own brands put further pressure on the manufacturers to innovate continually.

THE MEAL REPLACEMENT MARKET

By the mid-1980s the meal replacement market included a number of products:

(a) pot noodles;
(b) dehydrated complete meals (Vesta);
(c) savoury rice/soya products.

Overall the market had grown at around 15 per cent per annum, and was regarded as one of the most profitable sectors of the snack food sector – the raw materials were relatively cheap and the product could be effectively differentiated from the competition.

THE UK POT SNACK MARKET

Instant pot snacks were introduced in the UK in late 1977 by Golden Wonder, when its product, 'Pot Noodle', was launched in the Midlands. KP Foods had tested a similar product in 1976, 'Oodles', which was withdrawn due to product problems. The concept originated in Japan where it gained popularity for lunches at work due to the single disposable container in which the product was prepared and eaten. By 1980 there were around 400 million units sold in the Japanese market, which still remains far and away the main world consumer of pot snacks.

Pot Noodle sold out within two weeks, Golden Wonder having completely underestimated demand. The test market having progressed well, it was extended into the Midlands region, and a rolling launch followed soon after, which finished by October 1979. Heavy television advertising supported the brand, which together with the introduction of products from Knorr, Batchelors and KP, led to a substantial consumer trial until the market peaked at 108 million units in 1980, worth £36 million. At this time there were over thirty different varieties on the market, though there were only around five top selling lines, such as Sweet and Sour.

The following summary shows competitive changes over time.

1978 – Golden Wonder launched regionally.
1979 – Golden Wonder launched nationally. Batchelors and Knorr enter market.
1980 – Golden Wonder launches Pot Rice. KP enters market.
1982 – Golden Wonder launches Pot Casserole. Knorr withdraws.
1983 – Batchelors withdraws.
1984 – KP relaunches with quality improvements.

The total advertising expenditure level reached £4.2 million in 1980. Consumers were fairly evenly spread across age, sex and regional groupings but consumption of pot snacks is slightly biased towards the north, younger adults (up to forty-five), and to families with children.

The use of pot snacks depended on the occasion: a snack lunch at work was a

Table C12.4 Volume changes: pot noodle market

Year	Volume (million units)	Value (£ million)	Advertising (£ million)
1978	8	5	0.134
1979	41	15	0.475
1980	108	36	4.156
1981	98	35	2.551
1982	62	22	0.806
1983	46	23	0.893
1984	46	23	0.698

particularly appropriate moment for the consumption of pot snacks, whereas consumption in the home was fairly limited. In a fashion-dominated market, newly developed products should have been appearing on the market to consolidate it, but this did not happen and consumers considered that the market was regressing in product quality.

Many tried pot products only once, presumably due to a combination of poor quality and the high unit cost compared with other snack alternatives. This resulted in retailers delisting all but best selling varieties and the withdrawal of Knorr and Batchelors from the market in 1982/83. The spectacular growth and then decline of the pot snack market can be seen in Table C12.4.

Current users consider pots snacks to be filling, convenient, tasty and reasonably priced. However, even they had reservations – believing that pot snacks can be powdery, lumpy and gluey if not mixed properly.

Lapsed users believe that the quality of pot snacks is poor, and that there are alternative convenient snacks which offer better value and better taste. They describe pot snacks as:

(a) tasting unpleasant;
(b) looking unappetizing;
(c) cardboardy;
(d) plasticky;
(e) artifical.

Many lapsed users also dislike the idea of pouring water on to dehydrated food. The initial success, but lack of continued market progress, suggested that there might be additional market opportunities in the hot snack market that had not been fully exploited.

Advertising expenditure also dropped off as price competition continued. This pressure on margins turned the market inward, which led to a rapid decline, but by 1985 it had apparently levelled off at approximately 46 million cups in the UK.

In response to the poor image of pot snacks, KP relaunched its 'Quick Lunch' range, with improved recipes and a more appetizing appearance.

Golden Wonder, undoubted brand leader, was the only significant advertiser in the market: £893,000 in 1983 and £1.3 million TV advertising in 1984; and

Table C12.5   Golden Wonder distribution

Product	Numerical distribution	Weighted distribution
Pot Noodle	92	95
Pot Casserole	82	78
Pot Rice	78	82

Table C12.6   Pot noodle market shares by year (%)

	1981	1984
Golden wonder	58	91
KP	12	9
Batchelors	16	–
Knorr	14	–

conducted a very small test market of three pot desserts, with varying results.

In 1985 Golden Wonder sold a range of eleven pot snacks, retailing at about 47p each, mostly containing a base of beef or chicken flavouring in processed soya. Extensions of the product range into Pot Rice (1980) and Pot Casserole (1982) continued to maintain product listings in the supermarkets. The four new Pot Sweet varieties were nationally introduced in 1985: apple and blackberry crumble, spicy apple crunch, caramel crunch and peach dessert. This range has to date proved unsuccessful.

The KP 'Quick Lunch' range is smaller, consisting of four items similar to the Golden Wonder lines and which are about 10p more expensive.

Golden Wonder has been successful in maintaining wide distribution for the majority of its product lines throughout the 1980s (Table C12.5) and, by entering the market early, has managed to consolidate its market position when the market peaked and declined, as changes in market share over the 1981/84 period indicate (Table C12.6).

THE DEHYDRATED MEAL MARKET

Historically, this sector has been dominated by Vesta which still remains by far and away the market leader.

Vesta, produced by Batchelors (part of Unilever), was first introduced in 1960, and by the mid-1980s was achieving around 19 million units worth around £13 million at RSP (Table C12.7).

The product has changed concepts and ranges since its initial introduction.

Stage 1: Ready-to-cook gourmet meals at home.
Stage 2: Fun convenience food for occasional meals at home.
Stage 3: Standby meal products with 'exotic' varieties.

Research data showed those for whom Vesta had an appeal:

Table C12.7   Vesta sales

Year	Sales (million units)
1978	17
1979	19
1980	20
1981	17
1982	19
1983	21
1984	22

(a) bachelor households with limited time and/or facilities in which to cook (most products require two pans for preparation);
(b) small households wanting a basis for a more exotic meal.

The most popular varieties in 1985 were:

● Chow Mein
● Beef Risotto
● Paella
● Chicken Curry
● Beef Curry

There was greater competition in the market not only from supermarket own brands (Tesco, for example, tested its range in 1985) but from other entrants:

● Bernard Matthews
● Princes
● Lockwoods
● General Foods

Each of these product ranges was broadly similar to Vesta and priced at around 95–100p for a double portion, though some had moved towards the introduction of easy opening cans to reduce the amount of cooking time necessary, moving away from the dehydrated concept.

At the other end of the market, frozen food like the Menu Masters range from Birds Eye supplied another element in convenience meal competition, though the prices were considerably higher at around 160–180p for a comparable quantity to the Vesta range. Other companies quick to establish themselves in this sector included Findus, the Nestlé subsidiary, with its Lean Cuisine range. The frozen convenience food market was growing rapidly overall and by 1985 was estimated to be worth £150 million. The frozen convenience market was generally agreed to provide high margins, but required considerable investment in manufacturing and in research and develoment to ensure a consistent, cost-effective product. Distribution costs were also significantly higher for frozen products and as a result there were considerable advantages accruing to the main players in the market – Ross and Birds Eye.

All sectors of the market were influenced by the introduction of the microwave cooker, which made the frozen meal a far more viable proposition for the small household than had previously been the case, especially as ownership of fridge–freezers or separate freezers was also steadily increasing.

RICE, SOYA AND NOODLES MARKET

The market for convenience rice, soya and noodles products changed significantly over the 1970s and 1980s. Initially the market had been dominated by the Batchelors Savoury Rice range; supermarkets moved in with a variety of own-label products. Yet the market remained small both in volume (5 million units) and value (£2 million) since the products' introduction in 1970.

Crosse & Blackwell's share of the market was small – about 10 per cent. During the early 1980s the company had introduced a dried product called Pasta Choice, which had become established alongside the Batchelors range in the majority of supermarkets. The three products, based on pasta with a choice of sauces, retailed for around 50p for a single portion.

Growth in the instant rice and pasta market was estimated to be around 10 per cent per annum, though much of this was in the frozen varieties. Profitability in this market was not as high as that in the frozen convenience food sector.

The soya or textured protein market was both small and static. Established in the 1970s when the price of meat soared, the market had failed to establish any real consumer franchise because of quality problems associated with the sector and the stabilization of meat prices. Brooke Bond Oxo (another Unilever subsidiary) entered this market in 1984 with a soya product called Beanfeast, the concept being to provide a soya-based product which could be cooked with either rice or pasta in about twenty minutes. Beanfeast remained the market leader in a small market sector.

The market for noodle products has been explored by a number of companies in the snack food market; Batchelors, Kellogg's and Nestlé have all produced products in this small but fairly rapidly growing market sector, which was achieving a year on year expansion of around 12 per cent, though again there was a steady increase in the number of frozen products available from all major manufacturers.

The main features of the various products appear in Table C12.8.

THE PRICING STRUCTURE

The ingredient costs of Pot Noodle, dehydrated meals and soya-based snacks are fairly similar, with a general pricing structure given in Table C12.9.

Table C12.8   Summary of main features of pot snack, Vesta and savoury rice products

	Pot snacks	Vesta	Savoury rice
Varieties	28	10	5
Volume	46 million	19 million	5 million
Packaging	Plastic pot/foil lid	Sachet within box	Sachet
Price	50p (75 g)	110p (220 g)	45p (113 g)
Quality	Low	Reasonable	Reasonable
Cooking time	3–5 minutes	30 minutes	20 minutes
Equipment	None (except kettle)	Two pans	One pan
Media expenditure	£1.6 million	£0.1 million	Nil
User profile	C2/DE	C2/DE	C2/DE
Age	18–30	16–34	55+
Consumption time	Lunch	Early evening	Evening

Table C12.9   Pricing structure of pot snack, dehydrated meals and soya snack

Consumer price	100
Retail price	84
Manufacturer cost	56
Raw materials	25
Distribution	5
Packaging	26

THE CROSSE & BLACKWELL PROPOSAL

To become more firmly established in this growing market, Crosse & Blackwell developed a dehydrated meal concept called Snackatack, having four variants:

- Chilli con Carne
- Pasta Bolognese
- Chicken Curry and Rice
- Farmhouse Hot Pot

Snackatack was in a sachet and could be cooked in twelve minutes, using a single saucepan. Initially it was thought that the product could retail at 29p for a single portion (73 g), which would yield an acceptable industry norm margin. It would be positioned as a 'satisfying snack' with a target market of C2/DE aged between eighteen and thirty-four.

A comparison between the Snackatack concept and Vesta and Pot Noodles, identified as the main competition, yielded the results in Table C12.10.

The problem facing the Crosse & Blackwell management was to evaluate the likely success of the proposed Snackatack range in the market and to produce a marketing plan which would maximize the likelihood of success.

In common with all its other products Snackatack would benefit from the well-established Crosse & Blackwell salesforce and would be supported by

Table C12.10   Percentage preferring Snackatack over their current product

	Current Vesta users	Current Pot Noodle users
Prefer: Chilli	34	45
Pasta	42	55
Curry	55	48
Hot Pot	27	34
Snackatack a more satisfying concept?	36	48
Good value for money?	55	62

advertising and promotion, which would ensure its initial acceptance by the major supermarket outlets; the company would also be able to exploit any success that would be achieved with the sophisticated manufacturing plant that was available within the UK.

Case 13

GASCOFIX

INTRODUCTION

Gascofix was founded in 1984 by a fifty-two-year-old industrial chemist, Gurindar Shah, who developed the concept after several years of trial and error while working part time at a technical college in East London.

The product that was finally perfected was a new form of sealant for motor vehicle gaskets. Gaskets are seals between the engine block and the cylinder head to prevent the leakage of gases and water. They are made of a variety of materials – often asbestos with a thin steel or copper covering. The gasket must be fixed to the block with some form of adhesive, and this adhesive faces severe heat (ranging from $-20°C$ to $+250°C$), pressure and corrosion, which will often be sustained over a long period. The larger or more powerful the engine, the greater the forces on the sealant.

The new adhesive had two particular advantages over the competition – by using certain industrial waste as raw material in the production process it was substantially cheaper to manufacture and had greater resistance to both heat and pressure. Because of the basic nature of the product, the company could not take out a patent on the new adhesive, but Gurindar was of the opinion that finding the exact production process and combination of raw materials would require a substantial research programme, and the product was unlikely to be copyable in less than eighteen months.

THE PRODUCTION PROCESS

Gascofix could be simply produced from dry raw materials in 50 kg quantities in single air-tight reaction vessels, electrically heated and magnetically stirred over a

Table C13.1   Gascofix overheads (£)

Rent	2,000
Rates	750
Power	500
Telephone	300
Miscellaneous	1,000

five-hour period. The product could then be extruded via a simple filling machine into a range of containers ranging from 50 ml to 250 ml, or supplied in the reaction vessels themselves for local filling. Contact with air hardened the product which would then set rigid in two hours.

A 50 kg container of the finished product cost £100 including labour; the cost of tube containers ranged from 2p for a 50 ml tube to 5p for a 250 ml unit. Gurindar had facilities with the local branch of Remploy to fix these tubes on to instruction cards at 5p per unit. When established in a small warehouse in East London, the company had the ability to produce 100 kg per day, all of which could be successfully passed through the filling machine and fixed on to backing cards via Remploy.

Gurindar was able initially to handle the entire production process on his own but would be able to employ his two sons and other family members should production need to be increased.

Because of the nature of the production process overheads were very low (Table C13.1).

Gurindar had had no specific experience of running his own company, having been involved in research for most of his working life. He had been developing this process over a number of years and had to turn to the local authority for finance as he had no security to borrow money from the bank. The local authority had provided him with £7,500 start-up finance, repayable over five years.

COMPANY PROGRESS

Tables C13.2. and C13.3 supply details of the company's progress.

Table C13.2   Gascofix: monthly income and expenditure (£)

	1	2	3	4	5	6
Sales	450	650	1,300	2,200	2,600	2,800
Revenue	–	–	300	700	1,200	1,500
Materials	90	150	260	440	520	560
Rent and rates	1,375	–	–	–	–	–
Wages	500	500	500	500	500	500
Other	150	150	150	150	150	150
Interest and repayment	100	100	100	100	100	100
Equipment	1,500	–	–	–	–	–
Cash flow	(3,715)	(900)	(710)	(490)	(70)	190
Cumulative		(4,615)	(5,325)	(5,815)	(5,885)	(5,695)

Table C13.3   Gascofix: six-month
profit and loss account (£) (unaudited)

Sales	10,000
Materials	2,000
Overheads	2,200
Wages	3,000
Selling expenses	1,200
Interest	300
Loan repayment	300
Profit (loss)	1,000

THE MARKET

The market for a gasket sealant was potentially large, as the product could be used by both the manufacturer of the orginal engines and engine reconditioners and repairers. The main sectors within the UK are identified in Table C13.4.

A rough guide suggested that DIY repairs would use around 50 ml on each occasion whereas other users would use in the region of 150 ml.

The market was also clearly potentially worldwide, including the EEC, the United States, Japan and many other countries with well-developed road transport systems and fairly substantial vehicle repair sectors. Since the armed forces throughout the world required high specifications in their engine design and maintenance as a result of the greater demands for performance and reliability, this sector also provided favourable market opportunities.

Each of these sectors were serviced in different ways.

The OEM sector

This sector bought direct – a small number of large volume manufacturers such as Ford, GM, making up the bulk of the production of both cars and goods vehicles. These companies varied considerably in their degree of vertical integration (producing components in-house), but were all currently attempting to reduce the number of component suppliers with which they dealt. Because of the large

Table C13.4   Gascofix: potential market sectors

Sector	No. of vehicles per year
OEM (cars)	1,913,000
OEM (goods/transport)	116,000
OEM (others)	55,000
Reconditioners	500,000 (est)
Repairs (professional)	300,000 (est)
Repairs (DIY)	350,000 (est)

NB: OEM figures include imported and exported units.

volumes produced, OEM companies bought in bulk and demanded high quality specifications. It often took suppliers two or three years to be accepted as a potential source of components. The price at which these companies bought was uncertain but was thought to be around £10 per kilo. They also demanded highly favourable credit terms of around 100 days.

The overseas military market

This was handled by a number of international agents who co-ordinated the purchase of materials for the armed services throughout the world. The going price for this market was considerably higher than that for the OEM manufacturers, the product would tend to be available in small quantities with appropriate language instruction.

The reconditioning market

This market consisted of a large number of medium-sized companies with regional bases servicing the surrounding market. It was estimated that there were around 150 such firms in the UK, each handling between 200 and 1,500 engine repairs a year. They bought gasket sealant in fairly large quantities direct from the manufacturers, and were paying around £2.30 for a 250 ml tube. They were fairly erratic payers and average credit periods were of the order of 90 days.

The DIY repair market

This was serviced via retail and wholesale outlets. It was estimated that there were around 3,000 outlets that specialized in this market sector, the largest of which, Halfords – owned by the Ward White group – had an approximate 21 per cent market share. The rest of the market was characterized by independent retailers which bought either direct from individual firms, one of the five major distributors in the motor accessories market or via the growing number of specialized wholesalers. The price charged to the consumer was the highest, with competitive 50 ml tubes priced at £2.40 retail. This included a 35 per cent gross margin for the retailer and a 15–18 per cent wholesale margin. Credit terms varied according to the type of outlet, with 60 to 100 days being common. There was also a fairly high level of bad debts.

There were a number of independent sales agents who serviced the motor accessories market, making an income from a 15 per cent gross commission on the sales achieved, the supplier company taking all the credit risk involved for the particular account.

The professional repair sector

This sector was partly carried out in the 5,000 garages that provided a full service facility, and also via mechanics who serviced cars at home for individuals. Approximately 9 per cent of all repairs were carried out by a mechanic working on the car at the home of the owner.

The buying pattern of this group varied considerably.

1. Dealers were required to buy product direct from the manufacturers and only manufacturer-approved material could be used for repairs. This made up around 60 per cent of this sector.
2. Independent garages bought either direct or via the wholesale sector. There was no reliable information as to the percentage bought in either fashion.
3. Individual mechanics would on the whole buy direct from the retailer.

THE COMPETITION

There were a variety of companies producing gasket sealant, and a number which produced gasket replacement products that could be used for small gasket areas, but not in the case of the cylinder head. The market leader was Hermetite, a product produced by one of the major multinational chemical combines, which was estimated to have around 37 per cent market share. There were two other major forces in the market and then a number of concerns that supplied specific customers with product to their specification (the suppliers to the OEM sector, for example).

Because the production process used by companies currently in the market was broadly similar, pricing was fairly inflexible. Though there was no information as to the profitability of the competitive products it was considered in the trade that 40–50 per cent gross contribution on a typical retail product would not be unusual.

THE EXHIBITION

In early 1985 Gurindar had around thirty reconditioner clients to whom he was selling direct at around £2.15 for a 250 ml tube, though terms varied between each customer. He was also selling a small quantity of product through local retailers and via an advertisement in *Exchange and Mart*. As these selling activities were now taking up a considerable amount of time he decided to invest in attending one of the main motoring manufacturing exhibitions, the Motor Accessories Fair. After this event, and once potential customers had evaluated his product he received the following offers.

1. *Motor Spares Ltd* – one of the leading distributors in the country, covering 1,900 outlets with a salesforce of 15 – offered to distribute the product under its

own label and pay a royalty of 15 per cent. It estimated that a 20 per cent market share in the DIY and reconditioner market could be achieved within eighteen months. To achieve this it demanded exclusivity over a three-year period both in the UK and overseas, where it had some, though limited interests.

2. *Mazel Tov*. One of the leading international suppliers to the world arms market offered to buy the product in bulk at £4 a kilo for international distribution. It would initially want to take around 30 tons per year, but was not prepared to enter into a definite contractual relationship stating that Gurindar would not be able to pursue independent action overseas.

3. *Halfords* offered to distribute the product via its outlets as an own-brand provided it had exclusivity within the UK market. It would buy product in 50 ml tubes for £1.25.

A number of independent sales agents also approached the stand offering to represent the company in various areas throughout the UK.

D. Evans Associates, based in Dartford Kent, covered the south-east counties of England and claimed to sell to 400 accounts in Kent, Sussex and Surrey.

Arlex Ltd, based in Bracknell, called on around 600 accounts in Berkshire, Surrey and Hampshire.

James Motor Factors, based in Uxbridge, claimed to call on 800 accounts in the London area.

All these companies would be prepared to operate as wholesalers selling at an agreed wholesale price which they thought should be between £1.30 and £1.45 for a 50 ml tube, on which they would get 15 per cent gross commission.

Case 14

ADNAMS LIMITED

BACKGROUND

Adnams, a small family brewing company based in East Anglia, has just completed a five-year building programme doubling its brewing capacity. As the company continues to trade profitably, pressures to expand further become apparent. The current expansion programme, however, had left the company with fairly heavy borrowings and the directors were concerned about the implications further expansion would have for the company. Adnams was unconvinced of the value of a 'marketing approach' and sceptical about changing a strategy that brought steady growth and seemed likely to continue to do so in the future.

TRENDS IN UK BREWING

Prior to 1958, when the UK beer market began to grow at a rate of about 2.5 per cent per annum, it had fluctuated for a period of about thirty years. In 1959 the excise duty on beer was reduced, which in turn reduced the retail price. Many new beers also began to appear on the British market during the 1950s.

Over the next decade other factors boosted beer consumption: the 1960s were a period of major social change and economic growth when, for the first time, young people began to enjoy the benefits of high incomes spent on a wide range of consumer goods, including beer. At the same time, the number of young people had increased as the post-war population boom babies reached drinking age. Certain other factors were not so beneficial to the market: consumers' tastes were changing and beer came under increased competition from wines and spirits. Between 1959 and 1979, beer sales increased by 69 per cent while wine consumption grew by 428 per cent and spirits by 236 per cent.

Economic stagnation during the 1970s meant higher levels of inflation and unemployment. Heavy industry was hardest hit by recession and those who lost their jobs were traditionally good beer drinkers. To make things worse, in May 1979 the taxation on beer was increased when VAT soared from 8 to 15 per cent. Excise duty on beer increased in every subsequent budget so that taxation on beer was actually increasing at twice the annual rate of inflation. This had the inevitable effect on price and volume since the price of beer is 'elastic': the rate of growth of the market therefore slowed in the late 1970s and a downturn in beer sales was expected by 1980.

'GOING OUT FOR A DRINK'

The phrase 'going out for a drink' highlights some unique aspects of the UK beer market: the importance attached to pubs and clubs, to draught beer and the wide variety of beer available to the consumer. Social pressures such as drink/driving legislation, and the steadily increasing costs of certain products – especially spirits – were having a significant impact on the amount of drinking at home.

There are an estimated 60,000 public houses in the UK. Of these a considerable proportion are 'tied' to major brewers (Table C14.1).

Though beer has been consumed in the pub, inn or tavern for centuries, over the last eighty years the club has played an increasingly significant role in the pattern of the nation's drinking habits. The club is a peculiarly British institution – particularly the 'working men's' clubs, the British Legion clubs and now, more commonly, sports clubs. They are often owned by their members and provide intense competition to pubs in terms of price, flexibility of drinking hours and amenities. There are currently an estimated 33,000 clubs with bars (Table C14.2).

Table C14.1   UK 'tied' houses

Brewer	Outlets
Bass	7,500
Allied-Lyons	7,300
Whitbread	6,500
Watney (Grand Met)	6,600
Courage	5,000
Greenall Whitney	1,500
Scottish & Newcastle	1,400

Table C14.2   Clubs with bars (main categories, 1986)

Working men's	4,000
Political	2,000
British Legion	3,500
Sports	6,000

Table C14.3   Beer consumption
patterns (%)

Away from home	88
Pubs	62
Clubs	25
Hotels and restaurants	1
At home	12

Table C14.4   Percentage of beer
consumed in private homes

Eire	10
UK	12
Austria	40
Belgium	78
Denmark	78
West Germany	40
Netherlands	60
Norway	80
Switzerland	40
Sweden	85

Source: *Brewers Guardian*, June 1983

Table C14.5   Draught as a percentage of beer sales

UK	79	Japan	8
Australia	40	Mexico	1
Belgium	43	Netherlands	25
Canada	7	Norway	18
Denmark	1	Philippines	1
Ireland	89	Portugal	17
Finland	14	Sweden	10
France	21	Switzerland	30
West Germany	29	USA	13

Source: Brewers Society: *International Statistical Handbook*

Many clubs are effectively 'tied' to major brewing groups which, in return for the supply of free pub equipment, provide all the beer consumed on the premises. The average investment of the brewers in pub equipment per outlet is estimated at £800 with a payback of around eight to nine months. Estimates vary as to the percentage of outlets tied in this fashion but trade guesstimates put it at around 50 per cent. Recent changes introduced by the EEC have led to the brewers' ability to maintain the 'tied' system in public houses they do not own being replaced with a more informal system.

Distribution is vital to market share as the majority of beer is drunk in pubs (Table C14.3). The pattern emerging in Table C14.3 can be contrasted with the situation in Continental Europe where up to 80 per cent of the beer drunk is at

Table C14.6   Brewery market shares (%)

Company	Market share
Bass	18
Allied-Lyons	16
Courage	12
Watneys	13
Whitbread	13
Scottish & Newcastle	11
Others (regional)	17

home. Only in Ireland is the figure for home beer consumption lower than the UK – at less than 10 per cent (Table C14.4). Drinking in pubs can be linked to the British love of draught beer. Only Ireland has a higher percentage of draught beer sales than the UK (Table C14.5).

Ownership of outlets is directly related to beer market shares. As might be expected the big breweries dominate the total market (Table C14.6).

A wide choice of draught beer is available in the UK. A pub's or club's range will typically include a mild, two bitters, two lagers and a stout – a total of six different beers. Some outlets may offer different portfolios, depending on local drinking habits and tradition: two milds, three or four bitters or three or four lagers. With the reduction both in the number of staff employed in public houses and the decrease in their expertise at handling beer, the willingness of most landlords to buy stocks of beer and rack them professionally continued to decline during the 1970s and 1980s. The prevailing attitude was one requiring fairly rapid delivery of ready-to-drink product.

The growing popularity of pubs and clubs during the 1960s led to an increase in demand for draught beer. The quality of beer became more stable due to improvements in brewing technology. New brands appeared in the 1970s, many lagers became available in draught form, giving the consumer an ever-widening choice for draught beers. There was therefore a decline in demand for bottled beers, with different characteristics – colour, taste and strength – which had nevertheless been complementary to draught beers. Despite the high percentage of beer drunk away from home, the take-home market began to experience slow, but steady growth to the benefit of canned beer, though the increasing sophistication and acceptability of plastic bottles made from PET was taking an increasing share of this off-licence market. The off-licence trade demanded heavy investment in both packaging facilities and promotion and was in consequence the preserve of the larger breweries, which also owned a substantial proportion of the off-licence specialist outlets. The overwhelming impression of the beer market from the viewpoint of the small producer is that it is highly competitive mainly as a result of the domination of the big breweries in distribution and continuing investment in high levels of promotion.

Opportunities for British beer in overseas markets were fairly limited as the majority of other markets were dominated by lager-style products. By the mid-

Table C14.7   Brewery promotional
expenditure (1985)

Company	£ million
Bass	15
Allied-Lyons	11
Courage	8
Whitbread	4
Watneys	2

1980s the American market was showing signs of greater demand for heavier beers but this was still limited to an affluent fringe of the community, with over 97 per cent of beer still sold in lager form. Some of the major brewing groups were able to take advantage of this slowly developing trend because of their investment in canning and the types of beer that would can effectively.

Promotion in the beer market

All the major brewers spend heavily to promote both bitter and, more important the growing lager sector. Total expenditure levels for 1985 are in Table C14.7.

THE FUTURE OF THE UK BEER MARKET

According to market surveys, UK beer consumption is falling steadily resulting in heavy promotional advertising by brewers. A number of explanations have been put forward for the decline in beer drinking:

(a) the increased popularity of home brewing and wine bars;
(b) changes in leisure and therefore drinking habits;
(c) new tastes in drinking;
(d) the adverse relationship between the rate of inflation and the rate of increase of the price of a pint of beer.

THE BRITISH PINT: ITS CHARACTERISTICS

British beers cover a wide range of original gravities (OG) and alcoholic strengths, from about OG 1030 to in excess of 1100, with alchoholic strengths of 2.5 to 12.6 per cent by volume (Table C14.8). Sweet stouts, brown ales and some mild ales contain a greater proportion of residual sugar and less alcohol than average, whereas pale ales and lagers tend to contain less sugar and more alcohol than average.

The colour of beer varies from the pale straw colours of lagers and pale ales

Table C14.8   Average declared
gravity of UK beer

Year	Gravity
1974	1037.29
1979	1037.52
1983	1037.50
1984	1037.30

Source: The Brewers Society: *Beer Facts*
1985

through varying shades of orange-brown ales to the distinctive brown of brown ales and finally the black of stout. The colour is derived from the type of brewing malt used and special malts such as chocolate and black malts, roasted barley, caramel or any combination of these.

The foam or 'head' of beers varies from almost non-existent to creamy. This will vary geographically according to local tastes.

The bitterness of beers varies from 8 to over 80 EBU, most being between 20–35 EBU. The highest values are found in special strong ales and stouts.

THE TYPES OF BEER

A wide variety of different types of beer is available to the UK consumer. Each category of beer may also have subdivisions: mild may be dark or light, stout may be bitter or sweet. The market is far from static and while bitter still tends to be the major category, other traditional British beers have had to concede market share to lager.

The British have always drunk lager but until the late 1950s its place in the market was marginal. Since then there has been a phenomenal change in consumer attitudes towards it. During the 1960s lager became a fashion associated with young people. At the same time, there was a general switch from darker beer to the lighter and from warmer drinks to cooler: the good summers of 1973, 1975 and 1976 were timely enough to give a further boost to lager consumption.

The UK is traditionally well known for its cask-conditioned beers, that is, draught beers in which the yeast has carried out a secondary fermentation in the cask from which the beer is dispensed for retail sale. Such beers are usually the bitter or mild ale types. Types of beer may be categorized as follows.

1. The mild ales are the less bitter and sweet types of ale. Their colours vary from light to dark brown and their original gravities tend to be in the range 1030–1038.
2. The bitter, light and pale ales vary from straw colour to orange brown and have a bitter taste. Original gravities are in the range of 1030–1050.
3. Stouts are usually very dark brown or black and vary from a sweet caramel flavour to a dry, well-hopped character.

4. The lagers have the same wide range of characters of lagers found elsewhere in Europe, and cover a wide range of original gravities. Lagers demand more extensive storage and containment areas than other beers, and tend to be stored in refrigerated and pressurized containers.
5. Brown ales tend to have a sweet, caramel flavour with little hop character and original gravities of 1030–1042.
6. Most strong ales and barley wines are dark in colour and have original gravities in the range 1050–1100. They are full bodied and tend to have a sweet, fruity flavour.
7. The late 1970s saw the emergence of low-carbohydrate, low-alcohol and alcohol-free beers. Dietetic beers have increased with the growth of consumer consciousness about diet. Low-alcohol and alcohol-free beers are of obvious importance to the driver, and the 1980s saw further growth in this segment of the market (see Table C14.9).

ADNAMS

The Adnams family took over the Sole Bay Brewery, named after the bay off Southwold, in 1872. Adnams became a public company in 1890. The brewery prospered and expanded, taking over other breweries – C.J. Fisher of Eye in 1904; G. Rope & Co. of Orford in 1907; Flinton & Hall of Aldeburgh in 1924. This success was based on producing traditional beer using only the finest ingredients, barley from East Anglia – the light soils of East Suffolk being especially suitable for producing good malting barley – hops from Kent and a strain of yeast which has remained unchanged since 1943.

Table C14.9   Types of beer sold in the UK (percentage sales)

	1984	1983	1979	1974
Draught				
Bitter and stout*	43.2	45.2	47.6	61.2
Mild	7.0	7.3	8.7	–
Lager	27.9	26.0	22.1	12.6
Total	78.1	78.5	78.4	73.8
Packaged				
Light, pale and export	7.6	7.9	8.1	12.5
Brown ale	0.8	0.9	1.8	3.5
Stout	2.1	2.3	3.5	5.9
Strong ales and barley wine	0.4	0.4	0.5	0.6
Lager	11.0	10.0	7.7	3.7
Total	21.9	21.5	21.6	26.2
Total ale and stout	61.9	64.1	70.9	83.6
Total lager	38.9	35.9	29.1	16.4

*Bitter includes light mild

Source: The Brewers Society: *Beer Facts 1985*

Table C14.10   Adnams' sales (barrel equivalents)

	1978	1979	1980	1981	1982	1983
Draught						
Bitter	5,000	5,500	5,200	6,050	7,800	8,200
Mild	1,200	1,340	1,100	1,150	1,190	1,200
Old Ale	1,360	1,460	1,680	1,870	2,090	2,180
Bottle						
Champion	1,300	1,600	1,700	1,800	1,950	2,050
Nut Brown	800	600	500	430	420	410
Fisherman Brown	300	200	200	100	100	100
Broadside Pale	900	990	1,010	1,050	1,100	1,200
Tally-Ho Barley Wine	200	210	170	150	130	110

May 1985 witnessed the culmination of a five-year building programme of extension and redevelopment of the brewery. The rebuilding, carefully designed to blend in with the existing architecture and character of picturesque Southwold, enabled the brewery to double its production capacity whilst retaining its adherence to the traditional brewing process. There are no plans at present to instigate further production facilities, particularly the introduction of a canning line (cost around £600,000) or a PET bottling facility (£250,000) to enable the company to produce the product for the off-licence trade.

THE ADNAMS RANGE

Adnams produces four draught and five bottled products. Sales from 1978 to 1983 are given in Table C14.10.

Draught

1. Bitter – the now famous Adnams bitter is a full-flavoured, hoppy beer favoured by connoisseurs: original gravity 1036.
2. Mild – a traditional soft and slightly sweet country brew using the old X trade symbol to signify the guarantee of strength used by the monks of the Middle Ages: original gravity 1034.
3. Old Ale – a strong, dark, winter warmer with a rich malt flavour. Characterized as being like the beer that older drinkers used to get 'in their day': original gravity 1044.
4. Extra – a higher gravity beer (1050) introduced in 1985, with a planned volume of 1,280 barrels.

All the draught beers are conditioned in cask, not distributed under pressure like the leading brands. This has implications for the choice of distributors that could be used.

Bottled

1. Champion Pale Ale – this famous, prize-winning, bottled beer is dry and hoppy, light and clean. Named after the championship cup awarded by the National Brewers Exhibition to Adnams in 1936 for the best beer in Britain. The label shows one of the famous Adnams Percheron dray horses, in daily use for delivery of beers in Southwold: original gravity 1030–1034.
2. Nut Brown Ale – traditional, mellow, soft and slightly sweet bottled beer. The company was forced to change the original label of a squirrel nibbling whole acorns – it was implied that they were used to brew the beer – to an inset picture of an acorn: original gravity 1032–1036.
3. Fisherman Brown Ale – a bottled version of Old Ale and a traditional local favourite. The fisherman on the label has remained unchanged since first being used on show cards in the 1920s: original gravity 1040–1044.
4. Broadside Strong Pale Ale – a vigorous, full-flavoured, strong bottled beer appealing to connoisseurs. It commenorates the battle of Sole Bay in May 1672: original gravity 1064–1072.
5. Tally-Ho Barley Wine – the classic, sweet, barley wine in a bottle. Originally served as a strong, mulled ale before a hunt. Tally-Ho was the oldest brand of Adnams beer, first recorded in a photograph of 1880 when it was served in draught form: original gravity 1071–1079.

PROFIT MARGINS

Bottled beer was considerably more profitable on a unit by unit basis than barrels. Estimated current margins on the various Adnams product lines are in Table C14.11.

ADNAMS DISTRIBUTION

The company's tied estate has seventy public houses and two hotels, with an additional 550 direct accounts of which 500 are in East Anglia and 50 in London. In addition there are around 1,000 indirect accounts dealt with via wholesalers. Sales by region and distribution type are in Tables C14.12 and C14.13.

Direct accounts on average yielded £6,000 per annum, indirect accounts £2,000 (Table C14.14). The turnover in the tied outlets was considerably higher but varied considerably according to location. The cost of buying new outlets as they became available made such a policy extremely expensive, and Adnams ceased doing this in the 1970s, as the average cost of a pub rose through the £100,000 barrier.

Outside the direct delivery area in Norfolk and Suffolk, extra charges had to be made to allow for raised distribution costs and intermediary margins. The further the delivery, the higher the cost to the brewery, especially as the company could not

Table C14.11   Estimated margins on the Adnams range

Draught	%	Bottle	%
Bitter	25	Champion	28
Mild	20	Brown Ale	32
Old Ale	35	Broadside	36
Extra	37	Tally-Ho	18

Table C14.12   Adnams' sales by region and outlet

Region	% national population	% Adnams' sales
North	5.6	–
Yorks	8.9	–
East Anglia	3.5	65
Greater London	12.3	28
Other South East	18.9	7
South West	8.1	–
West Midlands	9.4	–
% sales by outlet type		
Tied	45	
Direct	28	
Indirect	27	

Table C14.13   Sales of product type by outlet (%)

	Bottled	Draught
Tied	25	75
Direct	12	88
Indirect	3	97

Table C14.14   Outlets and the salesforce

	1978	1979	1980	1981	1982	1983
Direct	450	475	500	525	550	555
Indirect	300	450	550	650	850	1,000
Salesforce	5	5	6	6	6	8

use third party delivery, since this had in the past led to unacceptable handling of the draught beer. A return lorry trip to the London area would cost around £200.

PRICING

The pricing policy that Adnams followed was to maintain prices at, or around, those of competitors. Examples of prices include (per barrel):

(a) Adnams – £121;

(b) Tetley – £117;
(c) Bodingtons – £123.

These market prices include the distributor discount (around 12 per cent) and the costs of physical distribution to the outlet.

PROMOTION

Adnams had not carried out significant advertising investment over the years except for free beer to public houses for introductory offer 'tasting evenings'.

ORGANIZATION

The salesforce of eight were split as follows (Table C14.14):

(a) three dealing with the 'direct delivery area', East Anglia;
(b) four dealing with agents and distributors;
(c) one for the London area.

There was no marketing department; the main board of directors carried out all the new product development and commercial functions.

Case 15

MEON PACKAGING

BACKGROUND

Meon Packaging was a small company, which had been operating for thirty years and which was run from a small rented workshop and warehouse in a trading estate. The founder of the business, now in his fifties, was the sole manager, helped by his wife, the company secretary. A workforce of six had been with the company for varying lengths of time:

1. John Norris, thirty-five. Worked for Meon for six years. Currently a foreman.
2. Brian Phillips, fifty-four. Longest-serving employee, with fifteen years' service. Mostly employed in the production of pallets.
3. David Murphy, nineteen. YTS trainee.
4. Paul Thompson, twenty-four. Worked for Meon for three years, mainly designing and constructing packaging units.
5. Alan Plunkett, thirty-eight. Worked for Meon for seven years delivering stock with hired lorries.
6. Martin Edwards, twenty-one. Worked for Meon for two years.

Jim Thrackford, the founder, had a long background in the timber industry, both his father and grandfather having worked for timber importing firms in the south of England. Neither of Thrackford's two sons had any ambitions to enter the business; one was a sergeant in the Cardiff police and the other an importer of artistic video films. Thrackford wanted, however, eventually to retire to the south-west of England and buy a small caravan park.

Meon Packaging initially operated as a supplier of fence-posts to the agricultural industry, but this source of trade had dried up in the early 1960s when, with increased mechanization, the fields became larger and larger. Since then the company had concentrated on the manufacture of custom-designed pallets, and provided a specialized export packing service for large industrial machinery exports. The success or failure of firms operating in the timber industry often hinges on the ability to buy effectively; to understand the strengths and weaknesses of different suppliers and how long timber from different areas of the world needs to be seasoned and matured before being used for various purposes.

THE PALLET MARKET

With the introduction of containers in the early 1960s, the unitization of loads increased steadily as automation in factories and warehouses led to a dramatic growth in the demand for pallets for stacking standard loads. The pallet market had been a non-standard one. Pallets had been custom-made for specific manufacturers and specific purposes. It rapidly became obvious that the benefits of standardizing pallets would be considerable, so that a pool of reusable pallets could become established. With certain exceptions, since the early 1970s there has been movement towards a European standard pallet 'concept' to which the majority of manufacturers have adhered. This had two consequences for the small supplier like Meon. First, because the pallet was no longer disposable but could be reused for a substantial period – unlike the milk bottle with an average of 23 journeys from dairy to home to dairy, the pallet can often be repaired with the most basic equipment (hammer and nails) – growth potential in the market substantially slowed. Second, the concept of standardization led some of the larger pallet manufacturers to mechanize production; and because of the low quality of materials normally used, many saw pallet production as an ideal method of disposing of sub-standard materials.

Both these trends meant that the market became increasingly competitive. Prices fell in real terms throughout the late 1970s and early 1980s. With the dramatic decline in manufacturing industry that occurred in the late 1970s and early 1980s, many of the larger pallet manufacturers were supplying at or below cost in order to survive in an industry worse hit by the recession than many others.

Other factors further depressed an already fragile market in the early 1980s. Increasingly the dominant retail multiples required that goods be delivered in knock-flat, metal 'cages' which could immediately be transferred to the shop floor. Furthermore, a number of container stuffing techniques developed and decreased the need for palletization. Metal pallets were being slowly introduced and these, made of aluminium, had a number of advantages over the wooden variants; although more expensive they were lighter, more durable, occupied less vertical space and weighed substantially less. Such properties allowed companies to fill containers more effectively than previously. These pallets were produced by metal working firms using their substantial investment in high technology equipment to enter a potentially attractive new market.

These new developments led to an increasingly diverse and segmented pallet industry with the various segments showing different growth rates (Table C15.1).

Table C15.1   Trends in the pallet market

Sector	Volume growth 81/85 (per annum)	Average price (£)
Standard pallets	−7%	4.50
Non-standard	−2%	7.50
Metal pallets	15%	22.50
Non-pallet techniques	20%	

MEON IN THE 1980S

The solution for Meon had been to seek out customers wanting specialized pallet designs or standard pallets of superior quality. By the early 1980s they had a customer base of around forty-five, largely built up by the founder, who had developed a number of personal contacts in the trade while his partner concentrated on maintaining production. These customers were based throughout the UK and had been gained by a mixture of direct mail followed by personal follow-up and local exhibitions. It was estimated that it took around three to four months and cost around £200 to establish a new customer. The amount of time required to find a new customer was estimated at twelve working days, taking into account the large amount of wasted time spent on non-productive visits. Once established, customers remained loyal to the company over a fairly long period, but an annual wastage of 15–20 per cent had been experienced over the last five years. The demand for pallets, though intermittent from individual customers, did not exhibit any substantial seasonality though there was a slight lull during July and August. Customers expected fairly rapid delivery of their non-standard pallets which meant that the stockholding of raw materials was at a high level because the lead time for timber purchase was of the order of four months, and five to six months was not uncommon for some particular materials. Meon employed two staff on the production of pallets throughout the year except when the demands of export packaging meant that the production line had to be closed down.

The move into export packaging took place in 1980 as a result of a discussion at the local golf club with one of the major machinery manufacturers in the area. The manufacturer sent the machinery for export to the Meon warehouse where the crates would be constructed on site. The orders varied in size considerably and occurred at two main periods in the year, February–April and September–November. Due to the space required, each order involved closing down the pallet manufacturing process while the export packing consignment was completed. These export orders were normally rush jobs – Meon would be told of them one or at most two weeks before they needed to be completed. The advantage was that Meon could ask attractive prices; but it had to hold further substantial stocks of raw materials to meet these rush orders. By 1985 there were fifteen customers placing intermittent orders. More staff were employed for the export packing because of the rapid turn-round the operation demanded.

Originally, Jim Thrackford had run the operation single-handed but by the middle 1970s he considered that the need for new business development made a partner essential. This was done but relations between the two were never harmonious and, by 1983, had reached breaking point. In the middle of that year the founder had decided to buy out the partner. To achieve this he remortgaged his house and raised additional loans on the company in the form of short-term bank borrowings.

THE MEON COSTING SYSTEM

Jim Thrackford costed each operation to ensure an adequate return to the company. He aimed to achieve a 40 per cent gross margin on the pallets and 65 per cent gross margin on the export packing operation. A typical costing approach would be as follows:

Price   A
Raw materials   X (all raw materials including power)
Direct labour   Y (workshop time directly involved in contract completion)

Export packing had come to account for a steadily higher proportion of the Meon turnover since the early 1980s (Table C15.2).

MEON'S PROBLEMS IN THE MID-1980S

When his partner left, Jim Thrackford had to spend more time at the workshop supervising both the production of pallets and the export packing operation. One unfortunate result of this was that the number of customers asking for special pallets started to diminish. Second, there was the financial collapse of two major customers which had accounted for 20 per cent of the orders for export packing, leaving debts of £10,000 outstanding. The loss of these major customers meant that turnover would drop during 1986. In addition to the loss of turnover, Meon found that its credit rating had been recalculated by the Timber Federation, which provided credit cover for timber importers – stock would increasingly have to be paid for with cash.

The problems encountered by Meon had led to an increasingly severe cash flow position which was summarized as a six-month projection to the end of 1986 (Table C15.3).

Table C15.2   Meon turnover 1980–1985 (£000)

Sector	1980	1981	1982	1983	1984	1985
Pallets	120	105	105	100	110	120
Packing	50	75	102	130	140	160
Total	170	180	207	230	250	280

Table C15.3   Cash flow forecast (£000)

	June	July	Aug.	Sept.	Oct.	Nov.	Dec.
Revenue	10.0	16.0	6.0	28.0	32.0	20.0	22.0
Materials	8.0	14.0	20.0	20.0	3.0	4.0	5.0
Wages	6.0	6.0	6.0	6.0	6.0	6.0	6.0
Rent/Rates	1.5	1.5	1.5	1.5	1.5	1.5	1.5
Miscellaneous	1.0	1.0	1.0	1.0	1.0	1.0	1.0
	(6.5)	(6.5)	(22.5)	(0.5)	20.5	7.5	8.5
Cumulative	(17.0)	(23.5)	(46.0)	(46.5)	(26.0)	(18.5)	(10.0)

Table C15.4   Garden shed market structure

Type	Retail price (£)	Market share (%)
Economy	200	20
Medium	300	50
Premium	400	30

As it was unlikely that either margins or the number of customers for either pallets or packaging could be substantially increased in the short term, Jim Thrackford considered either returning to the production of fence-posts or producing garden sheds for garden centres. The market for fence-posts had not improved since the 1960s and now appeared dominated by foreign imports. The market for garden sheds was estimated at £21 million, the majority of which were sold through the 1,500 independent garden centres throughout the UK. These garden centres were largely independently owned and would need to be contacted direct to establish a market presence. Retail margins for the sale of sheds were high, with garden centres making on average 35–40 per cent gross on the sale of each shed (Table C15.4).

Jim Thrackford estimated that he would be able to manufacture a premium-style product, substantially better than the competition, which, sold to the garden centre at £360, would yield around 60 per cent gross margin. The conversion of the large stocks of wood currently held would also yield valuable cash for the balance sheet (Table C15.5), and there would be no production problems as the techniques employed for crate and pallet construction could be easily converted to the production of sheds. Most of the manufacturers selling into this market were smaller than Meon and would not be able to offer the speed of production; this was a key point with the consumer wanting to erect a shed soon after ordering. Garden centres demanded on average sixty days' credit. Mail order was a possibility though demand in the mail order business was very seasonal and would conflict with distribution through the garden centres. The prices for mail order were also considerably lower than those obtainable through the garden centres, with basic sheds selling for £160–170.

Table C15.5 Meon balance sheet and profit and loss
account 1984/85 (£)

Profit and loss account	£
Turnover	280,000
Labour	88,000
Materials	102,000
Rent/rates	20,000
Interest	20,000
Hiring and leasing	25,000
Selling costs	15,000
Legal and professional	3,000
Insurance	2,500
Profit (loss)	4,500

Balance sheet	£
Assets	
Fixed	10,000
Stock and work-in-progress	85,000
Debtors	88,000
Cash	2,000
Liabilities	
Bank loans/overdraft	120,000
(Falling due within one year)	
Creditors	55,000
Current assets less liabilities	10,000
Capital and reserves	
Share capital	2,000
Share premium account	8,000

Case 16

DOORLARM LIMITED

INTRODUCTION

At the end of 1985 Doorlarm Ltd had been established for sixteen months, manufacturing and selling two entirely new products to the home security market. Through the efforts and skills of the three founder directors a great deal was achieved in a short time, but within eight months of the launch Polycell had introduced similar products and seriously threatened the new company's position. The fragmented nature of the market, however, meant that the company had a fair chance of success with a good product but limited distribution prevented it becoming a highly successful one.

The directors were aware of this weakness and had recruited John Hughes, an ex-manager of a car accessories company, as marketing director. Hughes was given a free hand as the founder directors felt they did not possess the necessary skills or experience to compete with Polycell.

Hughes was asked to study all the documentation provided and produce a new marketing plan with a justification as to why his new approach would be more successful than the company's current one. The other directors were particularly concerned about investment levels required to pursue any new objective, and sources of funding.

Hughes was asked to give particular attention to:

(a) distribution policy;
(b) promotional policy including all aspects of salesforce expansion.

The problems were acute as the company had grown rapidly. From its initial base in a small unit on an industrial estate in North Tyneside, Doorlarm had had to move within six months into a larger, 2,000 square feet unit. Full-time production staff had increased from two to eight at the time of writing. One salesman, a personal friend of the directors, was based in Newcastle, where he lived.

The directors had initially taken on positions as managing director, production director and sales director. All three had agreed, however, that the sales function was not as strong as it needed to be and Brown, the sales director, agreed to take on the new role of financial director to allow the position of marketing director to be filled by Hughes. They had differing views as to the potential direction of the company. The managing director, James Goodley, wanted to minimize overheads to ensure that investment levels could be maintained in new production development, which he saw as essential to the company's continuing success.

PRODUCTS

Doorlarm produces two products, both are easy-to-fit, external door alarms. They are battery-operated, emitting a loud 105 decibels when an external door is opened.

1. Doorlarm 1 (size 4″ × 1″ × 1″) is an easy-to-operate alarm using a simple on/off switch (recommended retail price £9.99).
2. Doorlarm 2 (size 5″ × 2½″ × 1½″) has an additional exit and entry delay alarm feature for operator use, and is operated by means of a key (recommended retail price £12.99).

Both products are made of attractive, heavy-duty white plastic and do not require wiring of any sort.

The end-users of the products are male householders in the B/C1/D socio-economic groups, and with a DIY orientation.

A third product, Doorlarm 3, is just about to be introduced. It is of a similar size to the Doorlarm 2 model but instead of a key control, a code-operated on/off facility is used. The alarm has eight push buttons enabling a personal four-digit code to be chosen from a selection of 1,680 different combinations. It has an additional feature of emitting a visitor entry bleep which would be suitable for shop or waiting room use (rrp £16.99).

THE HOME SECURITY MARKET

The market has grown significantly over the past five years thanks both to the increase in the number of households and the steady year on year growth of reported crime, especially in the area of household break-ins, which have escalated (Table C16.1).

The involvement of the insurance companies and the growing popularity of household watch schemes have contributed to the increasing willingness of the

Table C16.1   Trends in the security market

	1976	1977	1978	1979	1980	1981	1982
Households (million)	18	19	19	20	21	22	23
'Serious crime' (% growth)	17	5	6	7	11	13	11
Market size (£ million)	55	60	65	72	85	87	89
Locks/latches (share %)	90	89	83	76	70	68	66
Alarm systems (share %)	10	11	17	24	30	32	34

householder to invest in household security. Since the early 1980s some of the larger insurance companies have introduced schemes to reduce premiums in return for the installation of 'approved' home security devices.

Market shares and other companies operating in the market

There are three broad sectors identifiable in the market, each with distinct product attributes, namely locks and latches, alarm systems and DIY installations. The overall market is very segmented with over 200 companies having some form of national presence – in addition there are numerous locally based operations.

Locks and latches

The market splits into two sectors: cylinder locks, which are more DIY oriented, and mortice locks. Ultra-sophisticated, electronic lock systems have started to appear only in some prestige developments such as hotels, and are unlikely to pose any substantial threat for the rest of the decade. The market is dominated by a few large companies with large salesforces and wide distribution (Table C16.2).

ALARM SYSTEMS

Chubb and Automated Security Holdings (Modern Alarms) are believed to be the market leaders with around 15 per cent of the market each, followed by Securicor with 11 per cent and AFA Minerva with around 7 per cent.

A high level of customer service is required to operate successfully and many companies like Doulton Glass and Dolphin Showers entered and left the market as the going was tough. The insistence of insurance companies that clients install alarm systems had meant that this sector of the market had grown considerably during the 1970s and 1980s; whether growth would continue was of major concern to the large companies.

Table C16.2   Major suppliers of locks and latches

	Mortice (% value)	Cylinder (% volume)
Union	60	25
Yale	10	55
Legge	10	10
Others	20	10

DIY alarm systems

There are no market share figures for this sector. Companies in this sector supply mainly kit-type systems at around £140. In recent years companies like Hoover, Philips, Pifco and more recently Polycell have entered this market bringing with them their consumer-oriented marketing expertise.

Doorlarm is thought to hold an 8 per cent share of this sector in value terms. At present (besides Polycell), only a few small companies offer a product of a similar nature and their individual shares of the market are smaller than Doorlarm's. With the decreasing cost of electronic systems it is likely that the market will become more competitive over the next few years as the major companies, facing a downturn in office and shop installations, turn their attentions to the home market to maintain growth. This increased competition will inevitably affect pricing and profit margins. Such had been the experience in the institutional market, where gross profit margins fell from 65 to 30 per cent over three years.

The lock and latches and alarm systems sectors show only moderate growth. With current relatively low sales, it is the DIY alarm sector that is the potential growth area.

The growth rate in the security industry market is naturally influenced by the annual rate of burglaries and the gradual, if reluctant, consumer acceptance of the need for home security. The number of reported burglaries has steadily increased over the last decade. Recent figures show a 27 per cent increase between 1984 and 1985.

By 1985 Polycell was the largest competitor to Doorlarm, having introduced comparable products within eight months of the Doorlarm launch. The products are heavily branded and merchandised, fitting neatly into an existing range of security products such as Polycell window locks.

The presence of Polycell in this sector was not unexpected but the major obstacle presented is the company's well-established distribution network, enabling the competing products to gain shelf space alongside other items in the Polycell range within a very short time. Polycell has secured distribution through large DIY stores where it is usual to find an eight-foot rack displaying the extensive range of the company's home security products.

In addition to Polycell there are a few small companies which supply generally low-quality door alarms. These are, on the whole, badly designed and poorly packaged and do not pose a threat to Doorlarm Ltd.

PRODUCTION FACILITIES

Output is steady. Roughly 3,600 units of Doorlarm 1 and 5,400 units of Doorlarm 2 are produced per month. With the present workforce the maximum production capacity of the factory is roughly 11,000 units a month. This workforce can be increased to a total of ten before factory floor space available becomes a restricting factor. If the workforce were raised to ten, the maximum production capacity would be roughly 14,000 units per month.

Negotiations are presently proceeding with a manufacturer in Hong Kong with a view to importing Doorlarm products made under licence. It is expected that up to 20,000 units could be imported per month once an agreement was reached. This contribution is not expected to begin for at least another four months.

COMPANY FINANCIAL STRUCTURE

The ordinary shares of the company are now split according to the details in Table C16.3. The share allocation was adjusted to ensure that the marketing director had a personal stake in the business, to motivate and encourage commitment in the company's future.

At the time of writing, the first year's accounts are not yet published but the key points from the anticipated accounts are summarized in Table C16.4.

With its successful growth record, the company is favourably placed to raise a substantial sum of further loan capital from three interested northern entrepreneurs. The sum on offer is £100,000 for a 40 per cent stake in an enlarged company. Otherwise the company could borrow a further £35,000 from the local bank at interest of 16 per cent. None of the current directors can provide further capital to the organization as each has a fully mortgaged house.

Table C16.3   Doorlarm Ltd shareholding

Shareholder	%
Managing director	30
Production director	27
Financial director	27
Marketing director	16

Table C16.4   Doorlarm Ltd: anticipated end of year accounts

	£
Sales	460,000
Less	
Cost of goods sold	(160,000)
Gross profit	300,000
Less	
Overheads	240,000
Profit before tax	60,000
Less	
Taxation	(18,000)
Net profit	42,000
Ordinary share capital	16,000
	58,000
Fixed assets	24,000
Current assets	80,000
Current liabilities	(46,000)
Net current assets	34,000
	58,000

Table C16.5   Doorlarm pricing (£)

Product	Wholesale price	Expected mark-up (%)	Price to retailer (at 20%)	Expected mark-up (%)	Price (assume 40% mark-up)	VAT	RRP
Doorlarm 1	5.17	12½–25	6.20	33–50	8.69	1.30	9.99
Doorlarm 2	6.72	12½–25	8.06	33–50	11.29	1.70	12.99
Doorlarm 3*	8.79	12½–25	10.55	33–50	14.77	2.22	16.99

*expected launch price

PRICING STRUCTURE

Doorlarm had little information about price sensitivity in its market. What little evidence existed suggested that price sensitivity was fairly low, in the order of 2, which might allow an increase in the retail prices. Table C16.5 gives details of Doorlarm's pricing.

ADVERTISING AND OTHER PROMOTIONAL ACTIVITY

The only paid-for advertising used was an off-the-page campaign to generate direct mail order sales during the first six months. It was moderately successful with a positive return on media expenditure, an improvement in cash flow and a small increase in product awareness.

Local newspapers were used initially, followed by two national campaigns (*Daily Express, Daily Mail*) and the use of specialist magazines such as *Do-it-Yourself* and *Home Security and Insurance*.

Currently, an advertisement appears in every issue of *Home Security and Insurance* magazine due to its cost-effectiveness.

This medium has not been used to build up general awareness of the products due to the fact that the message that often comes across is one of a more generic nature – that of security products as a whole.

DISTRIBUTION AND INITIAL COMPANY PROGRESS

Mail order advertisements were used in the first six months to generate cash in advance of orders.

As the only effective salesforce in the company was one director and one salesman the coverage and distribution possible would always be limited. However, by concentrating on a broad area with a high concentration of wholesalers – Greater Manchester, Liverpool, Birmingham and surrounding districts – they had both achieved considerable success.

To encourage wholesalers to stock them, the new products were offered on a sale

Table C16.6   Doorlarm sales (units): months 11–16

Doorlarm 1	11	12	13	Month 14	15	16	Total
Mail order	95	90	94	80	65	70	494
Wholesale:							
Sale or return	2,200	3,000	4,100	2,000	3,600	3,600	18,500
Outright purchase	300	300	400	200	500	600	2,300
Specialist retailer:							
DIY	80	75	40	27	40	37	299
Hardware	50	85	116	30	41	40	362
Multiple retailer	–	–	–	–	–	–	–
Total	2,725	3,550	4,750	2,337	4,246	4,347	21,955
Doorlarm 2	11	12	13	Month 14	15	16	Total
Mail order	62	49	49	37	35	40	272
Wholesale:							
Sale or return	2,400	3,800	6,000	4,500	4,800	5,200	26,700
Outright purchase	100	300	100	200	400	400	1,500
Specialist retailer:							
DIY	60	47	40	39	48	29	263
Hardware	32	28	62	75	53	82	332
Multiple retailer	–	–	–	–	–	–	–
Total	2,654	4,224	6,251	4,851	5,336	5,751	29,067

or return basis. This proved to be a very good tactic for loading the trade but it has now become the norm for the majority of wholesalers in that region. Sales direct to specialist retailers and independents were achieved only in an area within forty miles of the factory, chosen to minimize travelling time from base but not cost-effective due to the small order quantities. Attempts by two directors to obtain sales through DIY and hardware multiple retailers were unsuccessful. Most of the problems were due to the directors' inexperience in dealing with buyers representing large accounts.

The sales achieved over months 11–16 are in Table C16.6.

THE CURRENT MARKETING PLAN

The current marketing plan is little changed from that given to the bank for the initial funding of the company.

Objectives

To establish a national distribution network enabling maximum exposure of the products to the end-user.

Goals

Short term   To maintain existing accounts profitably and introduce the Doorlarm 3 model to at least 70 per cent of existing customers.

Medium term   To obtain a national multiple retailer or mail order house account, and accounts with 40 per cent of hardware/DIY wholesalers and 10 per cent of the hardware/DIY/specialist retailers in the UK, selling the full range to all.

Long term   To achieve sales representing at least 80 per cent of production capacity (including imports) in the ratio 30 per cent national accounts, 70 per cent independent accounts.

Hughes considered the available strategic options to achieve these goals. Clearly a distribution-oriented strategy is required. Either a 'shotgun' approach is taken whereby distribution is gained in a broad and relatively uncontrollable manner, wholesalers for example, or by a 'rifled' approach concentrating distribution through selected channels, specialist retailers for example.

The nature of the product dictates that most can be gained from a 'shotgun' approach as it is a relatively simple product needing very little explanation and no after-sales service. One strategy therefore will be to obtain new accounts with the channels that offer the widest penetration possible.

Table C16.7   Doorlarm: available distribution channels

	No. of present customers	% of total sales volume
Multiple DIY retailers	–	–
Multiple hardware retailers	–	–
Independent DIY retailers	30	2
Independent hardware retailers	45	3
Specialist security product retailers	–	–
DIY wholesalers	30	40
Hardware wholesalers	35	50
Mail order houses	–	–
Mail order	–	5

A serious problem that could occur, which often affects many small businesses, is that of overtrading – taking on too many orders that cannot be produced and without the working capital to finance them.

Table C16.7 contains details of the available distribution channels.

POINTS TO CONSIDER

1. Multiple retailers and mail order houses. It is dangerous to tie up a lot of production capacity and capital with one buyer as it places the company in a very weak bargaining position and often places a reliance on that one company for business survival.

    Negotiations with the buyers of multiples are exhausting and require skill and authority – it may be too important an account for one salesman to tackle alone and is probably best handled by the directors.

2. Wholesalers. The products do not have a long sales history and wholesalers will require inducements to stock the products – sale or return conditions are presently used but increased margins for the wholesalers should be offered.

    Pre-selling to the consumer is not expected in this industry, where advertising can be counter-productive. The wholesalers' own salesforce will not have the time or inclination to promote the new products. The use of wholesalers gives cost savings in invoicing, credit and collection, order processing, delivery and selling costs over the smaller and more diverse retailers, but with a reduced margin.

3. Independent retailers. Although a far greater travelling time is involved covering each retailer, and the order size is normally very small, sales to the retailer enjoy a higher margin. If there is a restriction on productivity, i.e. the number of products that can be sold, then it may be worth spending more time obtaining more 'profitable' sales, despite the cost associated with such time.

4. A 'pull' strategy is an option but, again due to the effect of security product advertising, the expected 'pull' through the trade by consumers would not be strong. However, by approaching retailers using direct mail (promotional literature) a 'pull' factor may be generated by them against the wholesalers in their area.

5. A 'push' strategy is very feasible as in many ways it is the trade norm. This strategy will of course require a very high degree of personal selling, which brings with it further problems.

Tables C16.8 to C16.10 give information on potential sources of sales for Doorlarm.

Table C16.8   Major UK DIY retailers (multiple)

Retailer	Outlets
Magnet & Southerns	250
Jacoa Ltd (Ripolin, Decor 8, Ten Ten)	207
Art WallPapers (Homecharm)	200
B & Q DIY Supercentres	150
Texas Homecare	127
Payless DIY Ltd	59
Jewson	53
Timberland Ltd	48
W.H. Smith Do-it-All	45
Paul Madeley Ltd	40
Great Mills DIY Superstores	35
Homebase Ltd	14

Table C16.9   Major UK hardware retailers (multiple)

Retailer	Outlets
Wilkinson Hardware Stores	49
Knobs & Knockers	45
J.W. Carpenter Ltd (Shergolds)	40
Edmund R. Goodrich Ltd	38
Robert Dyas Ltd	33
Graham Ford Ltd	33
Lawson Fisher	22
Cato Hardware	15

Table C16.10   DIY wholesaler/independent hardware outlets/specialist outlets:
UK by region

	Wholesaler	Independent	Specialist
Scotland	94	800	64
North West	130	1,056	84
North East	114	898	72
Midlands	141	1,648	132
East	114	368	29
Greater London	149	2,416	193
South East	121	840	67
South West	104	1,046	84

Source: *Retail Directory 1985*

Case 17

YAMAZKA

BACKGROUND

One of the most successful new companies in the camera market, Yamazka is based in Taiwan. From its low-cost but highly sophisticated manufacturing plant, it produces a range of cameras which compete effectively with the major Japanese companies in the large American market. There the company carved out a 20 per cent market share, mostly at the lower end of the camera market, though it has the capacity to produce the entire range of camera types. For several years Yamazka has supplied the Magic Eye chain of up-market camera shops on the West Coast with their own-label premium items.

The company is evaluating expansion possibilities in the UK – its first European market.

THE UK CAMERA MARKET

Between 1981 and 1985, the UK camera market grew slowly (Table C17.1).

Within the total market there are clearly defined market sectors with different growth trends (Table C17.2). Each has specific features which appeal to particular segments of the camera buying public.

1. Single lens reflex or SLR. The SLR camera has a mirrored shutter allowing the user to see what is passing through the lens. This feature permits the use of a wide range of accessories such as telephoto or close-up lenses and is one of the main attractions of the SLR concept. Features such as automatic exposure and automatic focusing continue to make the SLR 'user-friendly' and this additional sophistication helped to widen the price differential between the top and

Table C17.1   Trends in the UK camera market

Year	Volume (million units)	£ million	Camera (%)	Accessory (%)	Film (%)	Developing (%)
1981	3.0	555	27	10	25	38
1982	2.9	565	27	10	25	38
1983	3.3	635	26	11	25	38
1984	3.3	660	28	9	25	37
1985	3.5	700	31	8	25	36

Table C17.2   Market share by type (%)

Year	SLR	Compact	110	Instant	Disc
1977	14	4	40	30	–
1978	16	5	50	20	–
1979	22	10	52	12	–
1980	18	15	55	10	–
1981	20	18	45	10	–
1982	20	20	40	10	10
1983	18	22	32	8	20
1984	16	26	30	6	20
1985	18	36	22	5	18

   bottom of the range. Two segments can be identified: the expensive electronic
   SLR; and the 'manual' SLR camera.
2. Compact 35mm cameras. This sector has grown substantially in the UK with·
   the emphasis on small, pocket-sized 'idiot proof' cameras with automatic focus
   and exposure, heavily promoted on television.
3. 110 cameras. These small cameras provide low-cost, unsophisticated holiday
   snapshot facilities with few additional features. One particular advantage of the
   110 camera type is the use of cassette films, which reduce the complexity of film
   loading.
4. Disc camera. Introduced in 1982, the disc camera takes photographs on a disc
   of film rather than a reel. Many of the products sold offer exposure control,
   flash, and automatic film advance.
5. Instant cameras. The Polaroid system created a new market segment in the
   camera market, though the main attraction was still to the 'amateur' photographer. Polaroid remains the sole company in this sector, having managed to
   win a legal battle against Kodak which had entered the market in the 1970s,
   forcing it out of the instant picture market sector.
6. Video still cameras. The gradual introduction of still frame video technology
   since 1985 has captured a small percentage of the total camera market, but has
   experienced more substantial growth in the United States.

   Different companies are established in the different sectors and tend to dominate
particular market segments. The main companies and their estimated market
shares are in table C17.3.

Table C17.3 Main camera companies and market shares in the UK

Company	SLR		Compact	110	Instant	Disc
	Electronic	Manual				
Canon	25		15			
Halina		9		45		22
Hanimex		3		12		18
Kodak				23		50
Konica	5					
Minolta	15		11			
Nikon	15					
Olympus	20	10	23			
Pentax	10	22				
Polaroid					100	
Praktica		40				
Ricoh			10			
Zenith		18				

The main companies operating in the market separate into fairly clearly defined groups.

1. Premium companies: five Japanese companies – Canon, Minolta, Pentax, Olympus and Nikon.
2. Mid-market: Kodak, Polaroid, Ricoh.
3. 'No frills': Halina, Praktika, and Hanimex.

DISTRIBUTION

Almost 12,000 retail outlets sell some form of photographic equipment. By far the most important outlets are the photographic specialists, which include probably the most important single outlet, Dixons. Dixons is estimated through its 283 outlets to account for 15 per cent of the total UK camera market. Other important specialist multiple outlets include Comet (102) and Greens (51) (Table C17.4).

Table C17.4 Percentage share of UK camera market by outlet type

Type of outlet	% volume
Photographic specialists	40
Chemists	25
Mail order	10
Discount chains	5
Department stores	5
Others	15

Closer analysis of purchase patterns reveals that low-cost cameras are usually purchased at chemists – especially Boots – and discount stores, whereas the purchase of the more expensive and complex products is concentrated among the specialist retailers. Film purchase and printing are, however, different. Customers go to the most convenient and cost-effective outlet available, and also subscribe to a number of mail order operations, such as Tru-Print, which provide rapid developing and low-cost films. Retail margins on the sale of camera equipment are high, averaging around 35 per cent of retail price. A special market characteristic is the number of special 'package' deals demanded by the major retail outlets. Both Dixons and Boots are eager to establish exclusive combined camera, accessory and film deals that would enable them to stand out from other outlets offering only individual items. This often means that retail margins are difficult to calculate.

As there are no wholesalers, distribution is direct either to the store (in the case of individual outlets) or into the warehouse of the multiple store. Physical distribution costs tend to be only a small element of the final price as the products are low weight and relatively high value. An average distribution cost of 30p per unit is anticipated by the majority of companies operating in the market.

The seasonality of the various sectors varies considerably. The lower end of the market tends to show two peaks of activity; Christmas and the holiday season together make up around 75 per cent of total sales. At the premium end of the market, seasonality is far less marked, even though the majority of cameras are bought from March to October. There appears to be little gifting in this sector of the market, in contrast to the lower-priced segment.

PRICING

Due to a world over-capacity of camera production, the UK market remains highly competitive on price and, in general, prices continued to decline in real terms throughout the 1970s and 1980s (Table C17.5).

Profit margins in each of these sectors varies considerably. Gross profit margins are believed to range from 15 per cent for the 110 cameras to around 65 per cent for the video camera. At the lower end of the range, companies such as Kodak sell cameras at low margins, intending to recoup on the eventual sale of films.

The market shows fairly distinct price elasticities. At the lower end, consumers buy on price 'functional boxes'. Within the premium sector the consumer tends to purchase more on features and reliability than purely on price.

CONSUMERS

Age and sex appear to have the single most important influences on the type of camera ownership (Table C17.6), though the use to which the camera would be put is also important.

Table C17.5 Camera pricing in the UK

Type of camera	Range of retail price (£)	Estimated margin (%)
110	10–20	15
Disc	20–35	20
Compact	30–90	35
SLR (manual)	80–150	40
SLR (electronic)	150–300	55
Video	600–900	65

Table C17.6 Demographics of camera ownership

Category	Camera ownership (%)	0	1–2	3–5	6–10	11+
Men	76	4	17	20	35	26
Women	71	3	25	32	29	11
Under 18	69	–	22	44	33	–
19–25	74	1	17	32	30	18
26–35	78	4	14	22	30	26
36–50	71	5	18	22	34	18
51–64	69	4	42	25	25	4
65+	60	17	67	–	17	–

(Films per year columns: 0, 1–2, 3–5, 6–10, 11+)

Camera manufacturers consider the number of films purchased per year to be a good indication of the type of camera the individual would use and the type of photographs taken. They identify three broad categories.

1. The 'snapshotter', who concentrates on holidays and family events, and would use around three films per year.
2. The 'interest' photographer, taking specific photographs of animals, scenic shots etc., who would use fewer than ten films a year.
3. The 'expert' photographer, who though amateur takes a keen interest in developing special effects, lighting and so on. These photographers would use a substantial number of films, in excess of ten and often more than fifty a year.

As might be expected the different user types buy different categories of camera (Table C17.7)

The different types of camera enthusiast cannot easily be fitted into socio-economic groups. The snapshotters tend to be in the lower socio-economic groups and buy their cameras through the multiple outlets such as Dixons or Boots. The interest and expert photographers tend to buy their products through the more specialist outlets and keep up to date via one of the main consumer magazines on photography (Table C17.8).

Table C17.7   Camera purchase by category

	Snapshotter %	Interest %	Expert %
110	79	18	3
SLR	50	30	20
Compact	71	18	11
Instant	79	15	6
Disc	79	5	16
Video	30	50	20

Table C17.8   Photographic magazines

Magazine	Circulation	Readership	Page rates (colour)
*Amateur Photographer**	90,000	735,000	£1,425
*Camera Weekly**	58,000	358,000	£900
Practical Photography	92,000	872,000	£1,488
SLR Camera	42,000	523,000	£1,100

*Weekly publications; the others are monthly.

Table C17.9   Yamazka: landed costs of cameras to UK

Camera	£
110	6.50
Disc	11.00
Compact	18.00
SLR (manual)	38.00
SLR (electronic)	60.00
Video	110.00

PROMOTION IN THE CAMERA MARKET

There is a high level of promotional activity in the camera market: Kodak spends an estimated £8 million a year, mainly promoting the sale of films. Many of the other camera companies enter into co-operative advertising arrangements with the retail outlets to ensure a continuing high level of consumer visibility. The average estimated expenditure by the major companies such as Canon, Minolta and Olympus is around £1–1.2 million a year. Different sectors of the market tend to use separate promotional channels – the lower end concentrating on television and newspapers (nearly always in combination with the retailer), the premium sector concentrating on the main magazines servicing the enthusiast (Table C17.8).

THE YAMAZKA PRODUCT RANGE

Yamazka can produce cameras suitable for the middle range of all UK market sectors and ship them into the market (duty paid) at the prices in Table C17.9. These prices will not include any profit for Yamazka as the UK duty position encourages companies to take their profits within the UK market.

POSSIBLE DISTRIBUTION METHODS

Yamazka pioneered the development of its own sales organization in the United States. By employing a part-time salesforce of high school student enthusiasts paid solely on commission it was able to gain nationwide coverage. This salesforce was replaced by a more permanent team once volumes had reached a sufficiently high level.

To Yamazka, the UK market will require either a distributor or its own sales organization. The cost of a local sales office employing five representatives – a general sales manager with responsibility for the national accounts, a service and distribution manager to deal with third party warehousing and all service problems, accounts and administrative staff – would cost the company an estimated £200,000 per annum, plus office costs of around £100,000. In addition the company would have to finance a substantial stockholding within the third party warehouse, which would cost in the region of £55,000 per annum.

Alternatively, the company considered the possibility of employing distributors within the UK market, and has been approached by two companies currently distributing camera products.

Allen Factors has been established for five years and employs three sales staff. It currently sells a range of East European professional box cameras to 450 specialist outlets throughout the UK. David Allen, the head of the company, worked for the Greens retail chain prior to establishing the company and has good contacts with other major buyers. Allen Factors currently works on a mark-up of 25 per cent on cost. The company is confident that it can achieve a 2 per cent market share for Yamazka in the first year by concentrating at the premium end of the market, and increase share to 5 per cent in the fifth year of operation, provided Yamazka is prepared to match the promotional investment in the market made by the other companies.

The other company which has approached Yamazka is Graham Camera. It has been established for far longer than Allen Factors and is a much bigger operation, with a sales staff of fifteen and a marketing manager recruited from Boots. It currently carries a range of products across the entire market, but is dissatisfied with relationships with the overseas manufacturers of its 110 camera and SLR ranges and is looking for new suppliers. Graham Camera works on a mark-up which varies according to the type of equipment, from 25 per cent at the lower end of the range to 35 per cent at the higher. It is more confident that an initial market share of 5 per cent can be achieved rapidly by concentrating at the bottom end of the market, which share would rise to 8 or 10 per cent over the five-year period.

Yamazka would, however, be required to invest heavily to produce special camera and accessory packages to tempt the multiple store buyer.

Case 18

BENJAMIN'S

INTRODUCTION

Benjamin Grove had chosen Alderbridge, a prosperous market town not far from Selby in Yorkshire, for a new restaurant, founded in 1983. He had decided after twenty years spent working for one of the main hotel groups in the country that he could use his expertise more effectively in the small business environment. At that time Alderbridge, with a population of 15,000 and an additional catchment area of 10,000, already had a number of establishments serving various kinds of food.

The two main hotels, the Swan and the George, served traditional English cuisine for lunch and dinner. Both had similar set menus and à la carte offerings which cost from £6.95 upwards for a three-course meal.

A wine bar – El Sporgese – had survived perilously for three years and offered dishes like paella and spaghetti at around £2.50.

The Bombay, the town's only Indian restaurant, operated both as a restaurant and a take-away, with meals starting from £3.75.

Two outlets offered Chinese food. One, the River Boat, had been redesigned internally to resemble a river steamer, with set meals starting from £10.50 per head or an expensive à la carte menu. The other, the Yangtse, operated as a take-away offering both English and Chinese food from around £2.50 a portion.

At each end of town was a fish and chip shop: the Tall Ship and the Jolly Friar. There was fierce price competition between them, with basic cod and chips available from £1.20.

Around a dozen of the public houses in the town also served meals of varying standards, mostly of the chicken in a basket type, with prices ranging from £2.00 per dish.

Table C18.1 Opening hours of competitive eating places

	8–11 a.m.	11 a.m.– 2 p.m.	2–6 p.m.	6–10 p.m.	10–12 p.m.	7-day week
Swan/George		●		●		●
El Sporgese		●		●		
Bombay		●		●	●	●
River Boat		●		●	●	
Yangtse		●	●	●	●	
Tall Ship/Jolly Friar		●	●	●	●	●
Public houses		●		●		●
Nickells	●	●	●			
Benjamin's	●	●	●	●	●	●

Table C18.2 Benjamin's 1986 tariff

Item	£
Burger	2.00
Fish	2.00
Pancakes (three)	1.50
Chips	0.50
Salad bar	1.20
Ice cream	1.00
Coffee	0.60
Cakes – from	0.60

Table C18.3 Benjamin's turnover by product 1986 (%)

Burgers	30
Fish	15
Vegetables	15
Sweets	15
Cakes	10
Drinks	15

Table C18.4 Benjamin's turnover

Year	£000
1983	60
1984	90
1985	150
1986	270
1987 (est)	297

Finally, next to Alderbridge's main church, the long-established café and coffee shop, Nickells, served basic meals to a predominantly elderly group of pensioners living in the surrounding area.

BENJAMIN'S

Benjamin's opened in a high street site, next to a public house and over one of the two supermarkets in the town. There was room for twenty tables – reduced to eighteen when the owner changed the decor to emphasize individual booths.

Benjamin's differed significantly from most of its competitors in many respects. First, it was open for far longer hours than most of the other eating places in town, opening at 8 a.m. and closing at midnight (Table C18.1). Second, it always followed a policy of not holding a drinks licence, but concentrated on the provision of a wide range of different coffees and teas together with all the various types of non-alcoholic wines and beers. Third, its menu was very different from its competitors'. Benjamin's had a salad bar, with fresh vegetables every day, a wide range of standard and exotic ice creams, pancakes, freshly prepared crisp chips, home-made burgers with a high meat content, and a variety of grilled fish, delivered fresh from the nearby port of Dillsand. During the morning and afternoon the restaurant concentrated on providing high-quality locally baked cakes and scones. Benjamin's postioned itself as a high-quality restaurant and this was partly reflected in the prices charged (Table C18.2). Benjamin kept a rough analysis of where the main bulk of his turnover came from (Table C18.3).

Occupancy rates had from the early days remained one of Benjamin's problems. Throughout the day the restaurant managed to maintain a high level of occupancy, as the customers tended to stay substantially longer in Benjamin's than in other outlets, particularly in the morning and late evening.

By the end of 1986 the restaurant remained full throughout the day, putting considerable pressure on the staff, and this trend continued in 1987. As might be expected, turnover had reached a plateau in 1986 and was unlikely to show any significant increase in 1987 (Table C18.4). The inability to handle more people was especially worrying as Benjamin's received the highest proportion of its turnover towards the end of the day (Table C18.5).

Table C18.5 Benjamin's turnover – percentage by time of day

Year	8–11 a.m.	11 a.m.–2 p.m.	2–6 p.m.	6–10 p.m.	10–12 p.m.
1983	20	30	15	20	15
1984	15	35	10	30	10
1985	10	28	12	35	15
1986	10	32	10	32	16
1987	8	30	14	29	19

The clientele varied with the time of day and Benjamin identified various key groups.

1. The affluent shopper. Of various ages but predominantly female, these were by far the main customers of the restaurant from 8–11 a.m.
2. The small business luncher. Lunchtime was mainly the preserve of the surrounding business community seeking lunch but there was still a high proportion of shoppers as well.
3. The family diner. The main evening customers from around 5.30 to 9 were the family diners, eating in groups of four or more.
4. The bachelors. The main late-evening (after 9 p.m.) clients were the young, eating in the restaurant either before or after attending other social activities.

As a result of operating to capacity, the considerable growth in profitability since the opening of the restaurant had also slowed (Table C18.6).

OVERHEAD COSTS

Benjamin Grove realized that in the early days the labour element of the restaurant would be the most likely cause of success or failure. As a result he had mechanized operations as much as possible, introducing large institutional dishwashers and food preparation machines. When he started the restaurant he and his wife carried out all the work involved. With the early success of the concept, he had brought in a cook and two part-time waitresses, but insisted on continuing to carry out all the food preparation to ensure that the high standards were maintained. Overheads, which Benjamin regarded as fixed, are included in Table C18.7.

Table C18.6   Gross profit (excluding labour and other overheads – see Table C18.7)

Year	£000
1983	30
1984	50
1985	90
1986	150
1987	140

Table C18.7   Benjamin's fixed overheads

Overhead	£
Wages (waitresses and cook)	15,000
Heating and lighting	3,000
Rent	7,000
Rates	1,500
Breakages/laundry	1,500
Insurance	500

Benjamin and his wife had from the start taken only living wages from the shop; in the early years, 1983 and 1984, in order to pay off the £40,000 bank loan they had taken out to refurbish the restaurant and buy the equipment, they had taken out only £5,000 in wages. Since the bank loan had been repaid, the amount of money taken in wages had increased, until in 1987 they were intending to withdraw £20,000.

The business now had a solid and healthy positive cash flow, and liquid assets (mainly cash on deposit) of around £100,000. The Groves were trying to decide what should be done with the restaurant now that it was full all the day and evening.

Because of illness in 1987, Benjamin Grove realized that the business could not effectively continue to be operated by himself and his wife, and that introducing more staff would have a significant deleterious effect on profitability.

As he saw it there were a number of options available to put the business on to a footing which could allow him to take his first holiday for four years.

1. To move to new premises outside the centre of town, which would double the number of tables. The only currently available site was near the town bypass about a mile from the centre. The move would mean that basic overheads would increase by around a third, allowing the recruitment of an assistant manager and two more staff to handle the increased work, which would add around £20,000 to the wages bill. The refurbishment of the proposed location would cost around £25,000.
2. To open another branch of Benjamin's in a similar market town, thirty miles away, with a slightly larger population. The competition in this location would, however, be more intense as there were well-established outlets of both a national pizza chain and a hamburger chain. The two possible sites, both situated adjacent to the town centre, were slightly larger than the current restaurant and would allow either twenty or twenty-five tables. Refurbishment would cost around £20,000. Benjamin thought that with two restaurants he would have to appoint a manager for each of the restaurants, at around £12,000 each.
3. To move the restaurant up-market by introducing higher charges and a more sophisticated menu and wine list. Benjamin estimated that this could improve turnover by around £100,000 a year, nearly all of which would be profit, provided occupancy levels remained the same. This would allow him to introduce the staff necessary to reduce his workload. He estimated the extra staffing costs to be around £35,000 (more waiters, chefs).
4. Franchise. A friend of Benjamin had suggested that he should consider setting up a franchise operation, offering his expertise to enable other entrepreneurs to set up similar outlets throughout the Midlands. After a comparison with other franchise operations it would appear that a reasonable franchise fee would be around £10,000, and income from the franchise operation would allow him to hire extra staff to manage the restaurant while he was away negotiating with potential clients.

Case 19

CUPCO

INTRODUCTION

CupCo is a well-established company operating in the drinks vending industry. It was one of the first companies to enter the beverage market, with a small operation centred around the supply of hot drinks to companies in west London, in the early 1950s. Since then it has grown to become a national organization operating in a number of market sectors. CupCo offers a complete drinks vending package, supplying both the cups with ingredients and/or the vending machines for their automatic dispensing.

The early 1980s saw the vending business becoming more competitive, with major catering groups (such as THF and Grand Metropolitan) offering large companies substantial packages of benefits, including the provision of vending machines, and a host of small companies offering low-cost vending machine support on a regional basis. As a result, CupCo has seen its profitability shrink and sales growth level off (Table C19.1).

MARKET SECTORS

There are three main divisions to the drinks supply industry, each with different purchase criteria.

The commercial sector includes all the suppliers of beverages to the public. The number of outlets is estimated to be around 200,000, with a wide variation in the annual volume of vending products sold. They include hotels, restaurants, sandwich bars and public houses (Table C19.2). On the whole this sector buys on price; margins on hot and cold drinks are a particularly important part of their turnover.

Table C19.1 CupCo turnover and profit margin by sector by year

	1982	1983	1984	1985	1986
Sales (£000)					
Commercial	85	82	83	79	73
Public	55	62	68	77	75
Industrial	267	302	312	322	327
Gross margin (%)					
Commercial	65	60	55	50	52
Public	35	35	37	38	35
Industrial	75	68	66	63	60

Table C19.2 Commercial drinks suppliers

Supplier	Outlets
Hotels/motels and holiday camps	12,000
Small hotels	41,000
Restaurants	14,000
Cafés	18,000
Sandwich bars and others	10,000
Clubs	35,000
Public houses	70,000

Table C19.3 Public sector

Supplier	Outlets
Hospitals/nursing homes	10,000
Education	15,000

The majority of these companies purchase their supplies either from delivered wholesalers or cash and carry outlets. The larger outlets tend to buy direct; Butlins at Minehead, for example, sells around a million hot drinks a season. Where labour costs are particularly important and drinks volumes high, vending companies such as CupCo manage to sell vending systems because of the convenience and reduced staff involvement. One of CupCo's initial successes was in selling cups and ingredients but not vending machines to the large number of bingo clubs throughout the country, and to follow this up with bowling alleys. The commercial sector is by far the largest single sector making up around 60 per cent of the total drinks volume consumed out of the home.

The public sector includes all institutions which provide catering services to the public, mainly hospitals and schools (Table C19.3). Budgetary considerations in the 1980s are making it increasingly important to minimize ingredient costs, and with a large labour force the convenience of a complete drinks vending package is less important. The public sector is estimated to supply 12 per cent of the drinks consumed outside the home.

The industrial sector provides the third element in the market. Firms with more than twenty-five employees tend to have some form of drinks vending system, generally set up to operate at a slight profit to the organization. The larger the organization, the more sophisticated the vending equipment tends to be, which reflects the need for greater volumes and higher dispensing speed. Firms employing twenty-five to fifty employees often use some form of manual vending system whereas firms with more than 100 tend to require some form of automatic vending system (Table C19.4). Because costs tend to be recovered the industrial sector is not particularly price sensitive, but reliability is crucial as the office management does not want to be involved in continual complaints from the office staff.

CUPCO PRODUCT RANGE

CupCo provides a wide range of hot and cold drinks and two machines, the X5 suitable for the small office and the X10 designed for the office with 100–200 employees. Both these units are now five years old, and are becoming uncompetitive with some of the more modern units introduced by the competition. The X5 is a basic low-cost, manually operated system with a separate sugar dispenser, and push-button hot water system. The X10 automatically dispenses hot water into the

Table C19.4   Industrial sector

Numbers per location	Outlets
25–49	69,000
50–99	33,000
100–199	18,000
200–499	10,000
500+	4,500

Table C19.5   Sales contribution by product line (%)

Item	1982	1983	1984	1985	1986
Black coffee	10	9	8	9	8
White coffee	32	29	28	23	20
Black coffee with sugar	5	4	3	4	4
White coffee with sugar	25	28	30	28	26
Tea (white)	7	9	5	7	6
Tea (white with sugar)	11	9	8	8	6
Lemon tea	6	3	4	2	3
Oxtail soup	4	1	1	1	1
Hot blackcurrant		5	3	3	4
Chicken soup		3	3	4	4
Cold lemon			4	5	10
Cold orange			3	4	8

pre-selected product. Neither the X5 nor the X10 dispenses cold water for the orange and lemon drinks.

The main selling lines, CupCo's coffee range (Table C19.5), use coffee supplied by one of the leading instant coffee manufacturers. This coffee is substantially more expensive than competitive products and, combined with the higher cup costs, this means that the purchaser will be paying on average 1.5p more for CupCo coffee than the lowest price offered by the competition.

In common with many other vending companies, CupCo makes no money on the sales of the vending machines, all its profit coming from the sale of beverages which could be vended only through its machines.

PRODUCT DEVELOPMENT

Due to the declining profitability CupCo is faced with some important decisions, involving changes to the product range, in order that the company can become more competitive. It has come to the conclusion that there are a number of alternatives, each of which has cost and timing implications.

1. Changes in vending machine. The company could introduce new vending machines, able to supply larger offices, and a wider range of drinks, especially cold. Such a development would require eight months' development work and cost around £100,000.
2. Broadening the product range. The company could look for further products to widen the product range by considering the introduction of chocolate and further soup products.
3. Changing the coffee range. The company appears to be losing market share because of the lack of price competition in the coffee products it supplies. A reduction in the quality of coffee could improve margins by 10 per cent.
4. Changes in cup design. The current CupCo cup is designed to provide greater insulation to the consumer than the competitive products, and as a result is substantially more expensive than the competitors'. Reducing the material content of the cup could improve margins by a further 10 per cent.

Case 20

ALONZO

INTRODUCTION

Alonzo sherry was one of the most successful drinks products introduced in the early 1980s. It established the new product category of sparkling fortified wine, capturing market share from the two previous market leaders, Croft (a subsidiary of Grand Metropolitan) and Harveys, a subsidiary of Allied-Lyons. Though sales came mainly from consumers who had previously drunk sherry, there was also a sizeable minority that had switched form sparkling wine, especially perry-style products such as Babycham.

During 1984 the parent company became dissatisfied with the service that its advertising agency MBG had provided, largely emphasizing the consumption of the product as a morning aperitif.

Alonzo's parent company, especially its chairman, saw the product as having a wider potential market in a number of areas.

1. As a long drink base for the youth market, possibly with greater usage in the restaurant and bar trade.
2. As a more clearly defined aperitif to accompany wine at meals, in addition to retaining the current market position.

The company decided to ask three new agencies for new advertising and marketing proposals for the £4.2 million account. The board of one of these, Creative Designs, is assessing the advertising brief provided, and is setting down the key features of the proposed advertising pitch.

It has to decide on the main issues.

1. Which target group to concentrate on and why?

2. The implications of this for promotional policy, in respect of the media channels and planning that would be required.
3. What other proposals the company would put forward for the development of the product, including any changes in the pricing or distribution policy.

THE COMPANY

Alonzo was founded by one of the new breed of Spanish entrepreneur. Don Manuel de Lopez de Perez-Aguear had built up his father's hotel business into an aggressive entertainment and development company, with thirty-five hotels, ten timeshare complexes and twenty-eight retirement villages. The catering subsidiary developed to service these residential outlets had expanded to provide British-style cuisine to a substantial number of hotels and other outlets along the Spanish coast. As a considerable proportion of the catering company's revenue came from the supply of drinks, Don Manuel had been interested in acquiring a drinks supplier in the Spanish market, and the collapse of the Rumasa group had allowed him to buy a variety of companies, one of which produced low-quality sherry. His contact with the British market had convinced him of the potential for novel and highly profitable drinks products, particularly one which appealed to the growing taste for lighter natural products, rather than the heavier spirits such as whisky and brandy, both of which showed continuing declines.

Market research confirmed his belief in the likely existence of a market gap, which he had exploited using an award-winning series of commercials based around Royal Family look-alikes, a series which had become established in the same fashion as the Brook Bond 'chimps' or the Oxo 'family'. In Spain his fruit and gin product, Cascata, was highly successful and it was likely that this would be the next product introduction into the UK.

Don Manuel held 90 per cent of the total company equity, and was well connected in Spanish political circles, his brother-in-law Enrique Carroza being the current Minister of Tourism in the Spanish government. The five-year progress of the M Group had seen sales rise from \$125 million to \$490 million and profit from \$25 million to \$91 million, and prospects for the future remained favourable, with the continued expansion of food and drinks interests into Western Europe and eventually the United States.

THE BRIEF

The product

Alonzo was the sole product in a new market category, sparkling fortified wine. Because of its composition it could not claim to be Spanish sherry as it fell outside the regulations imposed by the controlling body in Jerez on the production of sherry products. Alonzo did, however, use Spanish sherry as the base and incorporated CO_2 during the production process. Part of its success lay in the unique design of the reusable bottle cap, which maintained the fizz over a long period of time.

The range consisted of three product lines available in either 70 cl or 1 litre bottles.

1. Alonzo Pale – the dry version which used a Fino sherry base.
2. Alonzo Media – the medium sweet variety based on Amontillado.
3. Alonzo Cream – the sweet version based on a cream sherry.

The bottle had been specifically designed to stand out on the shelf, with a new glass moulding process combining green and yellow glass. The labelling of the bottle was achieved by a painting process which was then oven-hardened. The design was so impressive that it had won several awards, and appeared with frequency at village jumble sales modified into table lamps. The current sales mix showed that the 70 cl bottle made up the bulk of the sales with over 85 per cent of total volume, the 1 litre bottle selling through duty-free outlets and during the pre-Christmas rush.

Current positioning

Target group

C1/C2 females aged between twenty-five and forty-five.

Consumer proposition

The sparkling natural drink for the warming social occasion. (Sales and seasonality are shown in Tables C20.1 and C20.2).

Market definition

As a sparkling sherry, Alonzo operated in two markets, sparkling wine and sherry. For Customs and Excise purposes the product was treated as a fortified wine and in consequence paid duty at a different rate from champagne and other sparkling wine products. One of the main problems both sparkling wine (which included the champagne market) and fortified wine products face is the continually changing levels of duty imposed on various alcoholic drinks (Table C20.3).

The growth in both the fortified and sparkling markets was affected both by the level of duty and the disposable income of the relevant consumers. In recent years the wine market had grown spectacularly, particularly in response to pressure from the EEC to lower wine duties and raise those on beer so that the UK came closer into line with the Continent (Table C20.4).

Table C20.1   Market sales of Alonzo (at retail including tax and duty)

	1978	1979	1980	1981	1982	1983	1984
Sales (£ million)	50	70	85	90	100	105	110
Sales by type (%)							
Pale	25	23	22	20	18	19	20
Media	54	55	57	55	56	58	60
Cream	21	22	21	25	26	23	20
Profit (£ million)	6	9	10	11	12	12	12
Advertising expenditure	2	3	3	3	3	4	4

NB: Profitability figures are gross and do not include the staff costs for Alonzo in the UK.

Table C20.2   Sales seasonality (%)

Product	Month											
	1	2	3	4	5	6	7	8	9	10	11	12
Sherry	8	4	5	3	2	2	2	2	12	14	22	24
Sparkling wine	4	3	2	9	12	16	18	12	4	4	4	12
Alonzo	7	8	3	2	6	10	10	8	3	9	15	19

Table C20.3   UK duties per litre (£)

	1978	1979	1980	1981	1982	1983	1984
Sparkling wine	1.80	2.00	2.20	2.25	2.30	2.40	2.60
Fortified wine	1.20	1.40	1.60	1.80	2.00	2.00	2.20

Table C20.4   Market development (total market sales in £ million including tax)

	1978	1979	1980	1981	1982	1983	1984
Still wine	800	850	900	950	1,050	1,120	1,250
Sparkling wine	58	60	62	67	72	75	77
Sherry	350	360	370	380	390	400	450

Much of the growth in all three market sectors was the result of higher levels of alcohol consumption at home (the off-trade) rather than in pubs or restaurants (the on-trade) (Table C20.5).

Multiple grocers sold by far the largest proportion of all sherry consumed, whereas the specialist off-licences made up the bulk of the sparkling wine sales.

Consumption figures, however, concealed fairly dramatic variations in consumption patterns and the types of individuals who consume the various products. The consumer profile of the various markets was shown to be fairly distinct in market research Alonzo had carried out. Tables C20.6 to C20.8 show the findings of the research.

Table C20.5 UK alcohol consumption: off-trade and on-trade

Product	On-trade (%)	Off-trade (%)
Still wine	12	88
Sherry	18	82
Sparkling wine	21	79

Table C20.6 Alonzo research findings: consumer profile

| Product category | Consumption by age profile (%) | | | | | |
	18–21	22–25	26–35	36–45	46–55	55+
Dry sherry	2	10	30	35	15	8
Medium sherry	14	18	20	14	15	19
Cream sherry	2	25	25	25	15	8
Sparkling wine	18	45	21	7	7	2
Alonzo	8	22	38	15	7	8
All alcohol	15	20	30	15	10	10

| Product category | Consumption by socio-economic group (%) | | | | |
	AB	C1	C2	D	E
Dry sherry	88	3	4	3	2
Medium sherry	28	22	34	12	4
Cream sherry	15	21	38	22	4
Sparkling wine	75	12	7	3	3
Alonzo	22	45	32	1	–
All alcohol	20	28	29	17	6

| Product | Consumption by main TV area (%) | | | | | | |
	London	Mid-lands	North West	Yorks	Scot-land	Wales	South
Sherry	28	18	10	8	3	5	14
Sparkling wine	33	12	5	4	3	4	16
Alonzo	29	16	14	10	2	8	11
All alcohol	22	17	11	10	8	9	10

| Product | Male and female consumption patterns: total consumption (%) | |
	Male	Female
Dry sherry	70	30
Medium sherry	55	45
Cream sherry	77	23
Sparkling wine	42	58
Alonzo	32	68

Table C20.6   (*contd.*)

Product	Mid-morning	Aperitif	With meal	After meal
	Occasion of drinking (%)			
Dry sherry	18	75	7	–
Medium sherry	12	70	15	3
Cream sherry	36	29	13	22
Sparkling wine	28	22	45	5
Alonzo	43	29	15	13

Table C20.7   Alonzo research findings: importance of product attributes for various consumer groups

Category	1	2	3	4	5
			Segment		
Novel product	5	9	4	3	2
Taste	4	3	8	9	6
Sophisticated	5	9	7	4	2
Fashionable	6	9	6	2	1
High alcohol content	3	7	4	6	2
Natural ingredients	2	2	7	7	9
High-quality product	6	5	4	8	9

NB: Ratings are out of 10 (very important) to 0 (not important at all)

Table C20.8   Alonzo research findings: consumer perception of Alonzo

Analysis of the perceptions of Alonzo by respondents that were aware of the product

Category	% respondents agreeing
Novel product	75
Good taste	62
Sophisticated	45
Fashionable	33
High alcohol content	27
Natural ingredients	72
Quality product	66

Alonzo awareness (prompted awareness of name)

Age	% awareness
18–21	88
22–25	76
26–35	61
36–45	59
46–55	56
55+	45

Table C20.9   Main suppliers to the market and market shares 1983–1985

Product	1983 Price (£)	1983 Market share (%)	1984 Price (£)	1984 Market share (%)	1985 Price (£)	1985 Market share (%)
M & S	2.99	11	3.10	11	3.29	13
Harveys	3.10	15	3.40	14	3.95	11
Croft	3.05	11	3.35	11	3.95	10
Domecq	2.49	13	2.59	12	2.99	11
Alonzo	3.25	11	3.30	16	3.40	20
Other Spanish	2.29	22	2.49	17	2.49	18
Other sherry	1.99	17	2.19	19	2.29	17

Competitive products and market shares

There were three fairly distinct sectors of the sherry market. First, there were the premium Spanish sherries, such as Croft and Harveys Bristol Cream, that maintained market leadership on price. The middle of the market was occupied by other Spanish sherries and sherry from other countries, especially Cyprus sherries like Emva Cream. Finally, the lowest price sector of the market was occupied by British sherries such as QC (Table C20.9).

Consumer drinking types

Segment 1: The inexperienced drinker

These are typically men aged eighteen to twenty and women aged eighteen to twenty-three. They are likely to be conservative in their drinking tastes, sticking to beer (men) or low-alcohol products (women). This group can be summarized by the slogan 'I'd love a Babycham'.

Segment 2: The trendy drinker

This category of drinker is generally aged between twenty and thirty-five and is likely to experiment with the type of drink on offer, switching rapidly between the available brands. Real ale and Malibu cocktails would be typical drinks of this segment.

Segment 3: The social drinker

Aged between twenty and thirty-five, drinking as part of a social occasion, concentrating on small quantities of alcohol, particularly in long drinks. Gin and tonic and cider are typically consumed by this group.

Segment 4: The solid drinker

Typically aged between twenty-five and forty-five these were individuals who were heavy consumers of standard drink products: beer, whisky or wine.

Segment 5: The genteel drinker

These are individuals typically aged over twenty-five, who would consume alcohol at home either solitarily or in small groups. Sherry and liqueurs would be typical products consumed by this group.

Media and media availability

Table C20.10 gives 1985 advertising expenditure for Alonzo and its competitors.
Media availability with approximate costs and coverage are given below and in Tables C20.11 to C20.14.

Television

At peak viewing times ITV's share of audience is around 50 per cent, Channel 4 around 9 per cent. During 1984/85 the average number of hours' viewing per household was 5.75 hours per day.

Media costs vary throughout the year and between companies depending on the level of negotiating power the company wishing to advertise could exert. Regardless of this, television rates are higher for all operators at certain times of the year, especially around Christmas and Easter. For the purposes of evaluation it could be considered that costs would be around 50 per cent higher at those times than the average figures given in Table C20.11, and 50 per cent lower during the slack summer months.

Table C20.12 segments the population of each ITV area by socio-economic grouping.

Cinema

Cinema advertising is available on a TV region basis. The Cinema Audience Delivery Plan guarantees 1 million admissions for a 30-second cost of £16,000 (1985). The average audience profile of cinema admissions was:

● AB 25 per cent
● C1 29 per cent
● C2 27 per cent
● DE 19 per cent

Table C20.10   Competitive advertising expenditure (by category) 1985

Brand	Total (£ million)	TV (%)	Magazines (%)	Press (%)	Posters (%)
Croft	2.5	75	–	25	–
Harveys	3.2	51	23	26	–
Domecq	0.8	–	66	15	19
Alonzo	4.2	55	45	–	–

Table C20.11   TV advertising costs and coverage

Area	% households	30-second peak cost (list price) ITV (£)	C4 (£)
London	21	14,700	2,050
Midlands	16	7,500	650
North West	12	6,000	500
Yorkshire	11	6,000	450
South	10	4,700	750
Wales	9	3,400	200
East	7	3,000	500
Scotland	6	3,000	100
South West	3	1,500	80

Table C20.12   ITV areas by socio-economic group

Area	AB	C1/C2	DE
London	21	49	30
Midlands	12	45	43
N. West	12	47	42
Yorks	12	45	43
South	20	50	30
Wales	15	48	34
East	18	48	37
Scotland	16	48	37
South West	16	51	34

Posters

One poster site costs around £300 a month, according to location; campaigns can be run on a weekly basis. A minimum national campaign based on 800 sites would cost £30,000 a month, though there are a number of other options offered by the main contractors operating in the market.

Localized poster activity may be obtained through city transport authorities for bus and bus shelter exposure. Costs for the London Underground, for example, are from £5 to £350 per site per week depending on the size of the poster – escalator panels costing around £20 per week.

Table C20.13   Newspaper advertising costs and coverage

Title	Readership ('000s)	ABC1 (%)	Cost per page/colour (if available) (£)
Sun	4,000	24	23,000
Mirror	3,100	25	21,000
Express	1,700	50	19,000/44,000
Mail	1,800	56	19,000/35,000
Star	1,300	18	8,575/23,000
Telegraph	1,100	83	24,000/28,000
Guardian	500	79	14,000/18,000
Times	400	85	11,000/17,000
Financial Times	200	88	16,000
Today	300	48	3,600/7,600
Independent	300	75	7,500/10,500
Sundays			
News of the World	5,000	25	25,000
Sunday Mirror	3,000	28	22,000
Sunday People	3,000	26	20,000
Sunday Express	2,200	57	47,000
Sunday Mail	1,700	58	19,000
Sunday Times	1,200	78	29,000/45,000
Observer	800	76	18,500
Sunday Telegraph	700	75	18,000

Leaflet distribution

Using solo distribution with other leaflets, any particular area could be covered at the cost of £20.25 per 1,000 homes. There are 18.5 million households in the UK. Though there are facilities available to identify target populations for direct mail activity (for example the ACORN system) the use of leaflet distribution is for blanket distribution.

National newspapers

Newspapers naturally vary considerably according to their socio-economic readership. The standard population profile is 39 per cent ABC1, 61 per cent/C2DE. This compares with the percentages given in Table C20.13 for the different daily and weekly papers.

In addition to the national newspapers there are a wide range of regional newspapers that could be considered, with full-page black and white rates amounting on average to £15 per thousand of the population.

Magazines

These can be divided into general weekly (GW), general monthly (GM), specialized weekly (SW) and specialized monthly (SM), as analysed in Table C20.14.

Table C20.14 Magazine advertising costs and coverage

Title	Readership ('000s)	ABC1 (%)	Cost per page/colour (£)
TV Times (GW)	3,800	43	12,000/20,000
Radio Times	3,200	49	12,000/20,000
Reader's Digest (GM)	1,500	50	9,000/13,000
Woman's Own (SW)	1,000	n.a.	13,000/18,000
Woman (SW)	1,000	n.a.	11,000/16,000
Woman's Weekly (SW)	1,300	n.a.	7,000/10,000
Woman's Realm (SW)	600	n.a.	5,000/7,000
My Weekly (SW)	600	n.a.	3,000/4,000
Family Circle (SM)	600	n.a.	5,000/8,000
Woman & Home (SM)	600	n.a.	4,000/7,000
Living (SM)	400	n.a.	3,000/5,000
Cosmopolitan (SM)	400	n.a.	4,000/6,000
Good Housekeeping (SM)	300	n.a.	4,000/6,000

Case 21

CLARA

BACKGROUND

Clara, a German frozen foods group, has just acquired Home Foods, a UK firm, after a take-over battle which had been bitterly contested by the senior management of the British company. By a series of aggressive acquisitions, Clara had grown rapidly from a small Bavarian brewery into a group comprising a whole range of food activities. The Clara main board will shortly be discussing Home Foods's future within the group, including its potential as a method of expanding the sale of the company's bread and butter lines within the UK. Inevitably this process involves the examination of Home Foods's selling activity in the UK and overseas, its salesforce structure and their compatibility with the established experience of the Clara group, and the method by which all the products should be distributed.

The main board have asked for a series of recommendations concerning the reorganization of the salesforce and how the combined company should operate.

Currently the company has a Swiss sales director, Klaus Wunderlicht, and a Belgian marketing director, Wilhem Maertens. Wunderlicht is one of the original managers of the Clara group and his insistence on rigid salesforce controls has been highly successful in mass market rapid turnover product areas which make up the bulk of the Clara group's revenues. Maertens, a more recent arrival, has been instrumental in defining the identification of specific market niches and the necessary promotional requirements to meet the increasingly sophisticated consumer demands throughout Western Europe.

HOME FOODS

Home Foods, with its battery division and cheese division, could in many ways be described as two separate companies.

Cheese division

The company began manufacturing and selling processed cheese in the 1930s, but in the mid-1970s began a very successful diversification into hard and soft speciality British cheeses for sale at home and in major European cities, capitalizing on the expanding consumer interest in the return to original recipes. Cheese was exported to Denmark, Holland, Belgium and France. This operation was successful and remained a core activity for the firm, enabling it to withdraw from its early processed cheese market, which was declining throughout the 1970s and 1980s. The company became a market leader in the UK in the speciality cheese market and started to make substantial progress in the EEC. Both these markets were extremely fragmented with a large number of small manufacturers supplying the bulk of the retail market (Table C21.1).

Profitability was a major reason for the interest of the Clara group in Home Foods – margins at home were between 40 and 45 per cent; and 25 per cent for EEC sales in a more competitive market involving higher distribution costs. Though the group was highly profitable the amount of working capital tied up in maturing cheese stocks had always been substantial, and this led to a depressed return on capital employed.

Much of the market penetration had been achieved by concentrating on the major grocery chains, which were the main stockists of specialist cheeses in the UK. The main customers by 1984 were:

1. The Co-op (1,500 stores buying on an area basis).
2. Argyll group (1,000 stores buying centrally).
3. Dee Corporation (751).
4. Tesco (411).

Home Foods failed, however, to gain a foothold in three other main specialist retail outlets, Marks and Spencer, Asda, and Sainsbury's, being unwilling to supply

Table C21.1 Home Foods (cheese division): UK turnover

	1978	1979	1980	1981	1982	1983	1984
Turnover (£ million)	22	24	31	32	38	42	45
Gross margin (%)	20	21	19	21	19	22	24
Outlets ('000s)	12	13	15	17	19	20	20
Market share (%)	10	12	15	16	18	23	24
ROCE (%)	12	13	17	19	21	13	12

Table C21.2   Home Foods (cheese division): product range

Product range	Packs	Profit contribution (%)
Borzoi	5	14
Windsor	7	17
Flatford Mill	5	13
Carrimore	8	12
Erin	8	11
Yule	7	10
Plantagenet	10	11
Isis	10	11

Table C21.3   Home Foods (cheese division): UK distribution (%)

Outlet type	Hard cheese		Soft cheese	
	1977	1984	1977	1984
Major multiples	45	52	38	29
Independents	27	22	21	18
Specialists	28	26	41	53

own-label products. In the UK these main groups took 45 per cent of the total Home Foods turnover, with sales to the other types of outlets fairly evenly spread, but with substantial differences in their individual importance.

Product range and salesforce organization (UK)

Each geographically based sales representative handled eight main product lines, each with around five different flavours in a variety of pack sizes. There was a total range of sixty packs (Table C21.2).

Home Foods had followed a rapid innovation policy and, at the time of the take-over, three new ranges of soft herb cheeses were ready for introduction, increasing the total product range to around 100 lines. This product introduction was to take advantage of the rapidly growing demand for 'naturally' flavoured products.

The UK market had been slowly changing as speciality stores, including the delicatessen sector, became increasingly important soft cheese outlets (Table C21.3). Because of the large ranges of cheese the company sold and the requirement to mature the product correctly, Home Foods had always needed to maintain high stocks of its product range and this had always depressed the level of return on capital employed.

Specialist retailers were also becoming more important as suppliers of res-taurants and cafés, where an increasing quantity of soft cheese was being con-sumed. The specialist outlets were therefore becoming more concerned about product quality and more knowledgeable about the overall market.

Table C21.4   Home Foods (cheese division): customers' contribution to profit (UK)

Customers (% cumulative)	Profit (% cumulative)
10	30
20	50
30	60
50	75
70	85

At the time of the take-over there were thirty-five sales representatives each dealing with approximately 500 accounts. The four main multiple chains were handled on an *ad hoc* basis. The Co-ops and Tesco stores were handled regionally, with the Dee and Argyll negotiations the responsibility of the Home Foods sales director at national level. Each representative was responsible for around £700,000 of turnover, substantially above the industry average of £300,000, but which reflected the rapid growth of the company in the market. Each sales representative was allocated a call cycle that split customers into several categories.

Category A (weekly): approximately ten accounts.
Category B (bi-weekly): approximately 100 accounts.
Category C (monthly): approximately 200 accounts.
Category D (quarterly): approximately 200 accounts.

This system broke down with the rapid extension of the customer base, and was under review at the time of the take-over. Each call was estimated to take about forty minutes including travelling time. Home Foods had always followed a policy of concentrating on investing in sales representation rather than media promotion in what was a specialized market and this was reflected in its fairly wide spread of customers. Table C21.4 gives an indication of this spread.

Product range and salesforce organization (EEC)

In Europe progress had been achieved by some sales direct to groups such as Carrefour and Auchan in France, GB in Belgium and Makro in Holland. The majority of the trade was, however, handled through local sales agents or *multi-cartes* dealing with specific regions of the overseas markets. Home Foods had pioneered this type of overseas representation by not following the normal process of appointing overseas agents to develop sales nationally in overseas markets. This arrangment did, however, mean that Home Foods needed to use third party chilled distribution systems and pay relatively high commission rates to the independently employed *multicarte* agents. To supervise these 120 agents Home Foods employed an overseas sales management team of six, who spent most of their time on the road throughout Europe. The speciality cheese market was very different in these

Table C21.5 Home Foods (cheese division): EEC turnover

	1978	1979	1980	1981	1982	1983	1984
Turnover (£ million)	5	7	7	8	9	10	15
Margin (%)	18	17	16	18	17	22	21
Outlets	2,000	3,000	3,500	4,500	5,000	6,000	7,000
Market share (%)	2	2	2	3	3	3	4

Table C21.6 Home Foods (battery division): turnover

	1978	1979	1980	1981	1982	1983	1984
Turnover (£ million)	2	2	3	6	7	9	11
Outlets	1,000	2,000	3,000	4,000	4,000	4,500	5,000
Market share (%)	15	15	18	23	28	32	35
ROCE (%)	25	27	29	31	20	15	15

European markets and the skills the export salesforce had acquired were often unrelated to their previous tasks in the home trade. Because of the complexity of the market it was considered that it took over a year before an export sales representative became fully effective.

Table C21.5 gives details of EEC turnover, etc.

Battery division

During the period of uncertainty prior to UK membership of the EEC, Home Foods had acquired a small manufacturer of electrical batteries, then on the verge of bankruptcy. By reducing the scope of the operation, concentrating on producing a few, high-quality lines with a good reputation for durability, the company made the operation highly profitable (Table C21.6). These batteries were soon being exported to Spain, Portugal, Italy and Greece, though these countries at present comprised only 15 per cent of total turnover. Home Foods had, however, a number of plans under consideration for the development of this range overseas, and had started to exhibit extensively in the United States.

As the market was dominated by the volume manufacturers, Berec and Duracell, Home Foods had concentrated on a particular market segment – rechargeable batteries – where growth continued to be substantial. Demand was coming increasingly from the industrial sector, which could afford the initial substantial investment in the recharging systems (Table C21.7).

Product range and salesforce organization

Currently there were three products and twenty different packs (Table C21.8). Home Foods had more recently invested £20 million in a range of rechargeable

Table C21.7 Home Foods (battery division): distribution

Sector	1979 (%) Accounts	1984 (%) Turnover
Multiple grocers	10	2 (own label)
Independents	50	25
Specialist retail	35	28
Industrial	5	45

Table C21.8 Home Foods (battery division): product contribution to profit

Product	Packs	Profit (%)
Lightning	5	12
Thunderbolt	10	45
Dynamo	5	43

Table C21.9 Home Foods (battery division): customers' contribution to profit

Customers (% cumulative)	Profit (% cumulative)
10	20
20	35
30	55
50	70
70	82

sodium batteries which were half the weight of the competition yet provided an increased power output. An advanced manufacturing process being introduced into the Home Foods battery factor at Skegness would improve margins and overall company profitability in this area from 25 to 45 per cent gross and substantially lift market share. This enormous investment, coupled with the reduced return on capital in the cheese division due to the introduction of new variants, had allowed the Clara group to take the company over.

Each of the fifteen sales representatives employed in the battery division handled around 300 accounts. Call cycles were similar to those in the cheese division but the length of call had increased with the technical demands of the industrial market and each call now took around an hour including travelling time.

As the multiples were unimportant as outlets, the battery division also showed a wide customer base as the company followed its philosophy of concentrating its investment in the salesforce rather than in media investment (Table C21.9).

Overseas organization

To handle the overseas sales of the battery range, Home Foods maintained a standard export sales organization staffed by three managers. Business was conducted through agents and distributors.

HOME FOODS'S MANAGEMENT PHILOSOPHY

The two areas of activity remained quite separate up to the Clara take-over except that Home Foods, at the time of its first involvement in the battery operation, had decided on an integrated salesforce management policy. The company had realized it was losing some of its most talented staff to others partly because of the limited opportunities within the firm. The board acknowledged that because Home Foods was small, this would always happen to an extent, but that it was not fully exploiting the opportunities available to reduce the rate of loss.

The Home Foods salesforce policy subsequently adopted and in force at the time of the take-over had been strongly influenced by the need to motivate individuals and maintain salesforce morale. It was felt that certain measures would contribute to this end.

Organization

Because Home Foods's main business had been cheese, it was regarded as essential that those selling batteries should not be seen as poor relations. The sales structure adopted is in Table C21.10.

To set the pattern for the future, some of Home Foods's best salesforce performers were transferred to head the battery division. Terms and conditions of

Table C21.10 Home Foods: sales structure

	Sales director	
Battery division		Cheese division
Senior sales manager		Senior sales manager
Overseas sales manager		Overseas sales manager
Area sales manager		Area sales manager
Salesforce (geographically assigned)		Salesforce (geographically assigned)

employment were renegotiated to ensure that the retained members of the sales-force would be willing to transfer from one division of the company to another and that new recruits understood and accepted this as part of the company's personnel policy. The salesforce grew to accept the ethos that experience in both areas of the company's operations widened the options available to them in terms of movement within the company.

Training

Additional support was given through training programmes and in-house refresher courses for personnel about to transfer from one section to another. Language training was available for those interested, and included the opportunity to provide support for the overseas sales managers on trips abroad. A worrying factor was that the increasing technical demands of the battery division necessitated a steady increase in training investment.

Remuneration

To prevent serious anomalies arising over pay between the two sections, sales staff were paid a basic salary of £15,500, plus an index-linked cost of living award, and an additional lump sum payment for extra business acquired in excess of targets or during promotions.

This package achieved its goal of maintaining a highly motivated, flexible salesforce.

Recruitment

Home Foods continued to follow a policy of regional recruitment.

Appraisal

The growth in sales over the last few years meant that the appraisal system, often discussed at board level, had never in fact been implemented; it was felt that the similarity in pay throughout the salesforce decreased the need for such a system.

Policy effects

The success of these various policies was seen in the steady improvement in the company's profitability in the years preceding the Clara bid, and in the lower rate of salesforce turnover. The typical Home Foods sales representative stayed with the company seven years; the average age of the salesforce was thirty-eight. Surveys within the trade revealed that the Home Foods salesforce were the most highly regarded for their knowledge of and enthusiasm for the products they handled.

Outcome of the bid

It was not surprising that the Home Foods sales director had been among those most violently opposed to the Clara take-over. Its success had been followed by his resignation and that of two senior sales managers, four of the six area managers and the vast majority of senior members of the salesforce. Of the total salesforce of fifty-nine in the two divisions, twenty-two decided to stay and work for the new company. This included all the overseas sales managers, who felt that their expertise would be essential to the Clara group.

THE CLARA GROUP

The Clara group was made up mainly of companies engaged in producing, marketing and selling high-quality, speciality, premium frozen food, with activity concentrated in Europe. It had also recently established a sausage and cold meat manufacturing subsidiary, and its acquisition of Home Foods was an attempt to build up expertise in cheese as well as providing an entry into overseas markets. Clara's main markets outside Germany were, in order of importance, France, the UK, Switzerland, Austria, Denmark and Belgium.

A local subsidiary in each country bought from Clara manufacturing units and sold into the local markets, each subsidiary acting as a profit centre.

Turnover had grown rapidly from the early 1970s, though margins on sales had tended to stagnate and it was for this reason that the company was looking for improved margin business in new acquisitions. In its core markets the amount of own-brand activity from the supermarkets continued to grow, which was a further worrying feature of trends in the market (Table C21.11).

The Clara management structure is in Table C21.12.

Each subsidiary's survival depended upon its ability to contribute to group profits. Those group companies which had not been subsidiaries in the first instance had usually been acquired because they were involved with Clara in some way – usually raw materials suppliers in financial difficulty. Clara concentrated on high levels of return on capital employed as a key to success and tried to minimize stock levels throughout the group.

The only exception was Clara Export, which handled a small amount of business

Table C21.11 Clara group turnover

	1976	1977	1978	1979	1980	1981	1982	1983	1984
Turnover (£ million)	102	123	145	156	178	203	225	256	289
Sales margin (%)	11	10	9	10	12	13	12	11	12
ROCE (%)	32	30	28	27	25	27	23	20	20
Supermarket own brand (%)	5	7	9	11	15	17	21	23	25

outside Continental Europe. By 1984 it accounted for 10 per cent of turnover. It was seen as the development arm of the Clara group, with responsibility for trying new approaches to the market place.

Table C21.12   Clara group management structure

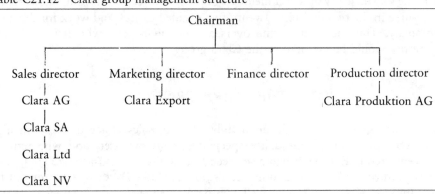

THE CLARA ETHOS OF SELLING

The Clara group shared a common approach to selling, geared towards achieving maximum distribution at the lowest possible cost. Strict control of sales costs was synonymous with a highly centralized system. Its highly sophisticated methods of cost calculation had revealed that in the product areas which concerned the group, the cost of achieving marginal distribution far outweighed the benefits.

Each company in the group therefore directed its sales efforts towards servicing key customers through a national accounts sales office. The use of EPOS systems by major chain stores had permitted further streamlining of the national accounts office and this was backed up with the increasing use of telephone sales services. The total number of staff engaged in selling in each company was therefore about four. Promotions were handled by the marketing departments with agencies providing the support staff as and when necessary.

The pattern of trade in each of their markets followed a similar form (Table C21.13).

Salesforce policy

National accounts sales staff were paid a basic salary; incentive payments took the form of reward for suggestions for improving efficiency. The average age of the national accounts salesforce was twenty-eight and they tended to stay with the company for three years.

Clara recruited its salesforce from outside the company by offering attractive salary and benefits packages, which resulted in the sales managers in Clara UK being paid around £22,000 a year. Because of their high salaries the Clara group did not pay any form of additional incentives.

The emphasis was on performance and flexibility. Individuals were expected to travel widely within their markets and the group maintained a structured six-monthly appraisal system that evaluated the salesforce against its share of national targets.

Table C21.13   Clara group
customers' contribution to profit

Customers (% cumulative)	Profit (% cumulative)
20	55
30	75
50	95

PROMOTIONAL POLICY

Clara was one of the major advertisers in Europe, and its emphasis on continual heavy advertising made it able to maintain distribution through the major chains. Product ranges were limited and the emphasis had mainly been on mass market goods.

THE HOME FOODS TAKE-OVER

The take-over had opened divisions in the Clara board. One group, led by the debonair Maertens, was convinced that the solution to the long-term problems facing the group lay in the re-evaulation of certain long-held articles of faith. The other, dominated by the dour Wunderlicht, continued to emphasize the success of the current policy.

RECENT DEVELOPMENTS

At the time of the Clara take-over the battery division of Home Foods – which had been exhibiting extensively in the USA – had been involved in negotiations with a major American distributor. Because of the acrimonious nature of the take-over, the Clara board had not been fully informed about the exact nature or true potential of these discussions. The American distributor has now placed a substantial order – the estimated sales value being about $1.5 million a year – with the Home Foods battery division giving potential access to a major proportion of West

Coast city markets and industrial markets. The proposal has now gone to the Clara main board for finalization. The distributor would have sole rights in the West Coast markets for a period of five years and Home Foods would set up a warehouse to hold supplies for the American market. The estimated cost of this investment was thought to be in the region of $0.8 million.

Another proposal concerning the battery division came before the board at the same time. An unknown group, backed by venture capital, had offered Clara $50 million for the division.

Following immediately upon the success of the Clara bid, the former Home Foods sales director, two senior sales manager and six area sales managers had formed a new company, Good Food. Having purchased a bankrupt dairy and buttery in Wales they had begun to produce own-brand cheeses very similar to the Home Foods range, and secured orders from Sainsbury's, Marks and Spencer, Dee and Argyll. Production capacity is already being expanded on the Good Food premises.

Rumours have reached the Clara main board that both the Home Foods cheese division and battery division export managers have been approached by their former colleagues at Good Food, who are now showing an aggressive interest in exporting. The Home Foods battery division export manager had been mainly responsible for negotiating the American deal and because of the Home Foods salesforce policy had good experience in cheese marketing overseas.

Case 22

ZENITH

BACKGROUND

The international charity, Pax, sold its publications division to Zenith Publishing in 1983. For many years Zenith had wanted to expand its overseas operations, and believed that there was an opening in the area of technical and specialist publications for Third World markets on subjects such as health, which had been mainly served by international aid agencies like Pax. Zenith had also previously published only journals; the Pax acquisition gave it access to a range of training manuals produced by Pax for overseas medical organizations.

Since Zenith had little experience in either publications markets overseas or the production of manuals it had also taken on the old Pax publications and information section to form the core of the new operation and appointed a sales and marketing manager, Abel Cornwallis, to take charge of the new Zenith Overseas section. Since some of the newly acquired publications were unprofitable Cornwallis was given a brief to develop a sales and marketing strategy to ensure that within eighteen months the operation was self-supporting, and profitable by the end of two years.

Conflict with the staff of the new publications venture had come to the attention of the main board and they had decided to review Cornwallis's proposals for restructuring the division. One hitherto unresolved issue was the question of the reporting structure of the ex-Pax publications. The chairman had been of the view that Cornwallis should eventually be promoted to the board and Pax made a full and separate division of the company.

ZENITH

Zenith had grown rapidly as a company by the production of magazines in specialized areas, and turnover had risen from £5.2 million in 1978 to £10.2 million in 1983, with profit increasing threefold over the same period. The company concentrated heavily on building up a portfolio of journals that would be mainly subscribed to by practitioners in industry, especially in the main growth areas of electronics and industrial health and safety.

The Pax acquisition (which had cost the comany £1.2 million) was seen by the chairman and initial founder of Zenith, David Wellington, as providing the impetus for the next stage of growth into the international market, an area in which Zenith had not, as yet entered. Furthermore, the development of expertise in the publications of manuals that were part of the Pax portfolio would enable them to 'feel' their way into book publication, which was seen by David Wellington as the most promising future sector for Zenith. Two other members of the five-man board were, however, extremely critical of the decision, for two reasons.

1. The price the company paid for the acquisition was extremely high, and it might well put a severe strain on company cash flow, already under pressure due to a £500,000 investment in new typesetting technology.
2. It was felt that Zenith lacked the management skills properly to exploit the market in which Pax publications had operated.

The current sales and profit of the various Zenith divisions are in Table C22.1. Each division operated as a separate profit centre represented at board level by a director. Within each division there were separate editorial and production staff, though the sale of advertising space was co-ordinated across the entire group. The main publications in each division are in Table C22.2. Each publication group analysed the market it serviced slightly differently, but a rough breakdown by customer type yielded the information supplied in Table C22.3.

The competition Zenith faced varied according to the market in which it operated. Pergamon Press was increasingly a major force in the industrial health sector and three major American firms had launched journals into the electronics sector in the past year.

The company now had net assets of £4.8 million and borrowings of £2.4 million (Table C22.4).

Table C22.1 Zenith current sales and profit (£ million)

Division	1978	1979	1980	1981	1982	1983
Electronics	2.4	2.9	3.8	4.6	5.3	6.2
	0.2	0.3	0.3	0.5	0.8	0.9
Engineering	1.5	1.2	1.4	1.8	1.7	2.0
	0.1	0.2	0.2	0.2	0.2	0.2
Industrial health and safety	1.3	1.5	1.9	2.0	2.0	2.0
	0.2	0.2	0.2	0.3	0.3	0.3

Table C22.2   Zenith publications

Division	Publications
Electronics	*Diagnostic Equipment News* *Electronic Measurement*
Engineering	*Control Systems Digest* *Cybernetics Quarterly*
Industrial health and safety	*Health and Safety* *Industrial Medicine*

Table C22.3   Zenith's customer profile (%)

Customer type	Electronics	Engineering	Industrial health
Companies	40	30	28
Institutions	25	34	42
Libraries	15	12	20
Professionals (architects, designers)	20	24	10

Table C22.4   Zenith: source and application of funds statement for 1983 (£ million)

Source	
Profit	1.4
Depreciation	.3
Application of funds	
Purchase of Pax	1.2
Fixed assets	.5
Taxation	.4
Stocks	.2
Debtors	.2
Creditors	(.3)
Funds required	.5
Increase in overdraft	.5

THE SITUATION IN 1983

On taking up his responsibilities for the Zenith Overseas section, Abel Cornwallis found that the company had taken over three distinct types of publication.

Global

Published quarterly, *Global* is a journal on development issues, which gives special attention to health matters – an area which Pax had traditionally made the centre of

Table C22.5 *Global* circulation by
profession (estimated)

Profession	%
Journalists	20
Aid administrators	30
Government officials	30
Libraries	12
Other	8

its operations. It cost about £500,000 a year to produce – in addition to the wage costs of the permanent staff – with a print run of 50,000 for each issue, each magazine costing £2.50. Currently the magazine was being produced on antique printing presses in north London, and Zenith proposed to bring the production in-house in its high-technology works at Swindon. This, and increasing the amount of writing by the permanent staff, would reduce production costs by 55 per cent, bringing the cost per copy down to £1.20.

The aim had been to give the magazine universal appeal, with articles by Third World writers rather than Western journalists, and it was published in English, French and Spanish, using in-house translators. In ten years Pax had been unable to sell the magazine – at the time of the Zenith take-over there were only 4,000 subscribers, 70 per cent of whom lived in the United States, who paid the full cover price of £2.50 plus postage (Table C22.5). Pax had achieved a high circulation by supplying bulk quantities to UN gatherings and other similar meetings free of charge. There was, however, a mailing list with 15,000 names in all parts of the world, a majority of whom also received the publication free of charge. With *Global* Zenith had taken on an editorial staff of three – two secretaries and a publications assistant. Wage costs ran at £65,000 per annum

Advertising revenue amounted to £25,000 a year, and came mainly from publishers promoting academic titles on Third World topics. *Global* had always avoided 'commercial' advertising of the type provided by banks, airline operators and drug companies. Initial research via Zenith's other publications strongly suggested that many of the multinational companies were starting to invest in corporate advertising to improve their public relations; hence *Global*'s concept of 'commercial' advertising was outdated.

Medical publications

A group of medical publications had been a particularly successful aspect of the Pax publications programme. The charity had made a name for itself by producing high-quality, easy-to-use publications for medical and public health personnel, written by acknowledged experts on the treatment of common health problems in the developing world. These publications, comprising a list of twelve titles, were regularly updated and well received and were available in English, French and

Spanish. Sales were achieved through the World Health Organization and through national health departments, which ordered them in bulk. They were, however, also stocked in specialist bookshops and bought by libraries. In 1979/80 Pax had sold 150,000 medical titles, producing revenue of £525,000 and a profit of £75,000 after allowing for wage overheads of £30,000.

The price of each publication had been fixed at £3.50, significantly undercutting the competing titles produced by American publishers, which had suffered throughout the 1980s from the effects of the strong dollar. Prices of American manuals were often over £9.00.

One of the reasons the Pax medical manuals cost so little was that acknowledged experts had written and edited them without charge to the non-profit organization. The attitude of the contributors now that the manuals would be produced by a profit-centred organization was unknown, but the relationship most of them had developed over the years with the editorial team at Pax was regarded as central to any change in the arrangements.

To support the medical publications a free newsletter, *Med News*, was published and distributed each month in English, French and Spanish. It had a mailing list of 20,000, and cost around £15,000 a year to print and distribute. An analysis of the readership showed that 25 per cent of recipients lived in the United States, 25 per cent in Europe, 10 per cent in Latin America, 15 per cent in India and another 12 per cent in Malaysia, Singapore and Hong Kong. The medical publications were the responsibility of an editor, two editorial assistants and a secretary.

In Brief

Promotional back-up for *Global* and the medical publications was also given by an additional free information newsletter, *In Brief*, which was distributed fortnightly to 7,000 recipients. By giving details and brief summaries of other publications and documents in the medical and aid fields, *In Brief* had acquired a name for accurate, reliable, up-to-date information which was distributed more frequently than other similar newsheets. In the three years in 1980 the *In Brief* mailing list had grown by 250 each year. Fifty-five per cent of the subscribers lived in the United States and 10 per cent in the UK. *In Brief* was produced by one individual with a part-time secretary. The production costs were low, around £20,000 a year, and the staffing costs ran at £15,000.

Each division of the former Pax publishing programme took a very independent stance. There was little if any communication between the editors, who had all been with the organization for more than ten years. As part of the take-over proposal Zenith had undertaken to guarantee the jobs of all staff for ten years. The reduction in other areas of the Pax headquarters staff had been achieved by voluntary redundancy, at an average cost of £18,000 per head. The expected cost of buying out any of the staff whose contracts had been guaranteed in this fashion would be considerably higher at an average of £70,000 per head.

THE MANAGEMENT STRATEGY

On the basis of this information Cornwallis made the following proposals as an initial strategy to begin at the end of 1983.

Global magazine

Free copies of *Global* would cease forthwith. The magazine would be available on subscription only and subscription tickets would be inserted into each of the magazines sent to the 15,000 names on the mailing list. There was no way that Zenith could distribute 200,000 copies of *Global* each year under the present circumstances. The print run should be reduced to 15,000 for all three languages, which would immediately cut the cost of production and postage.

It had been impossible to arrive at a clear reader profile for the magazine, which was something Cornwallis regarded as essential before any steps were taken to increase advertising revenue. The mail shot would help to supply some of this information, as well as information about response rates essential to attract further advertisers. Other mail shots would be inserted in the other publications to try to calculate the demand for *Global* in other areas.

As *Global* appeared to be read by influential decision-makers in the Third World, Cornwallis took the view from the initial research that substantial increases in advertising revenue would be possible, though the analysis of the readership would provide concrete evidence whether this would be achievable. Provisionally he had sketched out a programme for increasing advertising revenue (Table C22.6).

The task of selling the advertising space in the magazine would be handled initially by the experienced Zenith telesales force, but Cornwallis considered that by the second year one of the *Global* staff should be able to take over the function.

The editor of *Global* disagreed with this approach. *Global*, he said, had established an important place for itself at the international centres of decision-

Table C22.6   Programme to increase advertising revenue from *Global*

Source	Year 1 (£)	Year 2 (£)	Year 3 (£)
Publishers	25,000	27,000	30,000
Equipment companies	10,000	15,000	25,000
Banks	6,000	17,000	30,000
Construction	3,000	12,000	15,000

making, as an independent and impartial source of information. It would be a hopeless task to seek to change that by putting the magazine on subscription only and reducing its presence on the world stage. A more realistic approach would be to seek corporate buyers, UN organizations and international charities like Pax to buy and distribute large quantitites of the magazine. The reduction in the print run would make *Global* a far less attractive proposal to advertisers and would adversely affect the substantial advertising revenue it currently brought in.

Medical publications

Cornwallis suggested that the price for the medical manuals should be raised to £4.00. Coupled with the anticipated 25 per cent saving on production costs following transfer of the printing to Swindon, this should substantially improve profitability. Cornwallis appreciated that the market for these cheap, high-quality medical manuals was potentially very large and might possibly serve as an avenue for book publishers to promote titles overseas.

The success of the mailing list for *Med News*, currently distributed free, suggested that there were strong possibilities for selling advertising space to international drug and health care companies. Preliminary calculations indicated that Zenith could charge up to £3,000 a page. This would mean that if the number of pages were increased Zenith could more than cover the cost of the broadsheet, which could continue to be distributed free. A number of the major drug companies such as Merck, Schering and Sandoz had already indicated their willingness to take an omnibus page each, with descriptions of their ranges.

The medical editor was outraged that the impartial stance associated with the medical publications should be damaged by the taint of advertising. *Med News* more than paid for itself by successfully promoting other medical publications, and there were possibilities of further extending this coverage by broadening the scope of the publications unit into health, and disease control areas such as water treatment.

In Brief

To Cornwallis the steady rise in the *In Brief* mailing list over the past three years indicated that there was a demand for the information letter, especially in the United States. Examination of the mailing list had also revealed that 80 per cent of recipients were institutions – mainly libraries and research organizations. In other words, they could well afford to pay for the service. Furthermore, since the information supplied by *In Brief* was highly specialized it was believed that institutions would be prepared to pay a fairly high price for the service, as they did for similar publications. The provision of other information services built up around this concept fitted well with the expansion plans of Zenith, which had already developed an on-line database in the UK dealing with medical and engineering information. Cornwallis was of the view that a £1.50 cover price with an increased amount of information would be an acceptable first step, even though production costs would rise by around 15 per cent, even with the move to Swindon.

The medical editor again considered that this ran contrary to the established ethos that research data should be provided for those who needed it rather than for those who could pay for it. A third of the recipients of *In Brief* lived in the Third World, which was after all the main reason why Pax had built up its publications programme.

In contrast, the editor of *In Brief* – always regarded by the medical and *Global* editors as being of no account – was highly enthusiastic about the proposal, provided some of the staff on other publications could be transferred to help with the increased workload.

Part of the proposed streamlining required all staff to become familiar with the new technology Zenith used for its publications. This would involve intensive training on word processors and print-controlling equipment, none of which the staff had any experience of, and this was expected to take around three to four months. It would also mean regrading all staff, who would move on to managerial grades. Secretaries would be reclassified as assistant editors, assistants as editors and editors as senior editors, and all must move to the Swindon site. The regrading would not, however, affect current salaries.

Cornwallis was undecided as to the speed at which the staff should be transferred to the Swindon site, and was also considering whether it would make sense to reorganize the three divisions entirely as some streamlining of functions could be achieved without major changes in the way the staff currently operated. Part of the plan he had to present to the board would be his ideas on how the new division should be structured and how the current tripartite reporting structure could be simplified.

From the comments that he had received about his proposed changes to the operation of the Pax titles he also wondered about how to forestall or minimize the effects of likely staff resistance on the implementation of his plans.

Case 23

FANTSIS

BACKGROUND

Fantsis Ltd, a UK subsidiary of a worldwide fragrance company, had its main interests in women's perfume and cosmetics, hair products, and specialist bath products. In the UK, Belguim and France the company had also a sizeable men's toiletries operation, following an acquisition made as part of the company's international expansion, which had also provided the means of entry to the UK market. By 1985 worldwide turnover was £450 million.

The company was organized internationally on a product management basis and each division operated as a profit centre reporting to the international co-ordinator, based in Chicago, via the European group headquarters in Brussels.

Each division was headed by a general manager, with a team of three; a senior sales manager, financial controller and marketing manager. The numbers of junior, executive management and salesforce employed depended on the turnover of each separate divison. The corporate philosophy and main area of concentration of Fantsis had varied over the years, ranging from an initial marketing emphasis in the early 1970s, which had led to overseas expansion, followed by a sales drive in the late 1970s and early 1980s as market share had been pegged back following the growth in importance of the multiple chemists and grocers. Recently a slow-down in the earnings per share growth of the parent corporation and the acquisition of two large shareholdings by well-known Wall Street arbitrageurs had made the group tighten up its financial reporting and attempt to improve profitability.

In the UK Fantsis was divided into three divisions, which varied in size and profit contribution. The annual turnover of the group in early 1986 is given in Table C23.1.

Table C23.1   Fantsis UK 1986

	Women's perfume	Hair products	Men's toiletries
Turnover (£ million)	25	12	6
Market share (%)	8	6	4
Marketing staff	8	4	3
Sales representatives	10	4	4
Promotional budget (£ million)	2	1	2
Profit (£ million)	5	2	2

Table C23.2   Fantsis UK: turnover by outlet type (%)

	1975	1978	1981	1984
Perfume division				
Multiple chemists	12	15	15	25
Independent chemists	78	70	66	55
Multiple grocers	–	–	–	5
Independent grocers	10	15	19	15
Hair products division				
Multiple chemists	55	52	50	45
Independent chemists	10	7	6	5
Multiple grocers	22	27	35	42
Independent grocers	13	14	9	8
Men's toiletries division				
Multiple chemists	38	35	30	28
Independent chemists	40	33	27	22
Multiple grocers	22	25	22	30
Independent grocers	–	7	21	20

Table C23.3   Fantsis men's toiletries division: sales growth to 1986

Product	Annual growth £ million					
	1980	1981	1982	1983	1984	1985
Smooth hairspray	0.2	0.3	0.4	0.3	0.4	0.3
Smooth mousse	–	0.25	0.4	0.8	1.4	2.0
Total Smooth	0.2	0.55	0.8	1.1	1.8	2.3
Massif stick	3.1	3.0	2.9	3.0	2.8	2.7
Massif splash on	–	–	0.5	0.7	0.9	1.0
Massif spray	–	–	–	–	0.4	–
Total Massif	3.1	3.0	3.4	3.7	4.1	3.7
Total toiletries	3.3	3.55	4.2	4.8	5.9	6.0

In line with head office policy, these divisions had developed largely independent approaches to the market. The women's perfume division concentrated almost entirely on becoming established in premium outlets such as department stores and quality independent stores, whereas the hair products divison had concentrated on establishing a market presence via the multiple chemists and grocers. The men's toiletries division had varied over the ten years in the way in which it attacked the market. The hair products division had originally handled both male and female ranges, but it had been decided in 1979 that the specialist hairspray and growing styling mousse product range should be transferred to the male toiletries division. Hair products continued to sell Smooth shampoo and conditioner, which were seen as a separate market sector. One of the long-standing problems with the tripartite company structure was a considerable amount of sales overlap (Table C23.2).

MEN'S TOILETRIES DIVISION

Sales growth over the five-year period had been steady with turnover rising from £3.3 million to £6 million in 1985 (Table C23.3).

Management

The men's toiletries division was headed by David Grossman, aged thirty-eight, ex-Mars, General Foods, British American Tobacco and Xerox. He had been recruited to revitalize a division regarded by the Brussels headquarters as lacking initiative and drive. His background was that of sales and sales management, and he had little marketing or financial experience. His main experience in most of these companies had been putting together promotional packages for the major grocery multiples at national account level.

Marketing department

Reporting to David Grossman as head of the marketing department was Jeremy Davidson, aged forty-two, ex-Fabergé and Yardley. Davidson had been recruited by the previous management team to develop the Fantsis presence in the UK, and had been largely instrumental in increasing sales over the five-year period of the existing range of hair care products (the Smooth range), and stick deodorants and splash-on colognes (Massif). The initial new product introductions, styling mousse and cologne, had been successful and this had encouraged the product group to expand the range further.

The failure of the Massif deodorant spray, which had been variously described in the press as 'pungent', 'long-lasting', 'only for dog lovers' and – the *coup de grâce*, repeated on national television – 'for the man who has everything except lone-liness', had been the main reason why Davidson had been passed over for promotion when the general manager's job fell vacant.

Reporting to Davidson were David McAlister and Gynn Davies. McAlister, aged twenty-nine, had been in the division for five years and had previously worked for Birds Eye, the frozen food subsidiary of Unilever. He was brand manager responsible for the Smooth range. Gynn Davies, aged twenty-eight, had left Shulton – a major competitor of Fantsis – some eighteen months earlier to join the company and assume responsibility for the Massif range and the already well-advanced plans to launch the cologne.

Salesforce

The senior sales manager, Adam Kent, aged forty-four had been recruited five years earlier from the Avon Corporation, where he had risen to the position of area sales manager. He had been involved in building up sales via the national accounts of Boots, Underwoods, Superdrug and Medicare.

The remainder of the salesforce were split via television areas to cover specific geographical territories.

Mulan Akhtar, responsible for the London area, had joined the company after working as a sales assistant in the Underwoods chain; the remainder of the Home Counties and the TVS region were handled by David Divine, aged twenty-eight, who had worked for the company for the last five years. The northern sales representative, Hamish Mackintosh, aged twenty-six, had worked for the company for only six months, after a spell with Rowntree, the confectionery firm. He was responsible for the Yorkshire, Tyne–Tees, and Border areas.

The midlands sales representatives, James Smith, aged twenty-five, had worked for the hair products division before the hairspray and styling mousse ranges were transferred in the 1980s. There was no representation in Wales, Scotland, or the West Country as it was considered that the current turnover of the company could not justify the expense. This was one of the factors that would be continually reviewed as the division expanded.

All representatives called on a large number of outlets, with an average customer base of 1,000. In line with the Fantsis management style they were expected to make twelve calls a day, with a normal call cycle of two months per customer.

THE UK MEN'S TOILETRIES MARKET

The men's toiletries market had fluctuated considerably over the ten-year period to 1985, with a period of growth followed by decline in real terms and then renewed growth (Table C23.4).

Within this overall market there had been a considerable change in percentage market share. The roll-on and spray deodorant products had been replaced largely with splash colognes, the hairspray and hair treatment sector (Brylcreem, Vitalis) had been largely eclipsed by the rapid growth of styling mousse or gel products. Talcum powder had been the only market sector to remain fairly static in percentage share over the ten-year period. Recently the market had been showing signs of further restructuring with the introduction of men's cosmetics, and two

Table C23.4   UK men's toiletries

Year	Sales (£ million)
1975	65
1976	72
1977	77
1978	85
1979	92
1980	108
1981	115
1982	121
1983	130
1984	165
1985	190

Table C23.5   UK men's toiletries sale by sector (£ million)

Sector	1975	1976	1977	1978	1979	1980	1981	1982	1983	1984	1985
Roll on/spray	35	33	32	33	32	36	38	39	39	42	44
Splash	13	18	21	22	25	39	45	47	45	68	70
Hairspray	10	11	12	10	9	8	7	6	6	5	5
Mousse	–	–	4	11	16	14	13	15	15	23	24
Talcum	7	8	8	9	10	11	12	14	15	17	19
Cosmetics	–	–	–	–	–	–	–	–	–	–	1
Tanning	–	–	–	–	–	–	–	–	–	–	1
Total	65	72	77	85	92	108	115	121	130	165	190

Table C23.6   UK men's toiletries: 1985 sales by month (%)

Product	1	2	3	4	5	6	7	8	9	10	11	12
Roll on	2	3	5	7	10	8	8	7	8	7	6	29
Splash	3	5	7	6	11	12	12	11	7	6	5	15
Hairspray	5	5	4	3	4	5	4	11	12	11	10	26
Mousse	9	7	4	3	3	3	3	11	13	13	12	19
Talcum	6	6	5	5	7	9	12	14	13	5	6	12
Cosmetics	7	7	8	7	6	8	10	7	8	11	11	10
Tanning	15	16	13	2	3	2	2	2	1	11	17	16

N.B. Cosmetics and tanning based on American experience.

major companies – Schwarzkopf and Revlon – were testing men's 'face tanning' products in the south of England. (Table C23.5).

Historically, the market had been highly seasonal with the greatest proportion of product bought during the Christmas period, normally as a last-minute purchase falling into the 'I must buy something' category. Recently the changes in the product mix had meant that the degree of seasonality was reducing in the more recent product segments (Table C23.6). Thus, following American experience in cosmetics and tanning products, it was expected that the progress of the tanning product in markets where the sunny season was far shorter would change the seasonality pattern considerably and tend to increase consumption as well.

Market structure

The market could be divided into a number of sectors, each of which had specific distribution patterns, market segment and market pricing.

Superior

Products were highly priced, fairly limited in distribution. The market leader had been Aramis, but there were a steady number of brands in the sector such as Paco Rabanne, Cacharel, Dunhill, Yves St Laurent, Tabac, Yardley Black Label and Eau Sauvage. Prices in this sector varied considerably, ranging from £14 to £4 for 50 ml.

Premium

The premium sector of the market was the largest volume component with the most heavily advertised products, including Brut 33, Old Spice and Blue Stratos, Yardley Gold, Denim, Onyx and Insignia. Price for 50 ml within this sector of the market was around £3.00 by the end of 1985.

Standard

The standard sector of the market was characterized by own-label products, such as Lynx, Avon and Cedar Wood with prices from £2.80 to £1.50 for 100 ml.

Each product tended to be available in all possible variants. In other words, Blue Stratos would be available as a roll-on, stick and spray deodorant and as a talc.

All commentators on the market had noted the gradual movement of the market towards more expensive products during the 1980s and the proliferation of

Table C23.7   UK male fragrance market: share by type (%)

	1975	1981	1986
Superior	12	18	22
Premium	55	55	63
Standard	33	27	15

Table C23.8   Percentage of current users trying three or more men's toiletries products in single year

Age group	%	Socio-economic group	%
13–15	17	AB	45
16–20	60	C1	42
20–25	47	C2	28
26–35	21	D	13
36–45	12	E	8
45+	8		

(mainly) women's fragrance producers entering the market attracted by the steadily rising prices and profitability (Table C23.7).

As might be expected in a fashion industry, the market was not highly price sensitive, with brands holding their market position with high expenditure on both media advertising and sales promotions. The market showed a high level of brand switching, with consumers trying 2.8 products in the year on average. The amount of brand switching varied considerably with age (Table C23.8).

The Fantsis policy was to price at the top end of the standard market, just below the price of the premium products, in order to achieve sufficient margin to invest in brand-building activities.

The market was dominated by large, mainly international companies which were often subsidiaries of chemical or pharmaceutical combines. Though Fantsis was fairly large, it was dwarfed by comparison with the companies that operated in one or more sectors of the men's or women's toiletries market, including:

- Procter and Gamble
- Unilever
- Gillette
- Beecham
- Colgate-Palmolive
- Wella
- Schwarzkopf

During the late 1970s and early 1980s, the perfume trends had been away from lavender-based products towards stronger, more powerful fragrances based on musk and other aromatics. As a result market share had moved away from the original leader, Old Spice, towards Brut 33 and Blue Stratos.

Consumers

The men's toiletries market has changed – the type of buyer has changed as has the use of the product. In the 1970s women were the main purchasers of men's

Table C23.9   Percentage of adult population using men's toiletries at least once in last year

| Item | Socio-economic group | | | | | Age group | | | | | |
	AB	C1	C2	D	E	13–15	16–20	20–25	26–35	36–45	45+
Roll on	33	55	55	40	19	75	77	69	50	38	21
Splash	60	35	29	17	5	11	34	43	56	63	47
Hairspray	11	37	45	42	12	65	68	51	31	12	6
Mousse	31	25	20	11	7	55	65	55	45	18	8
Talcum	78	56	40	35	28	29	32	35	48	56	85
Cosmetics	14	8	5	3	1	56	31	16	9	3	1
Tanning	27	16	13	4	1	10	43	45	31	15	9

NB: Cosmetics and tanning based on American experience (West Coast).

Table C23.10 Percentage of population indicating usage who use men's toiletries more than twice a week

Hem	Socio-economic group					Age group					
	AB	C1	C2	D	E	13–15	16–20	20–25	26–35	36–45	45+
Roll on	21	25	22	15	7	56	61	55	34	22	19
Splash	43	17	19	12	2	5	25	36	37	38	20
Hairspray	7	21	22	25	5	26	45	17	15	3	2
Mousse	21	13	9	2	–	41	39	30	12	5	1
Talcum	62	45	34	22	18	13	17	23	35	42	65
Cosmetics	4	2	2	–	–	31	12	6	1	–	–
Tanning	15	11	8	–	–	3	18	23	25	14	4

NB: Cosmetics and tanning based on American experience.

Table C23.11 Profile of consumption by product category: men using toiletries (%)

Category	Socio-economic group					Age group					
	AB	C1	C2	D	E	13–15	16–20	20–25	26–35	36–45	45+
Superior	60	45	32	19	11	2	12	34	46	40	34
Premium	28	50	55	58	45	56	65	45	41	29	33
Standard	12	5	13	23	44	42	23	21	13	31	33

Table C23.12 Brand decisions (%)

Decisions made by	1975	1985
Women	45	15
Men	55	85

Table C23.13 Promotional expenditure by month (%)

Item	1	2	3	4	5	6	7	8	9	10	11	12
Roll on	–	–	–	10	15	15	–	–	16	25	20	9
Splash	3	2	–	7	9	12	2	3	12	17	27	6
Hairspray	9	8	–	5	4	–	–	4	15	14	13	28
Mousse	7	9	6	5	3	–	–	9	11	11	14	25
Talcum	–	–	–	8	12	13	15	14	11	10	7	10

Table C23.14 Market share by year (%)

	1975	1978	1981	1984
Multiple chemists	45	42	40	40
Independent chemists	50	32	23	15
Multiple grocers	3	20	31	37
Independent grocers	2	6	6	8

cosmetics, but by the mid-1980s it had become far more acceptable for men to be seen purchasing toiletries, and this coincided with the steady switch of toiletry product away from being solely received as gifts at Christmas towards a year-round consumption pattern (Table C23.9).

The usage patterns were also confused by the *frequency* with which the various groups used any product, and this showed considerable variation (Table C23.10).

Within the overall consumption pattern there was a fairly clear distinction between the age and socio-economic group and the type of perfume range purchased (Table C23.11).

The purchase pattern in the UK market had also changed substantially over the last ten years. Though women were still responsible for a large percentage of total purchases their involvement in the brand decision had considerably declined (Table C23.12). This change in the purchasing pattern was in line with the steady decrease in gifting as a component of the overall sales pattern.

Promotional expenditure in the UK market

As might be expected in a fashion industry, promotional expenditure was extremely high, especially around the peak buying period (Table C23.13).

Total expenditure on toiletries and cosmetics in 1985 was £86 million, of which men's toiletries accounted for around 12 per cent. As might be expected expenditure was concentrated mainly on roll-on/spray or splash products which together made up 66 per cent of total expenditure in the market sector.

The major companies' expenditure was estimated as follows (the estimates include the high common level of spending on consumer promotions).

- Brut   £1,100,000
- Aramis   £800,000
- Denim   £750,000
- Blue Stratos £700,000
- Old Spice   £600,000

Distribution in the UK market

The pattern of distribution in the UK market had substantially changed over the ten-year period. The aggressive growth of the multiple chemists led by Boots – but by the early 1980s followed closely by Superdrug, Underwoods, Medicare, Lloyds and other chains – had eaten into the share of the independents. Similarly, the multiple grocery chains such as Tesco, Argyll, Sainsbury's and Dee had all looked with interest at the high margins toiletries could provide as they sought ways and means of improving their overall profitability. The market audit, run by TGI market share information over the 1984/85 period, is given in Table C23.14.

The market was characterized by a very high percentage of direct sales; the independent chemists did not use wholesalers and expected the sales representa-

Table C23.15 Percentage of product brought direct by year and outlet type

	1975	1978	1981	1984
Multiple chemists	85	92	98	99
Independent chemists	96	94	95	93
Multiple grocers	100	100	100	100
Independent grocers	14	12	17	15

Table C23.16 Profit margins on men's toiletries by outlet

Outlet	Margin (%)
Multiple chemists	29
Independent chemists	36
Multiple grocers	28
Independent grocers	32

Table C23.17 Businesses and outlets 1986

Type of outlet	Businesses	Outlets
Large multiple grocer	384	18,632
Small multiple grocer	8,351	22,252
Single outlet grocer	73,890	73,890
Chemists	7,910	11,627

tives to call on them in person; the independent grocers had always tended to use wholesalers and continued to do so even though their market share was slowly increasing (Table C23.15).

Retailers bought direct because of the high margins achieved on all men's toiletries products (Table C23.16).

With the concentration of activity in fewer and fewer hands the number of outlets continued to contract at around 3 per cent per annum (Table C23.17).

Market share and price

Fantsis also used the TGI audit, which concentrated on the price and market share movements of the splash colognes, which held the largest market share and set the overall going market price for the remainder of the men's toiletries products (Table C23.18).

Experience of other markets

Fantsis, with its international network and its headquarters in the United States – one of the pioneering areas in the development of men's toiletries – was aware of

Table C23.18 Retail audit data (market share by outlet type)

1984 (by quarter)

Product	Chemists Multiple 1	2	3	4	Chemists Independent 1	2	3	4	Grocers Multiple 1	2	3	4	Grocers Independent 1	2	3	4
Aramis	3	3	7	6	10	11	10	11	3	3	3	2	4	4	3	3
Retail price (£)	6.50	6.50	6.80	6.90	6.85	6.85	7.05	7.05	6.50	6.60	6.70	6.80	6.80	6.80	6.90	6.90
Old Spice	13	13	13	16	15	11	12	11	13	15	13	14	8	9	8	8
Retail price (£)	2.35	2.35	2.45	2.35	2.55	2.55	2.55	2.55	2.45	2.65	2.65	2.45	2.35	2.25	2.45	2.45
Blue Stratos	15	16	16	17	13	13	13	11	13	13	13	11	4	6	7	4
Retail price (£)	2.05	2.15	2.15	2.45	2.25	2.25	2.25	2.55	1.95	1.95	2.05	2.25	2.30	2.30	2.30	2.40
Brut 33	22	18	17	16	14	14	12	12	29	27	26	25	38	32	29	27
Retail price (£)	2.00	2.20	2.40	2.45	2.30	2.40	2.50	2.50	2.25	2.45	2.55	2.65	2.35	2.55	2.65	2.65
Denim	5	6	9	8	3	4	5	6	7	7	8	8	2	3	4	5
Retail price (£)	2.35	2.35	2.35	2.35	2.45	2.45	2.45	2.45	2.05	2.05	2.05	2.05	2.40	2.40	2.40	2.40
Fantsis	6	6	5	6	3	3	3	3	4	4	4	4	4	4	4	4
Retail price (£)	3.75	3.70	3.80	3.85	3.90	3.90	3.90	3.90	3.75	3.75	3.75	3.75	3.95	4.05	4.00	4.05

1985 (by quarter)

Product	Chemists Multiple 1	2	3	4	Chemists Independent 1	2	3	4	Grocers Multiple 1	2	3	4	Grocers Independent 1	2	3	4
Aramis	5	5	5	5	10	9	9	9	2	2	2	2	3	2	2	3
Retail price (£)	6.95	7.05	7.05	7.15	7.15	7.25	7.25	7.25	6.90	6.95	7.00	7.10	7.05	7.15	7.15	7.25
Old Spice	15	14	13	12	10	10	10	9	13	12	11	10	7	7	7	7
Retail price (£)	2.45	2.55	2.55	2.55	2.75	2.75	2.75	2.85	2.55	2.55	2.65	2.65	2.45	2.55	2.65	2.80
Blue Stratos	18	19	19	19	10	11	11	11	13	12	13	13	8	7	7	7
Retail price (£)	2.45	2.35	2.45	2.45	2.55	2.45	2.45	2.55	2.25	2.25	2.35	2.35	2.55	2.45	2.50	2.55
Brut 33	16	15	18	26	12	12	12	11	22	20	19	18	25	23	23	20
Retail price (£)	2.50	2.60	2.60	2.70	2.60	2.70	2.70	2.80	2.65	2.65	2.65	2.75	2.65	2.75	2.85	2.85
Denim	8	8	9	10	7	7	8	7	10	9	10	11	5	6	7	9
Retail price (£)	2.35	2.35	2.35	2.35	2.45	2.45	2.45	2.45	2.05	2.05	2.05	2.05	2.40	2.40	2.40	2.40
Fantsis	5	6	6	5	3	3	3	3	4	4	4	4	4	4	4	3
Retail price (£)	3.85	3.85	3.85	3.95	3.90	3.95	3.95	4.05	3.75	3.95	3.95	3.95	4.15	4.25	4.15	4.25

Table C23.19   Market growth in the Western United States (£ million)

(By quarter)	1984				1985			
	1	2	3	4	1	2	3	4
Cosmetics	1.0	1.2	1.4	1.8	2.7	3.4	3.8	4.8
Tanning	2.2	2.7	2.6	2.9	3.7	4.9	6.5	8.4

Table C23.20   Projected growth in men's cosmetics

Year	Market share (%)
1984	0.2
1985	0.75
1986	1.5
1987	2.0
1988	4.0
1989	8.0
1990	10.0

Table C23.21   Current users of men's cosmetics/ tanning lotion as percentage of total consumers

Age group	Cosmetics	Tanning lotion
15–19	14	10
20–25	18	22
26–35	4	28
36–45	–	18
46–55	–	12
56+	–	3

the worldwide trends favourable to men's cosmetics and tanning lotions.

Market experience on the West Coast of the United States and Fantsis market research revealed that the market was rapidly expanding and the buying intention survey indicated that this growth would continue – a fact underlined by the growing use of some types of men's cosmetics by both pop and sports stars. In one recent report Cosmeta, the US-based toiletries research company, forecast that men's cosmetics and tanning lotions would be likely to make up at least 10 per cent of the US men's toiletries market by 1990 (Table C23.19).

The Cosmeta research indicated that the likely growth pattern for the Western United States would be along the lines indicated in Table C23.20. This research also showed that users of men's cosmetics would in the main be 'heavy users' of cosmetics, as consumption levels by current users tended to be higher than heavy users of colognes or deodorants (Tables C23.21 to C23.24).

Market research had shown that there was a considerable variation in the personality types of the potential consumer. Based on Fantsis's research the

Table C23.22 Current users of men's cosmetics/
tanning lotion by socio-economic groupings (%)

Group	Cosmetics	Tanning lotion
A	10	35
B	12	27
C1	6	15
C2	3	9
D	–	5
E	–	2

Table C23.23 Intended users of men's cosmetics/
tanning lotion as percentage of total consumers

Age group	Cosmetics	Tanning lotion
15–19	32	18
20–25	27	15
26–35	15	17
36–45	10	22
46–55	2	20
56+	–	12

Table C23.24 Intended users of men's cosmetics/tanning
lotion by socio-economic groupings (Question: 'Would you be
likely to use . . . under certain conditions?') (%)

Group	Cosmetics	Tanning lotion
A	34	55
B	21	52
C1	14	36
C2	9	21
D	5	15
E	2	8

consumption of men's cosmetics and perfumes appeared to be primarily associated with the 'pleasure-orientated' and 'achiever' groups in society, though in the United States the use of tanning lotions had reached a wider audience: that of 'he-man' and 'sophisticated man' (Table C23.25).

On another dimensional analysis exercise carried out on the VALS groups, it was found that those most likely to purchase tanning lotions and men's toiletries were the 'sustainers', 'emulators', 'I-am-Mes', and 'experiential' groups. It had been found that consumption of tanning lotion was likely to be acceptable to more groups than were men's cosmetics. It was, for example, noticeable in a proportion of responses from 'belongers' that tanning lotion was not immediately discounted as a potential purchase in the future.

Table C23.25   Profile analysis of male shoppers (US)

Group	% of adult male	Shopping style
Quiet family man	8	Practical, buyer of own brands
Traditionalist	16	Conservative, buyer of branded goods from well-known manufacturers
Discontented man	13	Price conscious
Ethical highbrow	14	Quality conscious; will buy fringe 'unusual' products
Pleasure-orientated man	9	Impulse buyer
Achiever	11	Status conscious, buyer of 'image' products
He-man	19	Buyer of masculine-orientated products
Sophisticated man	10	Fashion conscious, buys premium products

VALS LIFE-STYLE GROUPS

Survivors   The extreme poor who have come to terms with the fact that their station in life is unlikely to improve. The poorly educated, elderly and sick. Extremely conservative in attitude.

Sustainers   The poor who are trying still to improve their position. Younger, often part of the 'black' economy, with an often over-developed attitude to fashion of extreme types.

Belongers   The largest group of the population. 'Middle of the road', traditional, conforming, family oriented, patriotic. Their most important aspiration is to fit in rather than stand out.

Emulators   This group is attempting to copy the leading components in society. They will be interested in cost-competitive fashion.

Achievers   These are the individuals reaching the top of their particular activity. They are interested in displaying their achievement to others in their peer group, and conservative in attitude.

I-am-Mes   This group consists entirely of the young teenagers with their confusion of pressures from outside and inside.

Experiential   Similar in some respects to the achievers, they have high incomes but are more interested in personal hedonism than in impressing other members of the peer group.

Societally conscious   This group is primarily concerned with environmental issues, and the coherent development of society. It will be less interested in outward display than the other groups.

Integrateds   These are the individuals belonging to a small group who, according to the researchers, have 'put together the decisiveness of the outer direction with the penetration of the inner direction'.

THE FANTSIS DEVELOPMENT PLAN

Fantsis had tested the concept of both men's cosmetics and tanning lotion in the UK market as the test area most likely to be influenced by trends in the United States. The research had revealed a similar pattern to that established in the United States, with an increasingly high awareness of men's cosmetics and tanning lotion.

Due to its small position relative to its competitors, the company had decided that the introduction of a tanning lotion product to complement its current cologne range would provide the impetus to divisional growth, which had failed with the previous aftershave range. The company had carried out a small concept and perfume test to refine the proposed product further against the competition of Schwarzkopf and Revlon, and had come up with a product, pack and concept that were considerably superior. In the test 65 per cent of respondents preferred the Fantsis product to Revlon, and 82 per cent to Schwarzkopf.

The concept test had also come up with an appropriate brand name, which had the connotation of wind and rain and weatherbeaten ruggedness the company was attempting to portray – Tempest. The decision was taken on 1 April 1986 to hand over the project to the newly appointed product manager, Gynn Davies, to progress.

Production facility

The Fantsis product range in the UK, with the exception of the majority of the premium perfumes, was produced in a small factory in West London. Gynn Davies had received the following information on production capabilities and costing.

1. The facility could produce 8,000 dozen units of the new product per week in house. Any excess requirement would involve the use of outside packers, which would raise the cost by around 25 per cent, but would increase production by a further 12,000 dozen.
2. Storage of finished stock would not pose a problem though, in common with many men's toiletries products, the fragrance would slowly change over time and the production department therefore was keen to minimize stockholding.
3. The costs of the finished article would be:
   (a) perfume/lotion: £10.00 per litre;
   (b) bottle: £120 per thousand;
   (c) label: £20 per thousand;
   (d) carton: 20p per tray (containing ten units);
   (e) atomizer unit: 15p per unit.
4. As the most popular size of production on the market in the UK was 50 ml it was decided to concentrate initially on a single size, with an atomizer unit as a product to be sold in parallel. However, this would be possible only if the product were to be sold into the superior sector; for sales into other sectors, the

packaging mix would need to be reviewed and a 100 ml bottle introduced.

The introduction of any new cosmetic product required clearance from the DHSS, and there were various other time constraints on the production process that Gynn Davies was provided with (see following sections).

Table C23.26   Cost and timing information for Tempest launch

Item	Weeks required (n = notice)	Cost (£)
Product		
1. Check formulation for shelf life	12	–
2. Complete skin allergy trials	18	3,000
3. Gain clearance from DHSS	6	–
Pack		
1. Agency to produce pack design outline	2	–
2. Final concepts	3	1,000
3. Artwork of packaging	3	1,000
4. Bottle mould design	3	1,500
5. Bottle mould production	6	2,000
6. Testing production of final bottles	4	–
7. Carton design	1	400
8. Carton production	3	500
Sales promotion		
1. Agency to produce concept	3	500
2. Print material	6	400
3. In-store display racks	4	2,000
Salesforce		
1. Produce material for sales presenters	1	150
2. Book sales support for test market	8n	–
3. Sales conference	12n	500
4. Prepare presentation material	3	250
Media		
1. Brief agency	2	–
2. Finalize copy strategy	1	–
3. Approve storyboard/artwork	2	500
4. Pre-test advertising concept	3	2,000
5. Shoot and edit commercial	5	40,000
6. Book TV space	10n	–
7. Book magazine	10n	–
8. Book radio/cinema space	5n	–
Production		
1. Test run filling line	3	–
2. Advise third party filler	5n	–

Table C23.27   TV advertising costs and coverage

Area	% households	30-second peak cost (list price) ITV (£)	C4 (£)
London	20	12,400	750
Midlands	16	6,000	350
North West	12	5,000	200
Yorkshire	11	5,500	350
South	10	3,750	250
Wales	9	2,850	160
East	7	1,500	250
Scotland	6	3,675	100
South West	3	1,600	40

Promotional plans

There were a number of options open for promotional activity: cinema, television, magazines, newspapers and radio had all been used by Fantsis in previous campaigns; posters had always been regarded as unacceptable in that they were too unspecific.

Point of sale display had always been an important part of the launch of any men's cosmetics; the salesforce had also to be provided with support material and informed of the product in a sales conference.

Previously the company had occasionally used sales promotion, and public relations 'launches' for some of its products, outline proposals for which had been supplied by the advertising agency. The other uncertainty in the development of the promotional package was whether the company should go straight into national launch or carry out some test market activity first. The marketing manager supported the test market route, while the general manager wanted the product launched as quickly as possible to get into the shops ahead of the two current companies, Revlon and Schwarzkopf. To be realistic, the test market would need to run for at least six months.

The cost and timing information supplied to Gynn Davies is in Table C23.26. Media availability with approximate costs and coverage are in Table C23.27.

Television

At peak viewing times ITV's share of audience was around 50 per cent, Channel 4 around 5 per cent. During 1983 the average number of hours' viewing per household was 5.5 hours per day.

As a percentage of the total population in those areas in Table C23.27, 21 per cent of ABs lived in the London area, 21 per cent in the South, 17 per cent in the East, 15 per cent in the South West and 14 per cent in both Scotland and Wales.

Cinema

Cinema advertising is available on a TV region basis. The Cinema Audience Delivery Plan guarantees 1 million admissions for a 30-second cost of £12,800. The average audience profile of cinema admissions is:

- AB   25 per cent
- C1   35 per cent
- C2   25 per cent
- DE   15 per cent

Leaflet distribution

Using shared distribution with other leaflets, any particular area could be covered at the cost of £8.25 per cent per 1,000 homes. There are 18.5 million households in the UK.

National newspapers

Newspapers naturally vary considerably according to their socio-economic readership. The standard population profile is 39 per cent ABC1, 61 per cent C2DE. This compares with the percentages given in Table C23.28 for the different daily and weekly papers.

In addition to the national newspapers there are a wide range of regional

Table C23.28   Newspaper advertising costs and coverage

Title	Readership ('000s)	ABC1 (%)	Cost per page/colour if available (%)
Sun	4,084	24	22,000
Mirror	3,400	25	21,000
Express	2,000	51	14,000/40,000
Mail	1,800	55	14,000/30,000
Star	1,600	18	8,575/22,000
Telegraph	1,235	80	22,400
Guardian	472	77	14,000
Times	457	85	10,000
Financial Times	214	88	16,000
Sundays			
News of the World	4,698	23	22,610
Sunday Mirror	3,489	27	22,000
Sunday People	3,200	26	20,000
Sunday Express	2,500	60	34,000
Sunday Mail	1,600	56	14,750
Sunday Times	1,260	78	26,000
Observer	744	75	17,500
Sunday Telegraph	713	75	18,000

Table C23.29 Magazine advertising costs and coverage

Title	Readership ('000s)	ABC1 (%)	Cost per page/colour (£)
Club International	770	55	800/1,100
Fiesta	1,236	32	1,400/1,800
Knave	877	31	1,000/1,200
Mayfair	1,272	30	1,600/2,400
Men Only	1,112	15	1,500/2,100
Penthouse	1,077	25	1,100/1,850
Playboy	600	55	1,800/3,600
Smash Hits	2,244	n.a.	3,500/5,465
Melody Maker	397	n.a.	1,330/2,600
Sounds	515	n.a.	1,250/2,500
Record Mirror	404	n.a.	975/1,300

newspapers that could be considered, with full-page black and white rates amounting on average to £15 per thousand of the population.

Magazines

The details supplied by the advertising agency included magazines with a predominantly male readership, and others targeted at the younger age group. All magazines were monthly unless otherwise stated. The advertising agency was firmly of the opinion that half-page advertisements would not work effectively for the launch of a new cosmetics product, but could be used for later follow-up (Table C23.29).

Radio

Details for radio advertising on key stations only are in Table C23.30.

Public relations

Public relations was often extremely important in a high-fashion industry such as men's toiletries where personal recommendation was an influential promotional method. Fantsis would be able to hire disc jockeys and certain other personalities at around £2,000 per month. The company could also launch the product with a major press and client public relations 'event', as it had on previous occasions. This would cost around £4,500.

Sales promotion

The promotion suggested by the advertising agency revolved around the brand name 'Tempest'. The suggestion was to include a competition as part of the launch

Table C23.30   Radio advertising costs and coverage (key stations only)

Town	Adult audience ('000s)	30-second peak rate (£)
Birmingham	600	325
Bristol	150	63
Leeds	180	120
Liverpool	700	361
London (Capital)	3,000	750
London (LBC)	1,800	540
Portsmouth	200	83
Reading	150	80

(Adult audience refers to total weekly reach.)

package, with the prizes having an element of adventure and 'hardness'. These could include:

(a) a safari in Kenya;
(b) a raft ride down the Grand Canyon;
(c) a trip up the Amazon.

The cost of providing the prize and running the competition was estimated at £5,000 in addition to the leaflet costs.

The Brief

For 'Tempest', Gynn Davies was given the task of producing a marketing plan for Fantsis which would define:

(a) target market;
(b) distribution;
(c) price;
(d) promotion;
(e) expected market share;
(f) organizational issues;
(g) volumes;
(h) revenue;
(i) profit;
(j) test market or national launch;
(k) cash-flow implications.

Case 24

DRIVE-IN LIQUOR STORE

INTRODUCTION

The drive-in retail outlet is a phenomenon of many countries. In the United States drive-in restaurants are particularly common, and other facilities such as drive-in banks are becoming more popular. The phenomenon of the drive-in liquor shop is one of the features of the Australian retailing environment.

The licensing laws in Australia have made restaurant licences extremely expensive, which has led to most restaurants allowing customers to 'bring your own' (BYO) and charging a small corkage fee.

In the state of Victoria there are 1,400 hotels, of which 500 have separate drive-in liquor store facilities, open from 10 a.m. until 10 p.m. There are also a number of independent or multiple outlets which open from 9 a.m. until 6 p.m. These stores can survive only by offering substantial discounts to the hotel operations. This pattern of trade has had a considerable effect on the amount of liquor bought and consumed 'on-licence' in licensed premises compared with the amount purchased in off-licences.

The Liquor Commission for the State of Victoria, reporting in 1984, noted that

> 72 per cent of beer is sold for off consumption. Whilst it is not possible to ascertain the amount of wines and spirits sold by clubs or hotels for off consumption such amount would be considerable especially having regard for improved bottle shops and drive-in facilities installed by hotels in recent years. It thus seems likely that approximately 70 per cent of the litres of liquor sold is for consumption off licensed premises.

The drive-in bottle shops in Melbourne are usually situated on or near to a main road. The layout is similar in many ways to a petrol station, with a large forecourt, flags and awnings. Because the shop is often adjacent to a hotel there is usually parking space. The liquor is displayed in special packs leading up to and in front of the pay desk. Leaflets available at the pay desk contain a price list of available liquor and special offers.

The UK experience

By 1985 the number of drive-in operations in the UK was limited. There are three Kentucky Fried Chicken operations, of which two are franchised and the third – in south-east London – company-owned, having cost £500,000. The site was chosen for the following reasons.

1. There is a population of 70,000 within a radius of one mile.
2. The Old Kent Road is a major commuter route, with a road movement of 5,000 vehicles per hour each way at peak times.
3. Access is good and the site is clearly visible from both north and south.
4. There are few competitive fast-food or take-away facilities in the area.

The initial performance of the outlet was highly encouraging and the site achieved an acceptable level of profitability within six months of opening, despite little advertising or promotion, which appeared to indicate that the position of the outlet was crucial in the early success.

On the other hand, drive-in banks have proved unsatisfactory. Many of the experimental branches of the 1960s have closed, with no plans to open more.

THE ALCOHOLIC DRINKS MARKET

Total consumer expenditure on alcoholic drinks is estimated to have quadrupled in the period from 1973 to 1983, from £5.4 billion to £13.8 billion.

Expenditure on alcohol has remained a fairly constant proportion of household

Table C24.1   Household expenditure by sector (%)

Sector	1973	1983
Food	18.4	14.9
Drink	7.4	7.3
Tobacco	4.2	3.4
Clothing	8.4	6.6
Housing	12.7	15.0
Fuel	4.1	5.2
Durables	8.1	6.7
Transport	14.0	17.3
Entertainment	9.1	9.1
Other goods/services	13.5	14.6

Source: Family Expenditure Survey 1983/1985

Table C24.2   Leisure expenditure by activity (£ million)

In home		Outside the home	
Home electronics	5,150	Drinking in pubs/clubs etc.	8,715
Beer/wine at home	5,069	Eating out	4,475
Books etc.	2,736	Holidays	4,004
Total expenditure	14,485		21,200

Source: Family Expenditure Survey 1985

Table C24.3   Types of licence and numbers held

	Numbers held	
Type of licence	1973	1983
Full	63,878	69,136
Restricted on-licence	13,492	23,679
Licensed clubs	2,702	3,363
Registered clubs	24,593	27,192
Off-licences	29,710	40,853

Source: Retail Business Report 1985

expenditure over the ten-year period when compared with expenditure on food and durables (Table C24.1).

Many of these expenditure patterns have been influenced by government policy. The substantial and continuing drop in tobacco consumption is a result of steadily increasing tobacco taxation; fuel costs increased in real terms as the government moved towards privatization of both electricity and gas industries. As a major employer and export earner, the drinks industry escaped comparatively lightly with the rate of duty falling between the late 1970s and early 1980s in real terms.

The steady increase in the amount of leisure time available is an additional component in explaining the continued high level of expenditure on alcohol (Table C24.2).

The UK licensing system

The UK drinks market is regulated by a system of licensing which defines what an outlet can sell by the type of licence that it holds (Table C24.3).

The specialists' share of all off-licence outlets decreased from 47 per cent in 1972 to 28.5 per cent in 1982. Although specialists still accounted for over half the drinks turnover, the trend towards buying alcohol from grocery outlets is steadily increasing, and reflects the growth in the number of off-licences granted. The number of liquor stores on the high street has remained constant at around 10,000, but there has been a steady acquisition of off-licence outlets by the major drinks producers (Table C24.4).

The brewers' chain stores are characterized by a far higher level of turnover than

Table C24.4   Approximate numbers of off-licensed outlets held by major drinks producers 1983

Company	Subsidiary	Outlets
Whitbread	Thresher	800
Allied-Lyons	Victoria Wine	1,200
Bass	Galleon Wine	
	Augustus Barnett	1,000
Grand Metropolitan	Peter Dominic	800

Other drinks companies owned a further 1,200 outlets

Table C24.5   Structure of the off-licence trade 1982

Outlet	Numbers	Total turnover (£ million)	Per outlet (£000)
Big 6 brewers	3,109	690	221
Other brewers	3,574	602	168
Independents	5,083	431	85
Total specialist	11,766	1,723	146
Multiple grocers	3,451	819	237
Co-operatives	2,833	223	79
Independents	23,236	409	18
Total grocers	29,520	1,451	49
Total off-licences	41,285	3,174	77

Source: Retail Business Report 1985

Table C24.6   Alcoholic drinks outlets in London

Type	Numbers	%
Full on-licences	5,959	29.5
Off-licences	5,662	28.0
Restricted on-licences	4,595	22.5
Clubs	3,241	16.0
Others	0,000	4.0

Source: Mintel 1984

the independent outlets and often rival the multiple grocers' individual store levels of turnover (Table C24.5).

The market share of the multiple grocers is most marked in suburban rather than city centre areas. This is due to their concentration on larger suburban retail units, provided with parking, which can effectively be positioned only on the outskirts of towns in conjunction with the orbital road networks.

For London the pattern of licences is in Table C24.6.

Product changes

Beer sales peaked between 1979 and 1980, and have since declined with a small recovery in 1983. Sales of spirits followed the same pattern as beer but also had a shaky period between 1975 and 1976, although more was spent on spirits than on beer during this period. Except for a drop in 1975, and a small decline in 1980, sales of wine, cider and perry have been steadily increasing since 1973. Though the growth rates have been different, beer still accounts for over half the alcoholic drinks market, followed by spirits at 26.4 per cent and table wine at 12.5 per cent. Beer accounts for over 60 per cent of the on-trade's turnover, but just over 20 per cent of the off-trade's turnover. The off-trade is well ahead in sales of spirits and table wine.

Purchase patterns through off-licences

A survey carried out by the BMRB revealed that during the previous month 35 per cent of the total respondents had purchased beer, 31 per cent wine, 20 per cent whisky, and 12 per cent had purchased sherry. More men bought alcohol than women except for port and liqueurs but with the exception of beer, whisky and rum, men did not purchase alcohol to a greater extent than women.

Beer, cider and wine were shown to be more popular with the fifteen to thirty-four age group, while whisky and sherry were purchased most by those aged thirty-five and over. Beer and lager were bought predominantly by the middle to lower socio-economic groups, while port, rum, sherry, wine, gin and aperitifs were purchased more by the higher socio-economic groups. Whisky, brandy and liqueurs appeared relatively classless.

There is a definite trend towards lighter and milder (lower alcohol content) drinks, which began worldwide in the 1970s and is likely to continue throughout the 1980s and 1990s.

The drinking public have become more sophisticated and more experimental in their attitude towards products, and successful new product launches had opened up new sectors of the market.

1. Branded wine – Hirondelle, Piat D'Or, Blue Nun, Black Tower, Mateus Rosé.
2. Cocktails – Malibu, Bezique.
3. Alcohol-free beer – Barbican, Kaliber.
4. Cream liqueurs – Baileys Irish Cream.
5. Foreign lager – Foster's Hofmeister.

The increasing consumption of wine led to the growth of specialist outlets which provided higher than average quality and broader product ranges. The earliest of these ventures was Oddbins, which was eventually taken over by Seagrams, the Americans drinks multinational. In the mid-1980s the Majestic wine warehouses were successfully established in the London and Home Counties area, offering a

Table C24.7 Consumption pattern of alcoholic drinks by group (%)

Category	Beer	Brandy	Wine	Whisky	Port	Rum	Sherry	Cider	Gin
All	35	4	31	20	2	3	12	7	8
Men	44	4	31	22	2	4	13	8	8
Women	21	4	31	17	3	1	11	6	7
15–34	44	3	34	28	2	4	6	11	6
35+	28	5	28	34	3	2	19	5	10
ABC1	29	4	43	22	3	5	21	7	11
C2DE	46	4	22	19	1	1	6	8	5

Source: Mintel

Table C24.8 Specialist off-licence sales by product

Product	% of turnover
Alcohol	76.7
Tobacco	15.7
Groceries including soft drinks	4.1
Confectionery	2.5
Other products/services	1.0

Source: Mintel

discount service on case lots of premium wine. The large specialist stores and the multiple grocers were stocking a steadily increasing range of products. By 1985 the largest Tesco multiple in the London area was stocking over 200 different products, the product sectors broadly in line with the pattern of consumption (Table C24.7).

Off-licence sales are not limited to alcoholic drinks only, the range of non-alcoholic sales is widening all the time. The trend is towards larger outlets which can stock a wider range of goods. As pressure on profit margins increases, the off-trade has concentrated on new product areas with higher margins such as video, soft drinks, tobacco and confectionery (Table C24.8).

The overall sales figures disguise a considerable degree of seasonality, which affects the level of stock carried and the profitability of various types of product. For example, the vast majority of port sales are at Christmas and a well-managed multiple such as Marks and Spencer will stock the product throughout its stores only at this time of the year. In contrast, beer is sold throughout the year but achieves much higher sales levels during the summer months.

Changes in mobility

Much of the success of the drive-in liquor concept in the state of Victoria can be attributed to the high level of car ownership and the distances owners are prepared to drive.

Table C24.9   Car ownership by demographic group

Group	One or more cars (%)
Age	
15–19	74
20–24	72
25–34	76
35–44	83
45–54	86
55–64	63
65+	42
Socio-economic group	
AB	90
C1	79
C2	78
D	58
E	27
Area	
London/South	77
Anglia/Midlands	71
Wales/West/South West	77

Source: BMRB/Mintel Car Survey 1983

Car ownership in the UK has increased steadily since the 1970s, particularly in the twenty-five to forty-four age group (Table C24.9). It is thought likely to expand at around 1 per cent a year, with higher growth expected in the affluent South West and the twenty-five to thirty-four age group, the numbers of which will increase gradually until the mid-1990s, as the result of earlier 'baby-booms'.

FACTORS AFFECTING THE SUCCESS OF A DRIVE-IN LIQUOR STORE

Opening hours

Being able to open from 8 a.m. to 11 p.m. would be a major factor in the drive-in liquor store's (DILS) likely success. Regulations existing in 1985 would prevent the store opening all day on Sunday, but the proposed relaxation in the licensing laws would enable all-day Sunday trading.

Security

The large amounts of cash that may be held on site, together with the value of the goods themselves, would cause insurance and security costs to be extremely high, particularly as the site would be relatively remote from high street locations. The grant of a licence would pose few problems, as the main concern of the local police is to reduce under-age drinking and one must be seventeen to obtain a driving licence, and ownership of a car is unlikely below nineteen.

A substantial percentage of liquor sales would be by credit card and cheques (the industry estimates around 55 per cent of turnover). The cost of credit cards (approximately 4 per cent of turnover) would have a considerable effect on profitability but would improve security.

Location

The location of the DILS would have to be on one of the main commuter routes – not a motorway – into the centre of London. A position equidistant between the centre and the outskirts, such as the site occupied by the Kentucky Fried Chicken store, would be acceptable.

The site would have to meet the following criteria:

(a) no obstruction to traffic flow;
(b) no disturbance to local residents;
(e) it must be visually acceptable and fit in with surroundings.

The market that the DILS would attack would include both the non-commuting car owner and the commuter.

Within the London area there is a vast daily flow into the City from the suburbs, with 179,000 people commuting into Greater London between 7 and 10 a.m. The RAC, one of the main car breakdown services, estimates that the total flow of cars into London is of the order of 250,000 a day. Though there have been numerous attempts by the authorities to control the number of cars entering the centre by increasingly draconian regulations, traffic flow still grew throughout the early 1980s. The completion of the orbital motorway network, the M25, is expected to change the pattern of travel outside the central London area, and will affect heavy transport flow through the London conurbation. Initial research suggests that it is having little effect on car movements, which are largely radial journeys rather than circumnavigations of the urban area.

Research into the nature of London traffic flow suggests that the majority of car owners in the area are travelling up to two miles to shop, and some are travelling considerably further to work.

Size

The DILS must be of a size sufficient to:

(a) allow enough space for cars to drive in and through the facility;

(b) allow a wide enough range of product to be stocked.

To provide this sort of facility it is unlikely that a site much under 2,500 square feet will be viable.

Many of the main arterial roads pass through areas of decaying light industrial property where environmental considerations are unlikely to be important and where planning consent is unlikely to pose a crucial problem.

Layout

Display is a very important element in drive-in facilities. Large armoured windows would need to be provided both to display the product and provide the service point. Such windows could be introduced into most standard warehouse systems without too many complications. They would need to be of the toughest armoured glass available and installed behind a security grid.

Internally, the way the stock is organized within the store would need to be carefully monitored. It is likely that a large proportion of sales will be obtained from a few standard items, and these should be stocked close to the counter.

Product mix

As the DILS would be unable to service the impulse buyer, confectionery and other profit-earning products found in the typical off-licence would not be provided.

The product mix would need to be slightly varied from the typical off-licence, and directed more towards the car-owning population and reflect their buying patterns, with a reduction in the amount of beer stocked and an increase in the amount of wine (Table C24.10). The store would have to carry a considerable depth of product to compete effectively with the multiple grocers and the larger specialist stores – over 250 different brands would have to be stocked.

The DILS would have the potential to move large quantities of special offer products, especially wine, and this might lead to a reappraisal of the make-up of the product range, extending the range into soft drinks and mineral water.

Table C24.10   Changes in procuct mix: DILS and off-licence

	% stockholding	
Product sector	DILS	Typical off-licence
Cider	7	9.3
Beer	46	53.0
Spirits	14	9.6
Fortified wine	10	9.3
Table wine	20	17.7
Sparkling wine	3	1.1

Table C24.11   Comparative average case prices

Drink category	Price per case (£)	
	Wholesale	Manufacturer
Cider	9.84	8.52
Beer (112 cans)	32.20	27.72
Spirits	84.50	72.67
Fortified wine	44.94	39.55
Table wine	29.40	25.28
Sparkling wine	26.40	22.70

Pricing

The DILS would be able to buy direct from the manufacturers, without using wholesalers. The comparative saving per case would be of the order of 14 per cent (Table C24.11).

The DILS would have to undercut the prices offered in the local supermarkets, which the buying public would be likely to regard as its main competitors. This would mean that mark-ups of 22–25 per cent would be achievable on the bulk of the product range, though changes and re-evaluations of the product mix would enable this to be eventually increased.

Promotion

There would be a number of promotional channels available to the DILS to establish an initial consumer franchise.

Public relations

The introduction of a new retailing concept should allow the company to gain valuable local exposure.

Newspapers

Local newspapers are another possible option with a cost per thousand of a quarter-page advertisement of around £5.50 to £6.00. A typical quarter-page insertion would cost around £60.

Local radio

An introductory package on Capital Radio, London's main commercial radio, covering the entire Greater London area, would cost around £500 and provide a low cost per thousand (50p), The problem would be that of covering the entire area, only a small percentage of which would be likely to furnish potential customers.

Leaflet drops

The local area could be covered by leafleting, which might prove an effective promotional channel despite the high production cost per thousand. The cost would be around £400 for 5,000 leaflets (production and delivery costs included). These leaflets could also include a product price list and telephone number to enable customers to pre-order alcohol for collection.

External display

In the light of the experience of Kentucky Fried Chicken, the most effective promotional channel is likely to be a highly visible and well-designed exterior which would be noticed by the passing motorist. The cost of signwriting to this standard could be put at around £500.

Staff

Due to the long hours and the physical demands of the work, a full-time staff of five or six would be needed, divided into two shifts. The level of staffing would need to be reviewed once the target service time for each customer is determined.

Estimated start-up and running costs

Estimated start-up and running costs are supplied in Table C24.12.

The exact levels of stock costs and finance charges are an unknown quantity, but initial estimates suggest a stockholding of £20–25,000 would be necessary to obtain sufficient levels of discount.

Table C24.12   Estimated start-up and running costs for a DILS

Item	Cost (£)
Development costs (windows, access)	12,000
Alarm facilities	10,000
Rent for one year	4,000
Staff	30,000
Office printing, decoration etc.	15,000
Insurance	10,000

Case 25

AXE STORES

INTRODUCTION

Axe Wholesale Foods, a grocery wholesale cash and carry company, is a family-run private limited company with four warehouses in London. It employs about forty people but has no formal management structure, top management being heavily involved in day-to-day running operations. It experiences a high rate of employee turnover, the staff consisting mainly of women earning low wages – around 40 per cent below comparable salaries paid by the competitive wholesalers. Training is non-existent.

The two main directors, Mohammed and Walid Azarudinn, founded the company in 1970 with family money from East Africa. They continue to carry out all the buying and credit control functions. Now fifty-five and fifty-seven respectively, they faced the problem of succession and whether in the near future they should hand over to their three daughters, who had from time to time been involved in the business but were now all working away from London.

The company began trading in 1972 and achieved rapid growth at a time when the cash and carry industry was beginning steadily to contract. After a leap from £2 million sales in 1980 to £15 million in 1982, due to the acquisition of two nearby businesses which were failing, real growth in sales persistently declined.

Due to its location in north-west London the company benefited from rapid growth in property values over the five-year period to 1984. In consequence the mixture of freehold and leasehold properties owned by Axe has increased considerably in value, though the company faces continuing cash-flow problems, exacerbated by the continuing high levels of rates charged on businesses throughout the north London area; the Borough of Brent, in which the majority of the units are situated, had increased the rates fourfold since 1975, and further rises are likely.

Table C25.1   Axe: analysis of site sizes and operating details

Site	Size (sq. ft.)	Employees	Turnover (£ million)
1	10,000	13	3.0
2	16,000	15	4.8
3	6,000	6	1.6
4	20,000	16	5.8

Table C25.2   The Axe customer base

Customer type	Numbers (%)	Turnover (%)
Independent grocers	20	55
CTNs	50	15
Cafés/restaurants/pubs	10	20
Off-licences	5	5
Others	15	5

The company's four cash and carry sites (Table C25.1) are fairly close to each other. Site 1 is located in an industrial estate at Harlesden in north-west London; site 2 is four miles away in Wembley; site 3 is at the base of the triangle, in Cricklewood, four miles away from both the Harlesden and Wembley sites. Site 4 is in west London, six miles south-west of site 1.

Account base and product ranges

With nearly 1,330 accounts, all Axe products are sold through the four warehouses, each of which offers similar product lines competitively priced. Its customers are mainly drinks/CTNs and grocery outlets. Promotion is via a mail shot sent at three-weekly intervals and containing details of special offers, and listing three dozen or so key products which the stores are featuring during the month. As the mailing is sent to all customers it has become an significant element of the stores' expenditure. The customer base provides a varied level of total numbers and turnover (Table C25.2).

The customer split shown in Table C25.2 reflects the broad pattern of retail purchasing, with CTNs and grocers buying direct from the manufacturers less than other retail sectors.

Customers travel on average up to six miles to visit the cash and carry twice a week. Of these, 65 per cent of drinks/CTNs and grocery outlets purchase between £400 and £800 of goods in an average week. The purchasing patterns of caterers and public houses show a greater degree of fluctuation in purchasing patterns (Table C25.3).

Certain types of retailers do not often use a cash and carry: sellers of fresh and

Table C25.3   Buying patterns by outlet type

Customer type	Buying direct (%)	Using wholesalers (%)
CTNs/grocers	76	24
Caterers	67	33
Pubs/restaurants	80	20
Greengrocers	100	–
Electrical/DIY	93	7
Variety stores	75	25

Table C25.4   Axe account base

	1981	1983
Number of accounts	1,200	1,330
Number of active	800	700
Number supplying 50% of turnover	100	130

specialist foods, hardware and electrical goods, pet and toy shops, gift shops, florists, stationery and printing establishments. They either use specialist discount warehouses or purchase direct from suppliers, relying on the cash and carry only for odd items.

North-west London is a very cosmopolitan area. Large West Indian, Greek, Irish, Polish, Indian and Pakistani communities exist throughout the catchment area, with a range of ethnic restaurants and grocery outlets servicing each community.

Like other companies, Axe relies on a small percentage of its total account base for the majority of its business. A worrying recent development is that the overall number of active accounts dropped from 1981 to 1983 (Table C25.4).

Opening hours and organization

The four warehouses, all in good locations, open six days a week from 9 a.m. to 8 p.m. However, exits and entrances are poorly designed and customers wheeling trolleys sometimes find it difficult to avoid accidents. Further evidence of poor design is also evident in the warehouses, where display signs are sub-standard. Over the years the two smaller units performed less well than the two larger, due partly to the effect of the reduced aisle width of the smaller stores. None of the warehouses has been refurbished since acquisition, unlike the modern Makro store in the area and the refurbished Booker cash and carry. It is estimated that the investment required to upgrade each store is in the region of £5 per square foot and stores would have to be closed for an average of two months for the renovations to be carried out.

Particularly expensive alterations are needed to add further frozen cabinet space, where cost estimates are around £100 per cubic metre; expansion in this area and the installation of more racking for fresh vegetables would seriously reduce the two smaller warehouses' overall stockholding of other goods, causing problems with the minimum drops manufacturers are prepared to make.

Source of current turnover

The net profit margin has historically remained low, at 1 per cent of turnover. However, this is higher than some of the competition, though margins on sales in grocery retailing have traditionally been held at 4–5 per cent. The level of borrowings remains high and the company managers are concerned that the gross margins have dipped over the past two years to a level where it will become increasingly difficult to pay the interest on the loans (Table C25.5). This concern has increased with the opening of a giant Makro store in the centre of the Axe trading area (see below).

The estimated contribution from various sectors to Axe company turnover and profit in 1984 is shown in Table C25.6, and the sales history of each sector is shown in Table C25.7.

Table C25.5 Axe financial position 1980–84 (£ million)

	1980	1981	1982	1983	1984
Sales	2.9	8.2	15.7	14.8	15.1
Trading surplus	0.3	0.7	1.2	1.4	1.2
Salaries/wages	0.1	0.15	0.2	0.3	0.3
Interest	0.2	0.5	0.7	0.7	0.7
Net assets					
Fixed assets	0.8	1.0	1.2	1.6	1.8
Stock	0.3	1.4	3.0	3.2	3.3
Debtors	0.1	0.1	0.2	0.3	0.4
Net liabilities					
Creditors	0.3	0.5	0.7	0.8	0.7
Bank loans	1.3	3.0	4.2	4.0	4.0

Table C25.6 Contribution to Axe turnover and profit by sector 1984 (%)

Item	Turnover	Profit
Basic grocery	60	67
Fresh vegetables	10	6
Catering packs	15	13
Frozen	3	5
Alcohol	8	11
Tobacco	4	−2

Table C25.7   Axe five-year sales history (% sales by year)

Item	1980	1981	1982	1983	1984
Basic grocery	68	66	65	63	60
Fresh vegetables	3	6	8	10	10
Catering packs	9	10	11	12	15
Frozen	2	2	3	3	3
Alcohol	6	6	6	6	8
Tobacco	12	10	7	6	4

Table C25.8   Axe floor space allocation (%)

Item	Space
Basic grocery	75
Fresh vegetables	5
Catering packs	10
Frozen	3
Alcohol	5
Tobacco	2

Each store allocates the same percentage of floor space to particular areas of the business (Table C25.8).

THE INDUSTRY

Cash and carry grew rapidly to a dominant 60 per cent of the UK grocery wholesale trade at the beginning of the decade, and has since increased its share from 61 per cent in 1980 to 66 per cent in 1983, with a further 1 per cent in 1984 (Table C25.9).

Cash and carry outlets were, however, finding growth increasingly difficult to achieve, as the delivered trade continued to hold on to a substantial part of the market by providing credit, a very important factor especially for CTNs and grocers (Table C25.10).

The delivered wholesale sector has different operating criteria from the cash and carry industry. A typical delivered wholesaler such as ACS Automatic Catering Supplies employs a field salesforce and has a large fleet of delivery vans. The margins on which they operate must, therefore, be higher than those in the cash and carry sector, in addition to the cost of providing credit.

Given the concentration and rationalization for one-stop shopping, the need for large financial resources to carry stock and maintain credit in the delivered sector of the market is obvious. Companies with favourable locations and access to manufacturers enjoy the advantages of good trading terms through volume purchase. There is also cumulative experience accruing to established firms in terms of distribution, but the most conspicuous economies of scale lie in larger warehouses offering one-stop shopping.

Table C25.9 UK wholesale grocery trade 1980–83 (£ million)

Year	Total sales	Cash and carry	Market share (%)	Delivered trade	Market share (%)
1980	3,750	2,305	61	1,445	39
1981	4,989	3,166	63	1,823	37
1982	5,192	3,356	65	1,836	35
1983	5,593	3,685	66	1,908	34

Table C25.10 Importance of attribute in purchase decision from cash & carries (1 = low, 5 = high)

Store sector	Credit	Convenience	Price	Product range
CTNs/grocers	1	2	4	3
Caterers	4	1	3	2
Pubs/restaurants	3	1	2	4
Hardware/DIY	4	1	3	1
Greengrocers	4	3	2	1

Table C25.11 UK cash and carry sector

Company	Sales (£ million)	Market share (%)	Depots	Sales per depot (£ million)
Booker	656	16	109	6
Nurdin	516	13	31	17
Linfood	287	7	96	3
Lonsdale	145	4	13	11
Batleys	128	3	8	16
Makro (est)	120	3	6	20

THE CASH AND CARRY SECTOR

The trend towards larger and larger units is also happening in the cash and carry sector, which has changed over the last fifteen years from a very fragmented industry with a large number of small warehouses to steadily larger units owned by a smaller number of companies.

Nine companies accounted for 50 per cent of the sector's total sales in 1984, all but three either maintaining or improving their market position (Table C25.11).

With low bargaining power over suppliers many of the small companies like Axe have been forced out of business. Some have been compelled to form groups simply to gain volume discounts and good trading terms from manufacturers.

The larger groups are also able to invest heavily in a number of areas which are essential for long-term market survival.

Table C25.12   Cash and carry own-label lines

Company	Brand names	Approximate no. of lines
Linfood	Hallmark	375
ICCG	Sterling	309
N & P	Peacock	300
Lonsdale	ShopLocal	230
Makro	Aro	200
Consort	Consort	195
	Our Generic	50
Keencost	Maytree	150
Booker	Family Choice	100
Batleys	Batleys	60

Table C25.13   Major companies' average store size

Company	Average size (sq. ft.)
Booker	28,000
Linfood	29,000
Landmark	40,000
Nurdin & Peacock	70,000
Makro	140,000

Computerization

For the larger wholesale chains investment in microprocessor systems is fairly far advanced and companies like Makro consider this essential to maintain the high level of turnover required at the low margins on which they operate. The cost of installation, with the minicomputer necessary to monitor the stock levels, is about £120,000 per outlet. Its introduction means that companies can monitor inventories more effectively and no longer need to mark up goods individually in the warehouse, and also provides a speedier flow through the check-out points.

Own-label development

Major companies are also following the retail grocery trends by increasing investment in own-label produce, which is becoming an important contributor to both sales and profit (Table C25.12).

Increasing depot size

All the major cash and carry companies have been enlarging the average size of their depots, closing small units and opening newer and larger ones often in out-of-town locations (Table C25.13).

Table C25.14 Comparative prices of Axe and major competitors by key product line

Product	Makro	Tesco	Axe
Heinz beans	0.27*	0.27*	0.28
Persil Auto E20	2.25	2.40*	2.45
Smirnoff vodka	6.20	6.60*	6.40
Blue Nun	2.20	2.50	2.35
Gordon's gin	6.80*	6.85*	6.90
Echo margarine	0.14*	0.15*	0.14
Anchor butter	0.47*	0.48	0.49
5 lb frozen peas	1.20	1.18	1.32
Birds Eye burgers	0.55*	0.64*	0.68
Andrex (4)	1.00*	1.08*	1.15
Campbell's soup	0.24	0.25*	0.25
Mars (4)	0.63	0.69	0.65
B & H Gold (20)	1.42	1.45	1.51
Flour (2 kilo)	0.50	0.55	0.55

*Special offer prices.

The small cash and carry companies are, in contrast, unable to exert as much influence over their suppliers and so are steadily less able to compete on price (Table C25.14).

Changes in customer base

The customers buying from cash and carry wholesalers were also changing. As the giant multiples reduced the market share of independent grocers, retail buying groups like VG and Mace became more important.

For example, the number of independent retail outlets dropped from over 100,000 in the late 1970s to around 70,000 by 1984; CTNs had similarly declined from 50,000 to 35,000 over the same period.

The purchasing power of the major retailing groups was such that a rising percentage of outlets were buying from them rather than wholesalers for resale to the consumer. This applied to around 25 per cent of retailers in the London catchment area and 30 per cent of caterers. The retail giants offered lower prices and often, for the caterers, longer opening hours than those of the cash and carries.

Changes in the grocery market

Clear trends emerged in the grocery market during the early 1980s (Table C25.15).

1. There was a steady increase in the amount of frozen food (per capita consumption of frozen vegetables had, for example, increased from 0.9 kg per annum in 1980 to 3.5 in 1984).

Table C25.15   Consumption per capita per
annum (kg unless otherwise stated)

Product	1980	1984
Milk	132	125
Meat	56	54
Fish	8	7
Oils/fats	24	26
Sugar	45	46
Fruit	76	84
Vegetables*	72	81
Grain	70	67
Alcohol (litres)	130	130

*Excludes potatoes.

2. The amount of convenience food purchased was steadily increasing.
3. There was a movement towards larger packs of all items.
4. Sales of alcohol remained static overall even though there had been a growth in certain areas such as wine, up from 8 litres in 1980 to 11 litres in 1984 per capita.
5. Confectionery and tobacco sales continued to show a slow decline.
6. There was a steady increase in the consumption of both 'healthy' food and a wider range of exotic meals.

The local competition to Axe

In early 1983 a large 120,000 square feet Makro cash and carry warehouse opened in the centre of the Axe trading area. This added to the already extensive competition provided by a small Booker outlet (16,000 square feet) and four other wholesalers. The Makro catchment area was larger than that of Axe with customers travelling up to twenty miles to visit the store, which stocked both food and non-food items. The total number of card holders using the store rapidly grew to over 14,000, but many of these were individuals who acquired cards from positions in clubs and societies, which enabled them to do the weekly shopping through a cash and carry. The company carried out extensive mailings, concentrating on special offers both of own-label products and branded goods; the site also provided cheap petrol as a further incentive to visitors.

Further competition came from the new retail superstores opening on the North Circular Road and near the M1; Tesco, Asda and Carrefour all offered late-night shopping (up to 10.30 p.m.) and highly competitive prices.

Table C25.16   Results of Axe questionnaire – % customers interested

Service	CTNs/grocers	Caterers	Pubs/off-licences
Opening: 0700–2200	18	10	33
0900–1700	23	14	42
0900–2200	55	76	25
7-day week	59	20	25
Credit	21	17	–
Order planning	–	–	–
Wider range	49	40	–
Delivery service	29	20	–

Axe market investigation

To help find a solution to the increasing problems faced, Axe used a small questionnaire to ascertain the services that its customers would like a cash and carry operation to offer (Table C25.16).

The trading position was further complicated by the fact that a number of small customers were now preferring to shop in the three superstores in the area, Tesco, Asda and Carrefour, with their late-night opening and very competitive prices.

Current position

Barclays Bank, which had for many years provided the banking facilities for Axe, is increasingly concerned about the financial strength of the company, especially in the light of the high and rising level of group borrowings.

Recently the labour force became unionized by USDAW, and the two directors face an imminent strike for higher wages.

Case 26

BARNET PUBLICATIONS LIMITED

BACKGROUND

Barnet Publications Ltd was founded in 1963 by two partners, Robin Adamson and Richard Herdman, who had both worked in publishing for ten years. They had seen that the market for British and European technical and management textbooks was being inadequately filled, the majority of the material available being supplied from the United States in untranslated form. From their Surrey base they had actively recruited British and European academics to write authoritative texts in the main management areas.

The company grew slowly in the mid-1960s, achieving a £1 million turnover by 1976. After 1980 progress had been more rapid. In 1984 the company had taken over the technical list of another publisher, the *Factbook* range, to diversify into providing manuals for the business practitioner market. This expansion of titles had involved moving to new premises to bring distribution and packing, previously handled by third parties, in house. This acquisition and move unfortunately coincided with government higher education cut-backs, which led to a reduced level of sales for many of Barnet's main education texts. As a result, the company experienced a negative cash flow in 1984 (Table C26.1), and it became necessary to improve analysis of likely demand and pricing of the current and proposed book range.

The take-over of the additional list meant seeking additional financing from outside in the form both of increased borrowings and a change in the shareholdings. Barnet's West German distributor, a division of the multinational Bertelsmann Group, now held 30 per cent of the enlarged shareholding; its printer Octavo Press held 22 per cent; and the two founding directors 24 per cent each. Problems with cash flow had made the directors look much more closely at the entire list and

Table C26.1   Source and application of funds 1984 (£000)

From: operations and depreciation	470
To working capital	182
debtors	(2)
other provisions	(76)
fixed assets	324
cash element of take-over	196
taxation	60
Funds required	214

the way in which Barnet carried out its business. Barnet typically brought out around twenty new books each year and retired around ten with a net gain of ten a year. With the acquisition of the *Factbook* range the list had already been substantially expanded and every new project was being carefully scrutinized for pricing and profitability considerations.

Barnet continued to maintain an impressive record for retaining staff: of the thirty-seven employees, eight had been with the company since the late 1960s, and the average length of service was ten years.

In 1984 company personnel was as follows.

1. Four directors (including the founders as joint managing directors – Adamson, also finance director, and Herdman also marketing director).
2. Three editors.
3. Seven production staff.
4. Two accounts staff.
5. Four distribution staff.
6. Four UK sales representatives.
7. Two overseas sales respresentatives.

THE MARKET

The exact size of the market in which Barnet operated was hard to define. Statistics existed for broad divisions between 'professional' (which included all educational texts) and 'leisure' reading, which gave some indication of the broad value of the market sector (Table C26.2).

In addition to their UK sales, British publishers export around 40 per cent of their UK production, and Barnet was no exception, having a major market for its business books in West German academic institutions.

Before the *Factbook* acquisition, Barnet had concentrated on the tertiary education market both at home and overseas. By the 1980s there were around 840,000 full- or part-time students at university or college. Both the educational and practitioner markets were demanding increasingly up-to-date texts, and Barnet was finding that new editions were necessary every two years in most fast-moving areas of business management in order to compete with the other publishers in the sector.

Table C26.2   Market size and growth (£ million, manufacturers' selling price)

	1978	1979	1980	1981	1982	1983	1984
Professional	230	240	270	280	295	300	240
Leisure	450	475	465	502	550	640	680

Table C26.3   Market shares of Barnet's competitors (%)

Company	Share
McGraw-Hill	12
Macmillan	10
Longman Group	8
Gower	8
Wiley	5
Prentice-Hall	4
Addison-Wesley	4

THE COMPETITION

There were seven major competitors in what was a highly fragmented market, four American and three British. Market shares were estimated by the Barnet management to be very approximately those in Table C26.3.

In the early 1980s take-overs had started to concentrate the industry into a smaller number of large operators, and this was an additional reason why the original founders of Barnet had looked for funding from outside companies. Each company had specific areas of expertise and professional contact, tending to specialize in certain management areas and teaching levels. Barnet saw itself as operating at the premium end of the market and its purchase of the *Factbook* range was a further move in this direction.

DISTRIBUTION

The outlets for professional titles were limited to:

(a) forty-five university bookshops;
(b) fifty-five polytechnic and college of higher education bookshops;
(c) 300 academic bookshops in major towns.

The sale of academic books depended heavily on the personal recommendation of the lecturer on a specific course, and promotion tended to be limited to direct mail to individuals likely to be interested in particular titles and by the large-scale printing and distribution of catalogues.

BOOK PRODUCTION AT BARNET PUBLICATIONS

Barnet followed a procedure similar to other academic book publishers.

Each year an editorial panel consisting of the main board of directors and three outside advisers decided upon the direction of company publications and the broad areas where material would be commissioned. With this broad direction in mind, the three editors dealt both with unsolicited synopses and manuscripts and maintained contact with the academic and business world. This contact provided the vast majority of the eventual published material (over 80 per cent in most years).

Would-be authors were asked to provide a detailed synopsis of the proposed material, which normally took a month to complete. The synopsis was then considered by an internal review board which met every week and the author was then asked to prepare three sample chapters which, if approved, would supply the basis for a contract. This preparation period took an average of two months.

The three sample chapters were sent to a number of outside reviewers for comment, which were discussed at a weekly review meeting of the directors and editors. This process took a further month but could be longer, at the end of which provided the external and internal comments were favourable, the contract would be finalized. Sixty per cent of manuscripts submitted passed at the initial review stage. Of the remaining 40 per cent, half were accepted following extensive redrafting and a further review process, and the remainder were turned down.

On average, authors took nine months to complete a manuscript and rarely completed them on schedule. On receipt of the completed manuscript, editors could, and usually did, send the final draft to outside reviewers again. It would take one month on average before the draft had been returned by all the reviewers. Frequently their comments would necessitate further redrafting before the manuscript was finally ready for copy editing. Barnet found that it could take up to two months from the receipt of a completed manuscript to the start of copy editing. Editors exercised a key controlling influence on the length of this process.

Most publishers have a 'house style' and, once the final manuscript was accepted, the entire book was copy edited to make the presentation of the material consistent with that style; to check spelling, punctuation and grammatical mistakes; and to provide the printer with instructions as to headings, layout and other typographical detail. In the *Factbook* series, the house style was especially important as the aim was to achieve a consistent approach from volume to volume. The copy editing would therefore be an intensive and laborious exercise. The copy-edited material was then checked by the author. Copy editing took an average of two months but was expected to take three for the *Factbook* series.

Table C26.4   Barnet Publications' current list of titles

Title	Extent (pp.)	Price (£)
Finance		
F1 Finance for the Non-Financial Manager	224	12.95
F2 Training in Finance Management (2 vols.)	600	18.95
F3 Basic Accounting Factbook	1,056	26.95
F4 Presenting Accounts	500	18.95
F5 Using Cost Accounting	824	18.95
F6 Accounting for Managers	600	18.95
F7 Local Government Financing	140	8.95
F8 Government Financial Control	512	12.95
F9 Financial Markets	524	18.95
F10 Corporate Financial Policy	634	18.95
F11 Budgeting Decision Making	160	7.95
F12 Basic Financial Management	600	16.85
F13 Global Finance	394	22.95
F14 Financial Control for the Multinational	794	18.95
F15 Security Investment Factbook	600	26.95
F16 Individual Finance	300	14.95
F17 What is Money?	544	18.95
Computers in Business		
C1 Spreadsheet Applications for IBM	160	25.00
Spreadsheet Applications for Macintosh	176	25.00
Spreadsheet Applications for Apricot	152	25.00
C2 Using the Computer for Management	250	27.00
C3 Computer Logic and Programming	160	16.55
C4 Network Planning in Business	488	25.95
C5 An Introduction to Network Planning	460	24.75
C6 Linear Programming Factbook	600	26.95
C7 Chip Design Factbook	800	29.95
Economics		
E1 Understanding Economics	600	18.95
E2 Economics Today	400	12.95
E3 The Theory of Macroeconomics	500	14.95
E4 The Role of International Banking	300	13.95
E5 A Study of Exchange Rates	250	15.95
E6 Management of the Developing Economy	523	23.95
E7 Third World Industrial Development	400	18.95
E8 Economic Model Factbook	600	26.95
Organizational Theory		
O1 Dynamics of Management	350	12.95
O2 What is Management?	600	18.95
O3 Basic Management Concepts	650	15.95
O4 Job Satisfaction and Productivity	250	15.95
O5 Women in Management	350	15.95
O6 How Organizations Learn	300	12.95
O7 Organizational Development Strategies	150	8.95
O8 Organizational Change	100	8.95
O9 Systematic Organizational Change	150	8.95
O10 Modern Management and Organization	250	12.95

Table C26.4 *(contd.)*

Title	Extent (pp.)	Price (£)
O11 Analysing Organizational Structures	150	8.95
O12 Job Development Factbook	600	26.95
O13 A Model of Organizational Dynamics	100	8.95
O14 Strategic Issues of Personnel Benefits	250	12.95
O15 The Expanding Firm	100	8.95
O16 Careers: The Individual vs Organization	225	12.95
O17 Organizational Conflict	150	8.95
O18 Psychology and Physiology in Workplaces	400	18.95
O19 Automation: Office Manager's Factbook	600	26.95
Management Techniques		
P1 Effective Management in Government	200	12.95
P2 Business Culture and Personnel	350	18.95
P3 Management Control Systems	200	12.95
P4 Productivity and New Technology	400	18.95
P5 Business, Government and Unions	300	12.95
P6 Management Styles	250	12.95
P7 The Challenge of Japanese Corporations	300	12.95
P8 Business Management and Personnel Policy	400	18.95
P9 Management and Work	200	8.95
P10 Management Guide to Public Relations	300	18.95
P11 Achievers and Management	250	8.95
P12 Effective Business Presentation	150	8.95
P13 Personnel Development Factbook	500	26.95
P14 Team Development – Management Techniques	200	12.95
P15 Japanese Production Control Systems	260	18.95
P16 Industrial Relations Factbook	600	26.95
P17 Information Management Techniques	400	18.95
International Business and Marketing		
I1 The International Business Environment	600	18.95
I2 The Diffusion of Technology	400	18.95
I3 Small Business Planning	200	8.95
I4 Organizational Planning Models	500	18.95
I5 Business Law Factbook	780	26.95
I6 Selling Techniques	200	8.95
I7 Franchiser's Factbook	600	26.95
I8 Retailing Management and Strategy	700	18.95
I9 Modern Sales Management	300	12.95
I10 Industrial Marketing	250	8.95
I11 Marketing Factbook	550	26.95
I12 The Market Researcher's Factbook	909	26.95
I13 Business Statistics Factbook	600	26.95

After copy editing, the manuscript was sent to the printer for the production of proofs, which averaged a further two months as Barnet often used overseas printers to reduce printing costs. When received, proofs were checked by both author and publisher, a process taking about a month, and finally the book was printed and despatched to Barnet's warehouse, which process took a further three to four months. From the initial contact with the potential author to printed copy could take from eighteen months to two years. New editions required substantially shorter time scales – around eight months, unless the material was substantially altered in which case a year would be regarded as reasonable. Reprinting an existing work took only three months.

Table C26.4 gives Barnet's current list.

Barnet's forecasting system

Because of the individual nature of each title, the Barnet approach to forecasting and decisions on whether to commission new books was qualitative rather than quantitative. Each editor put forward individual titles and market pricing based on experience of individual market sectors and historical evidence as to how similar books had sold in the past.

Book costing structure

Books have low marginal production costs but require high levels of initial investment, which make further demands on cash flow. In consequence books are highly volume sensitive; long print runs lower the unit cost and hence significantly improve profitability. Barnet's costings for average investment are in Table C26.5.

Once the book was typeset, the additional costs of production were low, averaging 6p per page, including the cover and dust jacket. Further print runs incurred additional but lower 'set-up' costs at the printer, of around £400.

Other elements in the costing equation

Barnet sold very few books direct to the purchaser, the majority being sold by

Table C26.5   Barnet's costings for average investment per title

Item	£
Editorial panel cost	100
Review costs	150
Copy editing	400
Production of tables/illustrations	250
Proof editing	100
Indexing	100
Cover design	200
Author's advance	500
Printer's 'set-up' costs	800
Total	2,600

Table C26.6   List price and revenue (£)

	UK retail	Overseas
List price	15.00	15.00
Margin	4.50	6.00
Author's royalty	1.00	0.90
Barnet revenue	9.50	8.10

retailers or overseas distributors to bookshops. Normal retail margins were 30 per cent; overseas distributors worked on around 45 per cent. The agreed royalty payment to the author was deducted from the trade price. This varied according to the level the individual author was able to negotiate; normal terms were 10 per cent, but some authors commanded 12.5 or 15 per cent. The implication of this was that a book priced at, say, £20 would in reality produce substantially lower revenue to the company (Table C26.6).

For a typical £15 book with around 500 pages, Barnet would need to sell around 375 copies to break even. Each additional book would yield a profit of £5–6 depending on the split of UK and foreign sales.

Technology and book publishing

David Ortago, the new production director at Barnet and an appointee of Octavo, one of the major shareholders, had investigated the potential impact of the latest computer-based typographic and printing machinery on the production process. It appeared likely that time taken up by copy editing, proof production and final print runs could be substantially reduced to around two months on average, implying that new books could be produced from initial contact with the author in around ten months. The introduction of new technology would reduce the initial costs of a book by around £1,000.

Though the system had a number of advantages, it suffered from major limitations.

First, the cost was prohibitive for a small publishing operation. An integrated system for the full-scale setting and typography was estimated to cost around £750,000. Octavo was, however, in a position to consider seriously the acquisition of such a machine for its printing company based in Portugal, which currently serviced three other publishers in the UK market, all of which were in the leisure publishing sector.

Second, staff would have to be extensively retrained in the use of technology, which would take around six months, and there would be redundancies in the production department, where half the current twelve employees would need to be moved to other areas or be made redundant.

Third, the effectiveness of the new technology could be maximized only if authors could be persuaded to use word-processing systems and supply the company with material on disc that could be integrated immediately into the

Table C26.7   Business studies pricing segmentation

Segment	Price range (£)
1. Part time and preliminary studies textbook	5.95–7.95
2. Introductory and additional reading for tertiary education	8.00–8.95
3. Main text for major courses for tertiary education	9.00–14.95
4. Research texts for undergraduate and post-graduate students	15.00–19.95
5. 'Bibles' or complete reference texts for academics and professionals	20.00–29.95

publishing process. This would have a series of implications in terms of the supply of equipment to writers on loan or increases in royalty advances to allow authors to purchase compatible equipment. It could, however, mean that the production schedule for second editions would be further reduced, greatly enhancing the topicality of the book range.

Finally, improvements in technology would have no effect on the manuscript reviewing process, which was a major source of delay.

Barnet Publications and pricing

No research on pricing was available in the market, and Barnet followed a series of rough principles when arriving at a market price. The first key decision concerned likely market sectors for which the book was written. Barnet tended to follow the competition in perceiving the existence of market segments and priced books according to these notions (Table C26.7).

David Kornbluth, the new commercial director, an appointee of the Bertelsmann Group, disagreed with this philosophy and considered that the company should always follow a market-based pricing structure, obtaining the best market price and investing heavily to obtain it. In addition he was very concerned about the high level of stocks the company was carrying and wanted to see a substantial reduction, with consequent improvement in working capital.

Remaindering

Barnet followed the normal academic publisher's policy of not selling slow-moving products at a discount, the practice commonly followed by the rest of the trade. Historically the company had believed in carrying high stocks as the founders thought it essential that all the items in the range must be available ex-stock, because of the fickle nature of the book trade.

The two new appointees to the board took a slightly different stance, particularly in the light of the current cash-flow problems the company was experiencing.

Octavo offered Barnet the opportunity to sell off all its slow-moving lines through its city centre discount bookshops in Australia and New Zealand. This would interfere only marginally with current distribution arrangements. Octavo would take all the Barnet lines at 20 per cent of list price, in other words an 80 per cent discount off the current list price.

Table C26.8 gives a five-year sales summary, with current stocks, of the Barnet list.

Table C26.8 Five-year sales records (*indicates new edition)

Title		1980	1981	1982	1983	1984	Current stock
F1		2,000	1,500	1,800*	1,300	1,200	500
F2		1,100	800	300	450	250	300
F3					800	500	400
F4		1,500	1,300	1,450*	1,450	1,350	800
F5						1,250	1,000
F6		800	550	350	245	200	600
F7				1,700	1,300	1,300	1,300
F8			540	450	375	550	230
F9					300	150	850
F10		500	400	350	650*	450	230
F11		1,100	1,200	900	750	800*	700
F12				450	550	750	300
F13						1,800	980
F14		200	340	250	120*	600	150
F15		300	450	760*	880	660	780
F16						2,300	1,200
F17			450	850	230	600	180
C1	IBM			1,100	890	900	1,500
	Macintosh				780	550	300
	Apricot				200	180	800
C2				1,890	1,100	1,500*	800
C3					550	650	660
C4						2,100	870
C5					220	550	430
C6				1,200	1,680*	1,540	1,100
C7					880	1,230	330
E1		750	670	880*	670	550	760
E2		880	900	780	1,020*	860	660
E3			300	230	250	300	500
E4				550	400	120	480
E5			300	450	300	200	230
E6				1,200	800	980*	550
E7		600	760	670	800	600	200
E8				900	1,010*	770	300
O1		2,300	1,600	900	700	890*	500
O2		300	200	100	50	150	700
O3			600	300	450*	670	550
O4				560	670	800*	760
O5				300	470	900	650

Table C26.8 *(cont.)*

Title	1980	1981	1982	1983	1984	Current stock
O6	800	680	560	750*	500	550
O7	1,200	1,300	1,300	1,400	1,400	1,200
O8					1,200	1,100
O9	500	700	800	900	760*	800
O10					2,350	480
O11	450	340	550	600	550	350
O12			800	990*	750	750
O13			900	600	880	100
O14	600	760	550	400	300	250
O15		2,200	1,700	1,800	2,000*	1,100
O16	550	350	250	250	250	750
O17					4,390	490
O18	350	230	300	370	370	350
O19	1,200	1,100*	1,250	1,250*	1,300	1,000
P1			550	600	650	880
P2	750	540	500	450	350	550
P3	1,100	1,080	1,100	1,300*	1,200	1,100
P4			330	480	300	450
P5	450	550	650	450	550	650
P6		2,800	2,700	3,400	3,000*	200
P7	1,800	1,500	1,400	1,300	1,200	1,800
P8	300	200	150	450*	650	880
P9				550	450	250
P10	100	150	180	180	200	220
P11	1,600	1,500	2,000	1,500	1,200*	2,000
P12	670	450	470	480	550	600
P13			780	540	660	200
P14	330	100	80	50	60	1,080
P15	670	540	450	340	320	660
P16				780	430	760
P17					3,600	400
I1		1,200	600	450	800*	500
I2		780	660	800	900	120
I3			5,000	3,500	5,600	4,500
I4				1,500	1,200	1,100
I5					2,900	700
I6		6,000	4,500	3,500	2,500	1,100
I7					6,600	–
I8				1,700	1,500	200
I9		750	450	550	450	750
I10				800	900	1,050
I11				900	1,100	800
I12					1,500	–
I13					1,800	–

New titles

The new proposed titles for the Barnet range were:

Global Trends in Marketing: a 500-page book written by a practitioner for marketing professionals.

The Service Economy: a broad outline guide to the issues involved in the development of services; 180 pages.

Minicomputer Factbook: a 600-page guide to the detailed issues of minicomputer design and utilization.

Management and Information: how the information flow of a business should be organized; 250 pages.

Quality Circles Factbook: 550 pages of detailed analysis of the role and structure of quality circles.

Privatization in Europe: 350 pages on the issues of government privatization in the EEC.

The EEC and Business: the legal aspects of EEC policy towards business and multinational development; 300 pages.

Crisis Management: a popular management-style book of 180 pages, about the issues of companies facing rapid change.

Charts, Displays and Visuals: computer graphics and how they can be used in the preparation of business documents; 150 pages.

Government Aid and Business Development: an analysis of how government aid has affected business development; 350 pages.

Why Me?: a general interest management guide to decision-taking and decision-making; 150 pages.

Database Factbook: analysis of the uses and applications of databases; 600 pages.

The Growing Company and Personnel: an analysis of the issues of personnel function in the rapidly growing company; 280 pages.

Management and Customers: managing the interplay between company and customers; 350 pages.

Micro-economic Modelling: price evaluation in the company environment; 400 pages.

Environmental Audit: analysing the company's position in the market place; 420 pages.

The ChangeMasters: general book on successful business entrepreneurs; 200 pages.

In addition to these new texts, their pricing and production volumes, Barnet had to decide which of its previous titles to reprint and which required new editions.

Case 27

CASCADE

INTRODUCTION

Suzanne Neil, a young West Indian, had for two years been considering whether she could successfully produce and market a range of products for the ethnic hair care market. Suzanne had worked in a hairdressing salon for three years after being a self-employed sales representative for several cosmetic companies in the London area, and felt that she understood the market and the problems of selling to a specialized clientele. She had noticed that the vast bulk of the products available in the market were American, and the packaging and some of the formulations were not ideally suited to the European market. None of the formulations currently on offer was based on natural ingredients. She felt the continuing success of the Body Shop retail chain indicated a gap in the market, which would allow her to compete with the current UK-produced ethnic hair care products.

She felt that there was a major market opportunity for the development of a range of UK-manufactured products, and by working with lower overheads and ploughing the money back into promotional activity, the products could become firmly established in the market. This belief grew when, in the early 1980s, the dollar strengthened against the pound and American luxury products became more expensive.

To secure funding Suzanne approached two local entrepreneurs, armed with various pieces of information.

MARKET

The value of the ethnic hair care market was estimated at £18 million at manufacturers' selling price (msp) and was growing at around 15 per cent a year. It had established itself as a distinct sub-sector of the hair care market since the early 1960s, but it was not until the early 1970s that it accounted for any significant volume. The market was predominantly urban and concentrated in the South, with approximately 75 per cent of total sales (55 per cent in the London area), the remainder in Birmingham, Manchester and Liverpool. However, over the last five years the market had become steadily more national and the number of outlets stocking ethnic hair products of one form or another had doubled.

Consumers were mainly Afro-Caribbean in the eighteen to twenty-five age group, though there was increasing demand from older groups through specialist hairdressing salons. There had been a number of changes in the product mix over the five-year period (Table C27.1).

The most significant change in the market had been the replacement of the traditional hot oil treatment for curling and styling with a range of more modern styling mousses and gels; these had also marginally eaten into the share of the conditioners. The 'others' category included hair colourants as the major component.

As the consumer age profile suggests, the market was highly fashion conscious, and this decided Suzanne to market the range under the brand name 'Streetwise', and concentrate on image and appearance through sophisticated packaging design.

OUTLETS

The market was serviced through a number of distribution channels. Historically, the most important outlets had been the Afro-Caribbean hairdressing salons. They had declined in importance during the 1980s but were still a significant force in the market. These individually owned salons tended to buy direct, as Suzanne knew from her previous selling experience.

As potential customers, these outlets posed two problems. First, on the whole, they would not be prepared to buy consumer pack sizes, preferring to buy shampoo and conditioner in 500 ml rather than the largest consumer pack, around 175 ml. Salons also tended to buy on price, and to become established in this sector manufacturers would need to offer product at around £2 for a 500 ml pack, with similar discounts on conditioners and other product variants.

Table C27.1   Market share by product type (%)

Product	1980	1981	1982	1983	1984	1985
Shampoo	55	56	57	59	60	62
Conditioner	17	18	17	16	15	14
Hot oil	11	13	9	8	8	7
Relaxant	6	6	5	5	4	5
Styling mousse/gel	3	5	8	10	10	10
Others	8	2	4	2	3	2

Visiting salons was also a time-consuming business, and they would also have to chased for payment; realistic credit terms for the salon sector would range betwen 90 and 120 days.

A small but growing number of independent chemists stocked ethnic hair products, buying either direct or via the five specialist wholesalers. The chemists expected high margins from the products stocked, and this was easily achievable with all ethnic products. On the whole, chemists paid on around sixty days' credit. When buying direct the chemists expected to make around 23 per cent gross margin on their ethnic hair product lines (a 30 per cent mark-up).

Recently corner store grocers had also become a more important direct distribution channel in the market. Traditionally these outlets either bought from the wholesaler or the cash and carry outlet, but because few of the national wholesalers (Nurdin, Booker McConnell, Makro) stocked such products, many of these stores were buying direct from the manufacturers, provided that they could get good credit (sixty days) and delivery in small quantities – minimum drops of around two dozen mixed stock (shampoo, conditioner, gel, etc.). The grocery trade operated on lower profit margins than the chemists and, when buying direct, expected to make around 15–20 per cent gross.

Because of the importance of the specialist wholesalers, through whom 40 per cent of total market sales were made, it was difficult to estimate the market shares of the final retailers. From her experience Suzanne thought that the division given in Table C27.2 was a likely one. These wholesalers were able to negotiate strongly on price and credit terms; payment terms Suzanne discovered were from 90 to 120 days. To enable them to compete effectively with the companies supplying direct, wholesalers were looking for significant discounts – around 40 per cent off retail price – so that they could mark the product up and still present an attractive proposition to their customers. In common with the other distribution channels operating in the market, the margins were much higher than standard hair care products.

Over the five-year period it was estimated that the number of ethnic hair product outlets had substantially increased (Table C27.3).

COMPETITION

The pace of competion within the ethnic hair care market had speeded up over the past five years, though it remained predominantly American. The market leader, Revlon, had identified the potential of the UK market from its experience with products in urban areas in the United States, and had been instrumental in developing the market in the mid-1970s by heavy directed promotional expenditure. Since then a number of other American companies had established themselves in the UK market. All sold broadly similar ranges with imported American-style packaging. Estimated market shares are in Table C27.4.

By 1985 there were twenty manufacturers present in the UK; fifteen were

American. There were two UK suppliers serving the market, and the trade press had announced that a third was shortly to join them.

Table C27.2   Total sales by outlet type (%)

	1980	1985
Salons	60	40
Chemists	15	35
Grocers	25	25

Table C27.3   Ethnic hair products distribution outlets

Outlet	1980	1981	1982	1983	1984	1985
Salons	350	375	400	450	520	550
Chemists	80	200	250	310	320	330
Grocers	150	170	180	200	220	240

Table C27.4   Estimated market shares of major companies in ethnic hair products (%)

Company	Market share
Revlon	35
K-Co	15
Amaryllis	12

PRICING

All the products sold for substantial premiums over standard hair care products, with the Revlon range providing the general benchmark for competitive pricing even though some of the companies in the market continued to price above Revlon. Though there was no audit data to support the view, trade perceptions of the market considered that there were three price bands operating, with the central band – in which Revlon was positioned – accounting for by far the largest proportion of the volume: around 65 per cent. The top sector of the market, priced 25 per cent above Revlon, accounted for 15 per cent, and the lower end the remaining 20 per cent. As with the other cosmetic products, the lower-priced sector was slowly losing ground to the premium-priced products, which were more heavily promoted.

Though there was a substantial amount of price variation, average retail prices (including VAT at 15 per cent) for Revlon products towards the end of 1985 are in Table C27.5.

Table C27.5   Pricing of Revlon
ethnic hair products

Product	Price (£)
Shampoo	
150 ml	2.25
200 ml	3.10
Conditioner	
100 ml	2.00
Gel	
75 ml	1.80

PROMOTION

Promotional expenditure was heavy. Trade magazines estimated that on average the companies in the market spent around 20 per cent of their revenue on some form of promotional activity; this could include sampling (handing out free samples), demo-girls visiting salons, leaflets, and magazine and poster advertisements.

Three monthly magazines catered specifically for the Afro-Caribbean community, with average circulations around 30,000. The cost of a full-page colour advertisement in each was £750–800. Suzanne had received quotations for printing four-colour leaflets, around £300 for 5,000 excluding the costs of the photography, which would be part of the start-up expenditure.

The cost of demo-girls, essential for long-term development in the salons, varied considerably, but a realistic requirement would be £80 a day, enabling four salons to be covered. The cost of hiring an individual to hand out leaflets, a promotional approach which had been used by some manufacturers in key geographical areas such as Lewisham or Dalston, was less expensive at around £30 per day.

Two of the leading companies had experimented with both commercial radio and posters, one of which still used posters, with sites concentrated in the main consumption areas. Here, poster sites cost on average £300 a month, with the production cost of a poster at £25. Radio spots cost around £1,000 on Capital Radio but could reach around 60 per cent of the target population.

Following her work in salons, Suzanne was well aware of the importance of public relations in such a fashion-conscious market. For 'Streetwise' there were a number of possible approaches that could be used.

1. Investing in a launch party and inviting all the main journalists and fashion leaders – this would cost around £2,500.
2. Hiring one of the half dozen 'promoters' of Afro-Caribbean products. These individuals were closely in contact with the legitimate press and the pirate radio stations operating in the London area. Employing one would cost around £250 a month.

3. Using the services of one of the local PR agencies, which would cost around £5,000 a year.

The main problem with all these types of PR was that the final result would be uncertain, and the level of investment required was high for a low-overhead company.

PRODUCTION

Suzanne planned to subcontract all her manufacturing requirement, buying-in bottles which had already been silk-screen printed, either from a UK source or from an Italian manufacturer. The bottles would then be filled with product by another third party and packed into cartons by another.

Products would be in screw-top containers, with different variants identified both by the colour of the top – black, gold and silver – and the printing on the bottle, which would match the colour of the cap.

Because of the market trends, Suzanne decided to concentrate initially on three product variants, shampoo, conditioner and styling gel; these would together account for 85 per cent of total sales. The product formulation, produced by one of the suppliers to Body Shop, meant that the cost of the filled bottles would be more expensive than the competition.

Pack designs were by a professional who had previously worked both for L'Oreal and Schwarzkopf.

COSTING

Minimum quantities for both bottle manufacture and filling were 5,000 units, with payment initially in advance. Quotations had been received for 5,000, 10,000, 20,000 and 30,000 units (Tables C27.6 and C27.7).

Table C27.6   Bottle costs in pence per unit (including printing)

Item	5,000	10,000	20,000	30,000
Shampoo				
175 ml	10	8	6	4
250 ml	13	11	9	6
500 ml	20	17	15	11
Conditioner				
100 ml	8	7	6	5
200 ml	11	10	8	8
Gel				
50 ml	6	6	5	5
125 ml	10	9	9	8

Table C27.7 Filling costs in pence per unit (including raw materials)

Item	5,000	10,000	20,000	30,000
Shampoo				
175 ml	50	43	40	30
250 ml	70	60	55	50
500 ml	100	85	80	70
Conditioner				
100 ml	70	60	55	50
200 ml	120	105	95	90
Gel				
50 ml	100	85	80	70
125 ml	160	145	140	130

Table C27.8 Packing costs for 'Streetwise'

Item	Packing quantity (dozens)	Cost per pack (£)
Shampoo		
175 ml	4	3.00
250 ml	3	3.00
500 ml	2	2.75
Conditioner		
100 ml	6	4.00
200 ml	4	3.00
Gel		
50 ml	8	5.00
125 ml	4	4.00

PACKING COSTS

Each product would be packed in cardboard cases of varying capacity (Table C27.8).

OVERHEADS

Suzanne planned to start by working alone. Her estimated overhead requirements are given in Table C27.9.

There would be no delivery overhead as goods would initially be despatched by mail and third party carriers would be used for large orders. The cost per 100 ml delivered would average 7p. Suzanne would initially carry out all the selling activity, particularly in the London area, and estimated that she would be able to call on around fourteen outlets each day. In the future there would be the option of employing commission sales representatives, who would expect between 18 and 20 per cent gross commission on the amount of sales achieved.

Table C27.9 'Streetwise' estimated
monthly overhead requirements

Item	£
Storage (including rates)	120
Car (including petrol)	300
Wages	600
Telephone	100
Heating/lighting	30
Bookkeeping	200

Table C27.10 Estimated start-up
costs for 'Streetwise'

Item	£
Company formation	120
Design	1,200
Photography	750
Letterhead etc.	250
Legal costs	200

Because Suzanne was inexperienced in bookkeeping and accounts she decided to employ a local agency, and had included the costs in her overheads statement. The recruitment of the bookkeeper/accounts clerk was her first priority for additional staff; the current cost of this would be around £7,500.

START-UP COSTS

The company would incur start-up costs along the lines of Table C27.10.